*The Politics
of
Autonomy*

University of Massachusetts Press   Amherst 1976

The Politics
of
Autonomy

A Kantian Reading of Rousseau's Social Contract

Andrew Levine

*To the memory of my father, Arnold S. Levine,
and for my mother, Libby C. Levine*

Copyright © 1976 by
The University of Massachusetts Press
All rights reserved
Library of Congress Catalog Card Number 76-8757
ISBN 0-87023-215-0
Printed in the United States of America
Designed by Mary Mendell
Library of Congress Cataloging in Publication data
appear on the last printed page of the book.

Contents

Preface

This commentary is an intervention in the ongoing and always contemporary debate *The Social Contract* has elicited for more than two centuries. It is not, however, intended just for the Rousseau specialist or professional philosopher, but is also addressed to those reading *The Social Contract* for the first time. My main hope is that this guide to the text will illustrate for these readers why, in a time and place very different from Rousseau's, *The Social Contract* continues to be a very powerful—indeed, an inexhaustible—source of insight and interest.

What kindled my own interest in Rousseau was reading Marx, particularly the Marx of the early 1840s, of *The Economic and Philosophic Manuscripts* and *The Critique of Hegel's Philosophy of Right*. These early writings bear an obvious, though largely unacknowledged, debt to Rousseau's moral vision of the world, a profound conceptual affinity. However, what follows has very little to do with Marx, at least directly, and a great deal to do with Kant. My aim has been to produce a *Kantian reading* of *The Social Contract*, a reading that emphasizes the many respects in which Rousseau anticipates Kant and motivates his investigations in moral philosophy. This is not a diversion from my original interest: conceptually, Kant is the link between Rousseau and the early Marx. Reading Rousseau does help in understanding Marx, but only when Rousseau is read through Kantian eyes.

I do not mean to suggest that Rousseau was a full-fledged Kantian; far from it. It would be anachronistic, at best, to impose system—even Kantian system—on a thinker who is anything but systematic. However, the roots of Kantianism are in *The Social Contract*, whatever else is there, too; and while Kantian reading may not exhaust the text, it will draw out its principal historical contribution and, in my view, its continuing interest.

The connection between Rousseau and Kant has been asserted frequently. Hegel discerned it in *The Phenomenology of Mind* in the section entitled, appropriately, "The Moral View of the World." More recently, this historical thesis has come to be associated with the work of Ernst Cassirer.[1] Thanks to Cassirer, we know that Kant sensed a deep affinity with Rousseau and saw himself continuing Rousseau's work. However, the connection has yet to be demonstrated conceptually, and such a demonstration is the ulterior motive shaping this book.

The framework of concepts discovered by Rousseau and then explored by Kant underlies the 'deep structures' of the view of the world that emerged with the rise of the bourgeoisie to dominance and that continues to dominate our own sense of self, society, and being-in-the-world. Beyond its intrinsic interest, then, *The Social Contract* can be a means to self-knowledge, to knowledge of the concepts that shape our view of the world. To this end, paradoxically, contemporary social philosophy is seldom so germane as Rousseau; particularly now, when the cutting edge of the discipline has self-consciously regressed to the concerns of the English revolutions and Locke.[2]

Rousseau's Kantianism intrudes unabashedly on particular explications and on the general orientation of my remarks. Nevertheless, my overriding concern has been to produce a book that will be useful and fully intelligible even for those who know little or nothing of Kantian moral philosophy. For this reason, Rousseau's Kantianism is very seldom confronted directly, and Kant's Rousseaueanism is scarcely even invoked, though it still should be

1. Ernst Cassirer, *The Question of Jean-Jacques Rousseau* and, especially, *Rousseau Kant Goethe*.
2. The most recent expression of this tendency is Robert Nozick's *Anarchy, State and Utopia* (New York, 1974); but it is also evident in John Rawls's justly celebrated *Theory of Justice*, despite Rawls's claims to be writing in the tradition of Rousseau and Kant. See my article "Rawls' Kantianiam," *Social Theory and Practice* 3, no. 1 (Spring 1974): 47–64.

very evident, to readers familiar with Kant, that these themes are addressed constantly. A more explicit treatment would require a very different and, I think, less useful account of *The Social Contract*.

I suggest the reader take up the text of *The Social Contract* roughly in the order in which it is treated in this commentary: first, read all of Book 1; then chapter 6 of Book 2; then Book 2, chapters 1 to 5, and Book 4, chapters 1 to 3; then Book 3; and, finally, the remaining chapters of Books 2 and 4. When the text is read in this order, a coherence and logical development emerge that are otherwise lacking.

There is no standard English translation of *The Social Contract*, though the version most often cited is probably G.D.H. Cole's.[3] Cole's translation deviates considerably from the French and can be quite misleading. I have used the nineteenth-century translation of Henry J. Tozer,[4] but have modified it considerably in the interest of literalness. Except where indicated, all other translations from Rousseau's writings are entirely my own.

Since there are so many editions of *The Social Contract* in print, and since my translations correspond exactly to none of them, I have listed citations by reference to the book and chapter number of the text. Rousseau's chapters are short enough that concordance should be easy.

Needless to say, as in any reading, my conclusions are provisional, to be modified by further readings, my own and others. Perhaps this commentary will help to make future readings more productive.

3. G.D.H. Cole, trans., *The Social Contract and Discourses* (London: Everyman's Library, 1966). This translation was first published by Dent in 1913.
4. Tozer's translation can be found in Lester Crocker's edition, *The Social Contract and Discourse on the Origin of Inequality* (New York: Washington Square Press, 1967).

Acknowledgements

Of all the vast literature on Rousseau, I have learned the most from Louis Althusser's lectures on *The Social Contract*.[1] My very substantial debt, particularly in chapters 1 and 5, should be evident to anyone familiar with his work. I would like also to acknowledge the significant influence of my teacher, Robert Paul Wolff, Jr., under whom I first studied Rousseau, Kant, and Marx.

I have profited enormously from the criticisms and encouragement of D.G. Brown and Robert Rowan. George Kateb and Michael Teitelman have read the entire manuscript thoroughly and painstakingly; I am extremely grateful for their suggestions and support. Needless to say, only I am responsible for the errors that remain and for the particular theses I advance. Finally, I should like to thank all who helped in the preparation of this manuscript; particularly my typist, Heather Anne Prittie, for her skill and cooperation.

1. See "Sur le *Contrat Social* (Les Décalages)," in *Cahiers pour l'analyse*, no. 8, *L'Impensée de Jean-Jacques Rousseau*, which has been translated as "Rousseau: The Social Contract," in Althusser, *Politics and History*.

I
Theory

Introduction

The Social Contract provides an account of a cluster of concepts
that the emerging political reorganization of eighteenth-century
Europe had brought into conceptual crisis: above all, authority, the
state, and sovereignty. These concepts are mutually interdefinable.
Roughly, if by *authority* is meant the *right* (as opposed to the mere
power) to command or exact obedience, then the *state* can be
defined as those people who claim supreme authority or, equivalently, *sovereignty* over a given territory or population.[1]

These concepts have both a descriptive and a normative sense.
Plainly, their descriptive sense is unproblematic. Supreme authority or sovereignty is in fact claimed and acknowledged; *de
facto* states exist. Rousseau's aim is not to account for this fact, but
to inquire into its justification; or, rather, into its possible
justification, since he is not directly concerned with the claims
advanced by *de facto* states. Rousseau's problem is to provide an

1. The authority claimed consists in the right to coordinate at least some
individual activities through the use or threat of force. This is the sense of
the celebrated definition of the state formulated by Max Weber but capping
a tradition in political theory going back at least as far as the emergence of
the nation state itself: "the state is a human community that (successfully)
claims the monopoly of the legitimate use of physical force within a given
territory . . . a relation of men dominating men . . . supported by means of
legitimate (i.e. considered to be legitimate) violence." "Politics as a Voca-
tion," in *From Max Weber: Essays in Sociology*, ed. H.H. Gerth and C. Wright
Mills (New York, 1958), p. 78.

account of the *de jure* state, of the state that exists in right (whether or not it has ever existed in fact). He is tactful on this question, but his position seems to be that, while the *de jure* state certainly does exist conceptually, it has never been instantiated or even approximated.

To be sure, this problem would never arise but for the existence of *de facto* states. The fact that some people believe in God raises the similar question of the truth of their belief; but just as it does not follow that God exists because people believe in God, it does not follow that the *de jure* state exists because people acknowledge claims advanced by *de facto* states. In both cases, the facts of the matter raise the question, but no more. To its discredit, most contemporary political theory seems to ignore this obvious point, supposing that since there are states, the existence of the state must be justifiable. The classical tradition in democratic theory, and Rousseau particularly, at least face squarely the possibility of philosophical anarchism.

That the problem of *The Social Contract* is to inquire into the conditions for the possibility of the *de jure* state is announced in the opening sentence of the text: "I wish to inquire whether in the civil order it is possible to have some rule of administration that is legitimate and certain taking men as they are and laws as they might be made" (Book 1, introductory note). The point, in short, will be to investigate the principles of the right to rule (men as they are / laws as they might be made) and not how or why people in fact obey commands (men as they are / laws as they are). Roughly, the latter question defines the province of descriptive political science; the former question establishes substantive political philosophy, the theory of the *de jure* state. In *The Social Contract* these disciplines part ways radically.

Substantive political philosophy, then, is a part of moral philosophy, of a general theory of right and obligation. Because it does not theorize actual political practice, at least not directly, empirical evidence—including observation of *de facto* states—is irrelevant in ascertaining the viability of its concepts. The *de jure* state must be theorized *a priori*. To use Kant's expression, the *de jure* state requires a 'deduction,' a demonstration *a priori* of its coherence and possible application. This is precisely the task Rousseau undertakes: to give an account of the *de jure* state, "taking men as they are."

1

The "Fundamental Problem" of Political Philosophy and Its "Solution"

Rousseau's account of the *de jure* state is capsulized in an extraordinarily concise text: the sixth chapter of Book 1. The rest, one might almost conclude is commentary. For it is here that Rousseau poses and answers the question that, on his account, constitutes the fundamental problem of political philosophy: "to find a form of association that defends and protects with the whole force of the community the person and property of each associate, and by means of which, each uniting with all, nevertheless obeys only himself and remains as free as before." This, Rousseau tells us, "is the fundamental problem of which the social contract furnishes the solution." We must try to make sense of this question and to inquire how, indeed, "the social contract furnishes the solution."

The Solution Announced: Not from Nature, but from Convention (1:1)

It is significant that well before the fundamental problem is formulated, Rousseau announces its solution. In the very first chapter we read: "the social order is a sacred right, which serves as the basis for all the others. However, this right does not come from nature. Therefore it is founded on conventions." There is nothing new in this announcement. That the foundation of political society is in some sense or other "conventional" was very nearly universally acknowledged by the middle of the eighteenth century.[1] In form, at least, Rousseau never broke with this tradition. He used the contractarian idiom to express his own thought. But Rousseau's adherence to this tradition is problematic, for he did in effect break with the substance of contractarianism. *The Social Contract* is difficult, in part, because Rousseau thought new thoughts in old concepts, 'imported' concepts (to use Kant's expression), concepts inadequate to the thought expressed through them.

Within the contractarian tradition it was habitual to confound two quite distinct questions: the historical problem of the *origin* of the state, and the normative-moral problem of the *foundation* in right of the state (and so, of political authority and obligation). In the nineteenth century, contractarian thought declined, largely thanks to the increasingly evident untenability of the historical hypothesis. Nowadays, however, it is well understood that these questions are distinct, and that what infirms the historical hypothesis has nothing to do with the propriety of social contract theory in political philosophy.[2]

Contractarianism, in effect, is a methodological program for dealing with normative questions, for discovering the principles that determine how social and political institutions ought to be organized. The point is to generate these principles from a logically prior conception of the individual (abstracted from the social or political arrangements in question). Suppose, like Rousseau, we seek a theory of the *de jure* state. Then the contractarian program would have us begin by considering individuals—abstracted from their political relations—in "a state of nature." The normative principles that ought to govern the state are those that these individuals in a state of nature would choose.

1. In what follows I shall, like Rousseau, use *convention*, *pact*, and *contract* synonymously, except where a special emphasis is best suggested by one or another word.
2. For a comprehensive account of the history of contractarian thought and its decline in the nineteenth century, see J.W. Gough, *The Social Contract: A Critical Study of Its Development*. According to Gough, the final blow to contractarianism was the publication in 1861 of Henry Sumner Maine's *Ancient Law*. Maine argued that the development of society has been "from status to contract" and that the very notion of a legal contract comes into existence only very late in the history of civilization.

In suggesting that Rousseau accepts the form but not the substance of the contractarian program, I am suggesting that, appearance to the contrary, his social contract is not really the outcome of such a choice. Rousseau's starting point, we shall see, is not really the abstract individual but society or, more strictly, "social relations."

An important line of criticism directed against the contractarian program in general would deny the possibility of abstracting individuals from their social and political arrangements. Marx levels this point against Rousseau in one of his early writings, "On the Jewish Question" (1843). If I am right, however, Rousseau has anticipated this criticism, perhaps without realizing it. In any case, *within* the contractarian program—where Rousseau situates himself—everything depends on a correct characterization of the state of nature. For this reason, in an early note on "The State of War," aiming at Hobbes, Rousseau contends: "I have already said and cannot too often repeat that the error of Hobbes and the *philosophes* is to confuse natural man with those men they see in their eyes, and to transfer into one system, a being that can only subsist in another.... They know very well what it is to be a bourgeois of London or Paris, but they know nothing of what it is to be a man" (Pléiade edition, 3:611-2).

In addition to situating individuals in a state of nature, it is also necessary to motivate them to leave it. The state of nature must be so unsatisfactory as to guarantee a common interest in introducing the sort of institution the theory is supposed to justify. For Rousseau, what renders the state of nature onerous is what renders the way out desirable. There is thus a unique solution to the problem depicted.

Contractarianism presupposes that persons in the state of nature have a certain capacity for instrumental rationality, that they are able, to some extent at least, to adopt means to ends in order to realize their goals. The program could thus be viewed as an application of a theory of rational choice. However, in the eighteenth-century versions of contractarian theory (including Rousseau's), the choice problem is really too simple to warrant characterization on this level. It will, therefore, be best to focus on the options Rousseau presents, while leaving the notion of instrumental rationality largely unanalyzed.

It might seem odd to pose the problem of justification in this way. In Rousseau's time (and in his work), the rationale for doing so was never, to my knowledge, made explicit. Undoubtedly, the characteristic confusion of the normative and historical questions, the confusion of foundation in right and origin in fact, obscured the need for an explicit methodological discussion. Rousseau does provide an implicit account: an account that turns on his notion of freedom as autonomy. This rationale will emerge in the course of considering the formulation of the problem the social contract solves.

It is likely that Rousseau, at least some of the time, saw the social contract playing a strictly justificatory role. The clearest indication of this intent is to be found in the first chapter of Book 1: "Man was born free, but everywhere he is in chains. Those who believe themselves to be the masters of others, are nevertheless greater slaves than they. *How did this change come about? I do not know.* What can render it legitimate? I believe I can answer that question" (italics mine). The historical question, in other words, is to be bracketed; the "Subject of the First Book" is normative.

Kant, too, understood Rousseau to be engaged in a strictly normative enterprise. Speaking of the contractarian tradition in general but with Rousseau clearly in mind, he is unequivocal:

> We need by no means assume that this contract (*contractus originarius* or *pactum sociale*) based on a coalition of the wills of all private individuals in a nation to form a common, public will for the purpose of rightful legislation, actually exists as a fact, for it cannot possibly be so. Such an assumption would mean that we would first have to prove from history that some nation, whose rights and obligations have been passed down to us, did in fact perform such an act, and handed down some authentic record or legal instrument, orally or in writing, before we could regard ourselves as bound by a pre-existing civil constitution. . . . The social contract is in fact merely an *idea* of reason, which nonetheless has undoubted practical reality.[3]

3. Immanuel Kant, "On the Common Saying: 'This May be True in Theory, but it does not Apply in Practice,'" in *Kant's Political Writings,* ed. Hans Reiss (Cambridge, 1970), p. 79.

But What Convention? (1:2–4)

Rousseau, then, will not be arguing for the claim that the foundation of political society is conventional. That battle—directed historically against proponents of the theory of divine right—had already been won by Rousseau's time to a point where it no longer needed to be waged. Instead, Rousseau will argue *within* the contractarian tradition: against "illegitimate conventions." The question is in what sort of convention does society have its foundation? Chapters 2 and 4 examine and reject a number of illegitimate contenders. The examination is by no means exhaustive; nor is it systematic. What it represents is Rousseau's attempt to settle accounts with his predecessors by means of a critique, a critical reading of past political philosophy: of Filmer and Grotius, Pufendorf and Locke, and above all of Hobbes. I will not attempt to reconstruct this implicit critical history of political philosophy in detail. Rather, my object will be to exhibit the general features of Rousseau's critique in such a way as to prepare the ground for the formulation of the "fundamental problem" and the announcement of its "solution." "There are a thousand ways to assemble men together," Rousseau had written in the first draft of *The Social Contract,* "but there is only one way to unite them" (Pléiade edition, 3:297).

In chapter 2, Rousseau examines the contention that society has its foundation in the family.[4] At first glance, the family relation might appear a natural one, and not in any sense conventional.

4. This view had been proposed by Bousset in his *Politique* (1709) and again by Ramsay in the *Essai philosophique sur le gouvernement civil* (1719). However, the principal antagonist is almost certainly Sir Robert Filmer, whose chief work, *Patriarcha* (first published in 1680, though probably written some thirty years earlier), attempted a defense of absolute monarchy on the grounds of its inheritance of the powers conferred by God on Adam and his successors. The first of Locke's *Two Treatises of Government* is a direct reply to Filmer, as is the final paragraph of chapter 2: "I have said nothing about king Adam, nor about the Emperor Noah, father of the three great monarchs who shared the universe, like the children of Saturn, whom one thought could be recognized in them. I hope that my moderation will give satisfaction; for being a direct descendant of one of these princes, and perhaps of the eldest branch, how do I know whether, by examination of titles, I might not find myself the legitimate king of the human race." The analogy between political and paternal authority is in fact rather common in the literature. Other offenders, from Rousseau's point of view, though less blatant than Filmer, would include Grotius and even Aristotle.

Rousseau is quick to dispel this view: "children remain tied to their father only so long as they have need of him for self-preservation. As soon as this need ceases, the natural bond is dissolved. The children, exempt from the obedience they owe to the father, and the father, exempt from the cares he owes to the children, revert both equally to independence. If they remain united, it is no longer naturally but voluntarily; and the family itself maintains itself only by convention" (1:2).

Both the father of the family and the leader of a people have authority. However, the resemblance stops there. The state is not an extended family; still less is it the family writ large. The differences are qualitative.

The text of chapter 2 is singularly lacking in argument, but elsewhere Rousseau has treated the question more systematically—in the *Encyclopedia* article "On Political Economy" (1755) and in the fifth chapter of the first draft of *The Social Contract* (1761). In each case, Rousseau argues by assembling disanalogies. The father rules by "natural sentiments"; not so, the first magistrate. Property within the family "emanates" from the father or, strictly speaking, belongs to him; property, on the other hand, is "anterior" to the state. The family will branch out and eventually vanish into other families; the state, however, conserves its essential unity by incorporating new members. It would be tedious to continue elaborating disanalogies. The point is just that the family and the state are so unlike one another that no fruitful analogy can be drawn between them concerning the foundation of authority. "The functions of the father of a family and of the first magistrate of a state," wrote Rousseau in the *Encyclopedia* article, "tend in the same direction ... but by such different routes that their duties and rights are so distinct that one must not confuse them" (Pléiade edition, 3:243). That is, it is not profitable to regard the state as an extended family, nor as operating on the model of an extended family. It will not help for understanding political authority to understand paternal authority.

What, then, of the view that the state is the master-slave relation writ large? As Rousseau read them, nearly all of his predecessors, or at least those within the contractarian tradition, held some version of this view. And this view, he argues, is entirely mistaken. The argument is pursued polemically in chapter 4.

First, however, Rousseau establishes a prior point: that superior force does not constitute right, that compulsion is not a ground for obligation. This conclusion is relevant to the argument of chapter 4, but the point is more general. In a sense, it amounts to a restatement of the problem announced at the very outset: to conceive *legitimate* political power.

So in chapter 3, in language very reminiscent of Kant's, Rousseau attacks the view that might makes right.[5] "Force is a physical power," Rousseau notes; "I do not see what morality can result from its effects. To surrender to force is an act of necessity, not of will; it is at most an act of prudence. In what sense can it be a duty?" (1:3).

To hold that might makes right, Rousseau continues, is to believe "inexplicable nonsense." For then we should have to believe that whenever one force overcomes another, it "succeeds to its rights." This result would undermine the very notion of obligation: "as soon as one can disobey with impunity, one can do so legitimately, and since the strongest is always right, the only thing is to act in such a way as that one may be the strongest" (1:3). Force may give a prudential reason for compliance, but not a moral reason. It has nothing to do with duty.

If might made right, Rousseau could not even formulate the problem of giving an account of the *de jure* state; for inasmuch as existing states exercise a near monopoly on the means of coercion, existing states would *ipso facto* be *de jure* states. Then there would be no place for the investigation Rousseau undertakes. Political philosophy would lose its object; it would merge into descriptive political science. That might and right are radically different provides the starting point for Rousseau's analysis, and allows him to formulate the normative problem the social contract solves.

The failure to acknowledge this difference and its consequences rigorously is the primal sin of the writers against whom Rousseau inveighs in chapter 4.

Just as the political theory of Rousseau's day conceived the family relation not in natural but in conventional terms, so too the master-slave relation, which Roman jurisprudence had taken to be natural, was conceived as a contract. In chapter 4, having already

5. It is doubtful whether anyone since Thrasymachus in *The Republic* held this view seriously in the form Rousseau attacks it. But, if Rousseau is right, it does at least implicitly underlie a good deal of classical contractarian thought.

distinguished questions of power from questions of right, Rousseau proceeds to show how any contract through which one party becomes a master and the other a slave is illegitimate. The argument falls into two parts (following a distinction admitted by Grotius and Pufendorf): first, it is shown that it is never conceivable that one would submit voluntarily to become a slave; then, it is shown that there is no moral force in any convention that ratifies the effects of forced submission.

Strictly speaking, only the latter part of this demonstration presupposes the result of chapter 3. But there is, I think, a less systematic rationale for the placement of these chapters. The claim that the master-slave relation is not the basis of the state is an implicit attack on absolutism. "In insisting on the analogy between the pact that gives rise to monarchy and that which institutes slavery the jurists clearly aim to establish the legitimacy of absolute power. This is what Rousseau cannot allow. Thus the point for him is to prove, contrary to what the jurists suppose, that there is no analogy between sovereignty and the domination of a master, between *imperium* and *potestas dominica*."[6] The radical disjunction of might from right prepares the ground for this demonstration.

The question of voluntary submission turns on the possibility of the individual 'alienating' his liberty. Many of Rousseau's contemporaries and predecessors, among them Grotius, Pufendorf, and Burlamaqui, believed this alienation not only possible, but in some sense even necessary.[7] "If an individual, says Grotius, can alienate his liberty and make himself the slave of a master, why should not a whole people be able to alienate theirs, and make themselves subject to a king" (1:4). Rousseau's response is addressed to the supposition underlying Grotius's claim. The individual cannot (in right) alienate his liberty to become the slave of a master, and so neither can a people alienate its liberty to a king; because, Rousseau insists, liberty cannot be alienated. In view of that alienation

6. Robert Derathé, *Jean-Jacques Rousseau et la science politique de son temps*, p. 194.
7. The alleged right of slavery plays an important role in the political controversies of the seventeenth and eighteenth centuries. As Derathé has shown, Rousseau is not original in opposing pacts of voluntary submission. Among the predecessors from whom he borrows considerably are Jurieu, Locke, and above all Montesquieu.

of liberty Rousseau is to propose in Book 1, chapter 6, as the solution to the fundamental problem of political philosophy, we must examine this claim with care.

"To alienate," Rousseau tells us, "is to give (*donner*) or to sell (*vendre*)" (1:4). Now, man is "born free"; he has liberty. Thus, there is of course a sense in which it *is* possible for him to give it up or to sell it. But it is not conceivable that he would, Rousseau argues, for in principle there could be no *sufficient* reason to do so. We assume, in line with the contractarian program, that persons have, among other things, a capacity for instrumental rationality. When we look for a sufficient reason, this is the direction in which we must look. The argument is that it could never be *advantageous* (instrumentally) to alienate one's liberty. Hence, the alienation of liberty is unthinkable, and, in this sense, impossible or, as Rousseau would prefer, "vain and contradictory."

Plainly, it would never be advantageous to give one's liberty away. "To say that a man gives himself away gratuitously is to say something absurd and inconceivable; such an act is illegitimate and invalid, because he who performs it is not in his right mind. To say the same thing of an entire people is to suppose a people of fools; and madness does not make for rights" (1:4). If it is conceivable that liberty can be alienated, then, it can only be sold (and not given away). To sell something is to exchange it for something else. And that exchange, to be thinkable, would have to be advantageous. Otherwise, there would be hardly more reason to sell one's liberty than to give it away.

For what might it be advantageous to exchange one's liberty? For means of subsistence? Rousseau is scornful: "So far from a king furnishing his subjects with their subsistence, he draws his from them; and according to Rabelais, a king does not live on a little. Do subjects, then, give up their persons on condition that their property also shall be taken? I do not see what is left for them to keep" (1:4). Or perhaps, as Hobbes seems to suggest, it is advantageous to exchange one's liberty for civil peace. Rousseau's reply is no less scornful: "what do they gain by that, if the wars which his ambition brings upon them, if his insatiable greed and the vexations of his administration, desolate them more than their own dissensions would? What do they gain by that if this tranquility is itself one of their miseries? One lives tranquilly also in dungeons; is that

H. v. R:
H abandons liberty for peace.
R is not so hasty.

R: weak argument?

enough to make one contented there? The Greeks confined in the cave of the Cyclops lived peacefully while awaiting their turn to be devoured" (1:4).

That this reply is unfair to Hobbes, that it misses the point of his account of the state of nature as a state of war (to which even despotism is preferable)—an account Rousseau himself will shortly adapt to his own purpose—ought of course to be mentioned. But it is by no means fatal to Rousseau's position, for it is just so much rhetorical flourish. The real point is quite different and directly indicates the fundamental notion of Rousseau's political thought: the concept of liberty.

The real point is that *in principle* there is nothing that could be exchanged for liberty that would render the exchange advantageous. Because liberty is priceless; it has what Kant was to call *dignity* (*Würde*), as distinct from *price* (*Preis*). It is the essential characteristic of humanity, that without which the ends of man cannot be fulfilled. "To renounce one's liberty," Rousseau declares, "is to renounce one's quality as a man, the rights of humanity and even its duties." And he continues: "There is no possible compensation for one who renounces *everything*. Such a renunciation is incompatible with man's nature, *for to take away all freedom from his will is to take away all morality from his actions*" (1:4, italics mine). The end of man, his destiny, is to be a moral agent. To renounce one's liberty is to renounce the possibility of fulfilling this destiny. Thus, it is "to renounce one's quality as a man," to renounce one's essence.

In *The Social Contract* this thesis is simply declared. It is not argued for; still less is it proved. Yet it serves as the keystone of Rousseau's examination of authority and political obligation. It defines the parameters within which the fundamental problem of political philosophy is to be posed.

It is because liberty is priceless that the pact of voluntary submission is "vain and contradictory." It is obviously irrational to give one's liberty away. Now we are told it is equally irrational to sell it. But "to alienate is to give or to sell." Therefore, it can never in principle be rational to alienate one's liberty voluntarily. To do so is unthinkable; hence, impossible.

If the voluntary alienation of liberty is "vain and contradictory," the forced alienation of liberty would appear even more so, particularly inasmuch as might does not make right. However, the view that slavery—individual and political—has its justification in the right of conquest was a recurrent argument that Rousseau could not ignore. In Roman law, it was held that conquest in and of itself established the conqueror's right to mastership. Characteristically, the political philosophers of the seventeenth and eighteenth centuries recast this position in conventionalist terms, seeing the master-slave relationship as justified through a pact that, in effect, ratified the consequences of violent domination. It is this view that Rousseau, in the concluding part of chapter 4, seeks to refute.

The particular form of the argument considered by Rousseau is interesting in that it appears to avoid the problem with "advantage," on which the pact of voluntary submission faltered. The argument is taken from Book 3, chapter 8, of Grotius's *Right of War and Peace*. "Grotius and others," Rousseau begins, "... derive from war another origin for the pretended right of slavery. The victor having, according to them, the right to kill the vanquished, the latter may buy back his life at the expense of his liberty; a convention all the more legitimate in that it turns a profit for both" (1:4). In other words, if the conqueror has a right to kill the conquered, as Grotius asserts, then it is advantageous for all parties to contract together to establish the conqueror's mastership over the conquered. The conquered would lose his life (and, therefore, his liberty) anyway, the argument runs; thus he has nothing to lose and something—his life—to gain by becoming a slave. And since mastership is plainly advantageous to the conqueror, both parties have a mutual interest in the alienation of liberty. The exchange is advantageous and therefore rational.

Rousseau fixes attention on the premise of the argument: that the conqueror has a right to kill the conquered. In so doing, he resumes a line of argument undertaken earlier in the fragment "On the State of War." His express intention is to criticize the Hobbesian account of the state of nature as a state of war, and thereby to clarify his own account of the state of nature. The refutation of Grotius is an additional dividend. For Grotius's argument will work only if we do in fact accord the conqueror the right to kill the conquered. "If war does not confer on the victor the right to massacre the vanquished, this right which he does not have cannot be the basis of a right to enslave them. If we have a right to kill an enemy only when it is impossible to enslave him, the right to enslave him is not derived from the right to kill him. It is therefore an iniquitous exchange to make him purchase his life, over which one has no right, at the price of his liberty" (1:4).

Men are not naturally enemies, Rousseau argues. In the most primitive state of nature, there are no social relations sufficiently durable to constitute either a state of peace or a state of war. "It is a relation of things and not of men which constitutes war," Rousseau insists, "and since the state of war cannot arise from simple personal relations, but only from real relations, private war—war between man and man—cannot exist either in the state of nature, where there is no settled property, nor in the social state, where everything is under the authority of the laws" (1:4). In short, war is a relation not between individuals but between states. Hobbes has reversed the relation, since for him, human society arises out of a state of war. When states are at war, Rousseau contends, individuals are enemies "only by accident, not as men, nor even as citizens, but as soldiers; not as members of the fatherland, but as its defenders" (1:4).

If Rousseau is correct, the alleged right of the victor to kill the vanquished vanishes: the aim of war is the destruction of the hostile state and not its citizens. The defenders of that hostile state are enemies only insofar as they are its defenders. Rousseau concludes, "we have a right to kill its defenders only so long as they have arms in their hands; but as soon as they lay them down and surrender, ceasing to be enemies or instruments of the enemy, they become again simply men, and no one has any further right over their lives" (1:4). So, contrary to Grotius's contention, the victor has no right to slay the vanquished.[8] The alleged right of conquest collapses into the law of the strongest, which is, of course, no right at all. Thus, there is no justification in right to agree to become a slave.

We shall see later that Rousseau's rejection of Hobbes's account of the state of nature as a state of war is by no means unequivocal. For the moment, however, it is enough to point out that even granting the victor a right to destroy the vanquished, Rousseau still need not concede the case against the forced alienation of

8. Substantially the same argument had already been made by Montesquieu in *The Spirit of the Laws*, Book 15, chapter 2.

liberty. For "to renounce one's liberty," he has already told us, "is to renounce one's quality as a man." To consent to become a slave of another—whether voluntarily or by compulsion—is to consent to a living death. And a living death, Rousseau might argue, is scarcely an advantage over death *tout court*. This is perhaps his intention in remarking how "in taking an equivalent for his life the victor has conferred no favor on the slave; instead of killing him unprofitably, he has destroyed him for his own advantage" (1:4). The master has not acquired any authority over the slave, but simply compelled compliance through superior force. Therefore, no matter what the circumstances compelling a person to consent to become a slave, that consent cannot in principle create an obligation. Or, as Rousseau would have it, "these terms *slavery* and *right* are contradictory and mutually exclusive" (1:4).

We should pause on this concluding remark. There is more substance here than just some criticisms of Grotius and Hobbes. The rejection of the master-slave relation as the model for political association carries with it, implicitly, a number of substantive claims. Up to this point, however, the text has been strictly negative: we have been told only what the foundation of the *de jure* state cannot be. Indeed, it is not until Book 1, chapter 6, where Rousseau finally formulates "the fundamental problem of political philosophy," that these substantive claims become explicit. It will be useful, however, to consider the positive elements of his theory here, on the basis of the negative results obtained thus far. In this way, it will be possible to anticipate the result of the relatively fresh start Rousseau is about to make in chapter 6.

As a first approximation, it is fair to say that the rejection of the master-slave relation (and also of the family) as the model of political association amounts unsystematically to a rejection of any form of unequal political association. Unequal power gives rise to domination, not right.[9] The notion of right presupposes a fundamental equality among persons.

9. The case of domination within the family is an exception. Although Rousseau conceives the family as a voluntary association, where authority relations are conventional, the ground for this association is plainly natural sentiment. In view of what Rousseau says in chapter 4, however, it would take substantial argument to show that there is any moral force underlying

But equality in what? There has so far been no mention of property except in chapter 4, where we are told that in a state of nature there is no "settled property." That is, there is simple possession of goods (*biens*), but not real ownership (*propriete*). Indeed, there is only one genuine possession named so far, which is a gift at birth ("Man is born free") and a priceless possession. The unequal relation Rousseau criticizes, the master-slave relation, is essentially a relation of unequal liberty. It is thus reasonable to suppose the positive content of chapters 1 to 4 to be that a *de jure* state will be one formed by convention from an original position of equal liberty.

But this is not yet complete. For liberty is the defining characteristic of humanity, its essential trait. Since liberty is priceless, it can never be alienated for a sufficient reason. Moreover, liberty is 'indivisible'; either one is free or one is in chains. No partial alienation of liberty is conceivable.[10] It follows that the individuals who form a political association from an original position of equal liberty can never rationally forfeit their liberty or any part of it. A *de jure* state, in other words, will be one that preserves and maintains freedom. Insofar as "man is born free," the establishment of the *de jure* will leave him *as free as before.*

The problem, then, is to reconcile authority (the *right* to compel obedience) with liberty. Shortly, Rousseau will tell us that to be free is to obey only oneself (1:6).[11] To reconcile authority and liberty in this sense would appear to be a hopelessly paradoxical task. Rousseau's formulation in chapter 6 will attempt to finesse this paradox—we shall see, however, with what success.

---

this natural sentiment. Lacking such argument, Rousseau ought in all rigor to regard the domination of the father over the family (that is, over women and major children) as equally illegitimate as the domination of the master over the slave. He stopped short of doing so.

10. Rousseau has not so far drawn this conclusion explicitly, though his account in chapters 2 to 4, and also in chapter 6, presupposes it. The warrant for treating liberty as indivisible does not begin to be introduced explicitly until Book 2, and, accordingly, it will be discussed further on. A possible position, it should be noted—and one Rousseau is to reject—is that individuals alienate only part of their liberty. Locke, for example, so concluded.

11. This definition, which should not be confused with the liberal view of liberty as (roughly) the absence of coercive restraint, bears a striking resemblance to the key notion of Kantian moral philosophy: autonomy. We shall see further on that these notions are, in fact, identical, that Rousseau's problem is to reconcile authority and autonomy.

These substantive points may now be summarized more systematically. The argument of *The Social Contract* in its positive aspects through Book 1, chapter 4, has the following structure:

1. Man is born free. Hence, a necessary condition for being human is being free; "to renounce one's liberty is to renounce one's quality as a man." This claim is not argued for; it is simply declared. It is the fundamental premise on which *The Social Contract* rests.

2. A *de jure* state will be one chosen by convention from an original position of equal liberty. This is Rousseau's application of the contractarian method to (1);

3. The only sort of state it would be rational to choose from the situation described in (2) is one in which the liberty of each individual is preserved. This follows directly from (1) and (2) and leads to the following problem, a sort of first approximation to the problem Rousseau will formulate in chapter 6 and call "the fundamental problem of political philosophy";

4. The problem is to find a form of association that will preserve (equal) individual liberty; or, equivalently, to reconcile liberty (obeying only oneself) and authority.

A First Convention (1:5)

We must be clear, finally, about precisely what individuals in the state of nature are supposed to establish. Rousseau is critical of Grotius and others for confusion on this point. In the seventeenth and eighteenth centuries, the notion of a social contract covered two quite distinct, though often confused, kinds of convention: that by which individuals living in a state of nature agree to form an organized "civil society," a *pact of association*; and that by which individuals already in civil society elect a government, a *pact of government*.[12] Rousseau is unequivocally interested in the former only. In pointing out Grotius's confusion, Rousseau declares: "Before examining the act by which a people elects a king, it would be good to examine the act by which a people becomes a people. For

12. See Gough, *The Social Contract*, pp. 2 ff. As a good example of a pact of association being turned into practice, Gough recalls the covenant of the Pilgrim Fathers when they landed from the Mayflower in 1620: "We do solemnly and mutually in the presence of God and of one another, covenant

this act, being necessarily anterior to the other, is the real foundation of society" (1:5).

This pact can only be unanimous. It cannot, for example, be established by majority-rule vote (as Grotius imagined); for the decision to arrive at collective choices by majority vote—or indeed by any procedure—must first be established. This agreement on constitutions, on means of arriving at collective decisions, Rousseau argues, must be unanimous. Without unanimous agreement, "where would be the obligation of the minority to submit to the choices of the majority? And whence do the hundred who desire a master derive the right to vote for the ten who do not desire one? The law of the plurality of votes is itself established by convention, and supposes unanimity at least once" (1:5).

If we add this result to the conclusion of the last section, the problem we face may be resumed as follows:

5. It is necessary to form a pact of association that will establish authority without sacrificing the (equal) liberty of any individual associate. This pact must be unanimous.

Recall, though, that the individuals who form this pact are outside society, in a state of nature. To motivate (5), then, Rousseau must look to the state of nature; he does so as a new point of departure in Book 1, chapter 6.

The State of Nature

The opening paragraph of chapter 6 recapitulates and continues the argument of Rousseau's account of the state of nature in *The Discourse on the Origin of Inequality*. Man is originally solitary and isolated; he lives by and for himself alone. He has, however, a certain natural pity (which he shares with other animals) and a capacity for intellectual development (which other animals lack). Most important, he has liberty, and therefore certain (still undeveloped) moral capacities. In the course of time, these endow-

---

and combine ourselves together into a civil body politic." A well-known example of the pact of government, also cited by Gough, is that "original contract" between the king and the people which James II was supposed to have broken. "Properly this has nothing to do with the foundation of the state," Gough remarks, "but presupposing a state already in existence, it purports to define the terms on which it is to be governed."

ments suffice to give rise to a certain minimal level of social intercourse and a modicum of technological development. Obligations and duties as such do not exist, but individuals may occasionally band together to the extent that it proves advantageous to do so.

Technological development, though largely fortuitous, has momentous consequences, of which the most important is the introduction of metallurgy. Eventually, a more settled form of existence succeeds the older, nomadic wanderings of primitive man. The family replaces solitude and grows into the tribe. Population grows. And fixed property—in the form of simple possession—comes into existence and begins to dominate human life: "The first man, who after enclosing a piece of ground, took it into his head to say, *this is mine*, and found people simple enough to believe him, was the true founder of civil society" (Pléiade edition, 3:164). With fixed property in existence, life becomes increasingly a struggle for its acquisition. And so, the essentially solitary existence of the first men is transformed into an increasingly competitive struggle for scarce resources in which opposed and often antagonistic social relations dominate.

At this point Rousseau resumes the argument. "I suppose," chapter 6 begins, ". . . that men have reached a point where the obstacles (*obstacles*) that endanger their preservation in the state of nature, prevail over the resistance of the forces (*forces*) each individual can employ to maintain himself in this state. Then this primitive state can no longer subsist and the human race would perish, unless it changed its mode of existence (*sa manière d'être*)" (1:6). We are, in short, in Hobbes's generalized state of war. Recall the account Hobbes offers of this "primitive condition" in chapter 13, Book 1, of *Leviathan:*

> As the nature of foul weather, lieth not in a shower or two of rain, but in an inclination thereto of many days together; so the nature of war consisteth not in actual fighting; but in the known disposition thereto, during all the time there is no assurance to the contrary. . . .
>
> Whatsoever therefore is consequent to a time of war, where every man is enemy to every man; the same is consequent to the time, wherein men live without other security, than what their own strength and their own invention shall furnish them

withal. In such condition, there is no place for industry; because the fruit thereof is uncertain; and consequently no culture of the earth; no navigation, nor use of the commodities that may be imported by sea; no commodious building; no instruments of moving and removing such things as require much force; no knowledge of the face of the earth; no account of time; no arts; no letters; no society; and which is worst of all, continual fear and danger of violent death; and the life of man, solitary, poor, nasty, brutish and short.

In the state of nature, "every man is enemy to every man" with the result so incommodious as to render desirable literally any "solution" that will guarantee stability and order. Rousseau, too, saw the human condition—abstracted from its political institutions—in this light. To be sure, for Rousseau, man is not by nature warlike, as Hobbes sometimes appears to suggest; but the advent of property does make man warlike. And so the state of nature becomes, in effect, a generalized state of war. We ought perhaps not to call it so, in view of Rousseau's insistence, remarked above, that war can pertain only between states and not between men. But if the state of nature is not strictly to be called a state of war, it surely amounts to the same thing. Rousseau's state of nature is Hobbesian. Man enters into the social contract to escape an unbearable situation; a state of nature become, let us say, a state of universal opposition.

For Hobbes, the state of universal opposition is unbearable because it is incommodious—life is "solitary, poor, nasty, brutish and short." While Rousseau, too, finds the state of nature incommodious, he sees in its development an inevitable crisis: "this primitive state can no longer subsist and the human race would perish, unless it changed its mode of existence" (1:6). The state of nature become a state of universal opposition is a limiting point, a critical moment in the existence of the human race. There is nothing in Hobbes that corresponds to this critical moment. For him, the motivation to leave the state of nature is a constant exigency of human life. And so it begins to appear that Rousseau has given a new dimension to the Hobbesian account. As a first approximation, we might say he has historicized it. We shall return to this point shortly. First, however, there are points to clarify. What are these "obstacles" and "forces" we are told are in mortal opposition? And precisely what does this opposition threaten?

The obstacles of which Rousseau speaks are not natural obstacles. The struggle with nature is a constant factor in the life of the human race and is little affected, at least at first, by political association. That struggle is not a moment in its history; still less a critical moment. Were these obstacles natural obstacles, there would be no reason to hypothesize their intensification coalescing into a critical conjuncture in which "the human race would perish unless it changed its mode of existence." Nor do these obstacles come from already constituted human groups outside the state of nature. Such groups, by hypothesis, have yet to be formed. These obstacles can only be *internal*, then, just as they were for Hobbes. They are the products of those pre-political social relations that constitute the state of nature.

Against these obstacles, Rousseau tells us, each individual possesses certain "forces." Clearly, in the state of nature, these "forces" can only be one's own person and one's possessions (*biens*). That possessions are to be included among the individual's forces has not yet been made explicit, though it is clear enough from what has already been said, particularly in the light of *The Second Discourse*. Three chapters later, however, Rousseau *is* explicit: "Every member of the community at the moment it is formed gives himself up to it, just as he actually is, himself and all his forces, of which the goods (*biens*) he possesses form part" (1:9). These forces—and liberty (at least, potentially)—are all that individuals in the state of nature possess. It is with these that they must face the obstacles that endanger their preservation in that state.

The inclusion of possessions among these forces is crucial for understanding the antagonism Rousseau depicts between forces and obstacles. With the inclusion of possessions, a new category is introduced by means of which the social contract will be conceptualized: private interest (*intérèt particulier*). Private interest, we shall see shortly, renders the social contract both necessary and possible. In Rousseau's account in the opening sentences of Book 2: "if the opposition of private interests has rendered necessary the establishment of societies, it is the agreement of these same interests that has rendered it possible" (2:1). With the introduction of possessions, private interest replaces or, better, supersedes the self-love (*amour de soi*) Rousseau describes in the opening pages of *The Second Discourse*. Self-love becomes rational egoism (*amour propre*), which is, then, a creation of that universal opposition Hobbes called a generalized state of war. Or, what amounts to the same thing, private interest is a product of social relations internal to humanity in the state of nature.

It is private interest, therefore, that allows us to conceive the antagonism Rousseau depicts between forces and obstacles. Forces and obstacles—because of the inclusion of possessions among our forces—are two aspects of the same entity, two sides of the same coin. Indeed, in a state of universal opposition, one man's obstacles are another's forces. There are not really two different entities— forces and obstacles—in conflict at all; rather, there is a single entity—the social relations of humanity in a state of nature— developing an internal opposition.

True to the contractarian tradition, Rousseau conceives this internal opposition by depicting individuals with forces, confronting obstacles. However, it is clear that the concept Rousseau uses is inadequate to its content; the real starting point of his account is not the individual at all, but the *social relations* of persons in the state of nature. This point, I think, Rousseau learned from Hobbes. To be sure, both Rousseau and Hobbes use an individualist idiom: in Rousseau's case, the appeal is to a mortal opposition between an individual's forces and the obstacles the individual faces; but these forces and obstacles are each just manifestations of the real starting point, social relations. Like Hobbes, Rousseau effectively revolutionizes the sense, if not the form, of the contractarian schema.[13]

It should be noted how paradoxical it is that the category *private* interest should elicit this transformation of sense, from the individual to the social. On the face of it, private interest would appear to be an eminently unsocial, individualist notion. Yet it is grounded in social relations. We shall encounter this curious situation again, in connection with the opposition Rousseau will depict between private wills and general wills.

13. Marx's criticism of Rousseau in his early essay "On the Jewish Question" (1843) takes Rousseau to task for assuming individuals can be abstracted from their social and political arrangements. While this criticism may well apply to true contractarian writers, I think I have already shown that Rousseau implicitly anticipates this objection. However, the main force of Marx's argument is hardly vitiated, for it is not so much Rousseau's methodology that Marx attacks as the *partiality* of his solution. For the young Marx, the state does not put an end to the universal opposition of the state of nature. It simply *dislocates* it—into civil society—thereby even intensifying universal opposition. That Marx never realized his debt to

Finally, it should be noted that the antagonism between obstacles and forces (properly understood as an internal opposition, an opposition *within* social relations) warrants the suggestion that Rousseau is describing a "dialectical contradiction," in the Hegelian sense. That is, a single essence, a totality—in movement—develops internal oppositions, structural instabilities within the totality. The totality stands divided against itself and in mortal danger, unless "it changes its mode of existence." That this is precisely the situation Rousseau depicts for social relations in the state of nature will be further corroborated as we reflect on what, according to Rousseau, the opposition of obstacles and forces threatens.

"The human race," we are told, "would perish [at this critical point in the development of universal opposition], unless it changed its mode of existence." Is it then the physical existence of humanity that is threatened? Does the state of nature, become a state of

---

Rousseau, and persistently assimilated him to the contractarian tradition, is clear from the opening sentences of the 1857 *Introduction* to *A Critique of Political Economy:*

> The solitary and isolated hunter or fisherman, who serves Adam Smith and Ricardo as a starting-point, is one of the unimaginative fantasies of eighteenth century romances a la Robinson Crusoe; and despite the assertions of social historians, these by no means signify simply a reaction against over-refinement, and reversion to a misconceived natural life. No more is Rousseau's *contrat social*, which by means of a contract establishes a relationship and connection between subjects that are by nature independent, at all based on this kind of naturalism. This is an illusion and nothing but the aesthetic illusion of the small and big Robinsonades. It is, on the contrary, the anticipation of 'bourgeois society', which began to evolve in the sixteenth century and in the eighteenth century made giant strides towards maturity. The individual in this society of free competition seems to be rid of the natural ties etc. which made him an appurtenance of a particular, limited aggregation of human beings in previous historical epochs. The prophets of the eighteenth century, on whose shoulders Adam Smith and Ricardo were still wholly standing, envisaged this individual—a product of the dissolution of feudal society on the one hand and of the productive forces evolved since the sixteenth century on the other—as an ideal whose existence belongs to the past.

Marx's curious insensitivity to Rousseau, as well as his unconcious debt to him, has been remarked by a number of Marxist writers, among them Della Volpe and Colletti.

universal opposition, threaten mankind with physical annihilation?

This seems to have been Hobbes's view. At any rate, Rousseau understood Hobbes this way, and took him to task for thinking so. For example, in the piece "On the State of War," with Hobbes clearly in mind, Rousseau writes:

> This unrestrained desire to possess everything is incompatible with the desire to destroy one's fellows; and the victor, having killed everybody else, would have the misfortune to be alone in the world where he would enjoy nothing even though he possessed all. What good are riches that cannot be communicated? What use would it be to possess the whole universe if one were its sole inhabitant? What use? Would one's stomach consume all the fruits of the earth? Who would bring together for the victor the products of all climates? Who would bear witness of his empire in this vast uninhabited solitude? What would he do with his treasures? Who would consume his products? By what eyes would be measure his power? I understand. Instead of massacring everyone, he would put everyone in irons, so that he might at least have slaves. But that immediately changes the entire sense of the question; and since we are no longer dealing with destruction, the state of war is annihilated. [Pléiade edition, 3:601]

In a state of universal opposition one seeks to dominate one's fellows, not to destroy them. There is no advantage in annihilating one's rivals. Thus, it is inconceivable that a state of universal opposition should result in the physical annihilation of the race.

In what sense, then, would the human race perish? The passage just cited already indicates the answer. The result of a state of universal opposition is not the physical destruction of the vanquished, but their reduction to slavery. The state of nature would transform humanity into masters and slaves, and, ultimately, into a single master and a race of slaves. In short, not our bodies but our liberty is threatened by the state of nature. It is not physical death that threatens us but moral death: the loss of that priceless and essential trait that allows us to fulfill our destiny as moral beings. The human race would indeed perish: it would lose its *humanity*.

And in losing its humanity, it would lose its "essence." Here we have in adumbrated form what Feuerbach and the early Marx, the best disciples of Rousseau after Kant, were to conceive as *aliena-*

tion: separation of Man from his essence.[14] Man's essence, his liberty, is alienated in slavery.[15] And the state of nature, a state of universal opposition, would reduce everyone to masters and slaves. The state of nature thus denies man his liberty: it threatens his essence, and only incidentally his person and property.

Thus the suggestion hazarded above, that the opposition of obstacles and forces be regarded as a dialectical contradiction, is corroborated further. The state of universal opposition that defines the social relations of individuals in a state of nature can now be called, with justification, a state of alienation. It is alienation that engenders the dialectical contradiction between obstacles and forces. Alienation is the 'motor' that works itself out through the development of internal oppositions. And these oppositions, as we shall see shortly, give rise to their own supersession (*Aufhebung*) in the social contract. Rousseau has produced, in effect, a Hegelian reading of Hobbes.

In other words, Rousseau took the Hobbesian account of the state of nature as a state of war a step further by recasting it as a "moment," a critical moment, in the development of humanity. For what Rousseau realized was what Hobbes, with different philosophical preoccupations, failed to see: that this state of universal opposition that Hobbes regarded—wrongly, according to Rousseau—as a state of war threatens not life, but liberty. The state of war threatens humanity itself, its essence and its destiny. The state of nature thereby separates man from himself; it is a state of alienation that renders humanity unable to "become what it is": a race of free moral agents. Instead, humanity, reduced to slavery, is "everywhere in chains," and those who believe themselves masters

14. This concept of alienation is familiar enough from Marx's *1844 Manuscripts*, though its most systematic elaboration may be found in Feuerbach's *Essence of Christianity*. The subject—Man—expresses the predicates which constitute his essence in an external object. This object becomes alien to him, and so the essence of man is passed into an alien being. Alienation, then, is *separation*—of humanity from what it really is, from its essence. The process of externalization of this essence is not developed by Rousseau, and so it would be an exaggeration to attribute the full Feuerbachian-Marxian theory to him. But the fundamental figure of separation is nearly explicit.

15. In Book 1, chapter 4, Rousseau expresses himself in these very terms. To be sure, by *alienation* he there means "to give or to sell." But as in the famous chapter on Alienated Labour in the *1844 Manuscripts*, this very prosaic, commercial sense of *alienation* effectively glides into the metaphysical sense of *separation*.

of others are the greatest slaves (1:1).[16] The point, then, is to recover one's freedom: to break the chains of slavery and to become a citizen. Or, to speak anachronistically but fairly, the point is to overcome alienation. The state of nature is an alienated condition; hence the motivation to escape it. The social contract is the means for effecting that escape.

The Formulation of the Fundamental Problem (1:6 continued)

The fundamental problem of political philosophy, already implicit in the polemical argument of chapters 2 to 4 is to be posed within the limits of the mortal contradiction of obstacles and forces. In the second paragraph of chapter 6, Rousseau makes this exigency explicit: "Now as men cannot create new forces, but only unite and direct those that exist, they have no other means to preserve themselves than to form by aggregation a sum of forces which can overcome the resistance, to put them in action under a single motive, and to make them act in concert" (1:6). The solution is to be found within the givens of the problem, within the world of alienated social relations of which individuals in the state of nature are both authors and victims. Posed this way, only one sort of solution is conceivable: to change one's "mode of existence."

This, too, is a Hobbesian motif: the refusal of any external solution. No new forces may be introduced; no salvation from without. The only resolution to the contradiction between obstacles and forces—an expression of alienated social relations—is to change "the disposition of forces"—the social relations—already present: "to form by aggregation a sum of forces which can overcome the resistance"—of alienation.

The fundamental problem of political philosophy is thus to be formulated in terms of individuals and their forces. Whence paragraph 3: "This sum of forces can only be born out of the gathering together (*concours*) of many; but the force and the liberty of each man being the chief instruments of his preservation, how can he pledge them without injuring himself, and without neglecting the cares that he owes himself (*sans négliger les soins qu'il se doit?*)" (1:6). Forces (including property) and liberty constitute the individual's private interest. Therefore, "the cares that he owes him-

16. This thought, too, has a Hegelian resonance. Recall the chapter on "Lordship and Bondage" (4,A) in *The Phenomenology of Mind.*

self" can only be protection and respect for life, property, and liberty. The two strains of argument—the one based on a critique of political philosophy (chapters 2 to 5), the other on an analysis of the state of nature as a state of alienation (chapter 6, paragraphs 1 to 3)—converge into the fundamental question of political life: "To find a form of association which defends and protects with the whole force of the community the person and possessions (*biens*) of each associate, and by means of which each, uniting with all, obeys only himself (*n'obéisse pourtant qu'à lui-même*) and remains as free as before" (1:6). Earlier, on the basis of the "negative" results of the first five chapters, it was suggested that the task was "to form a pact of association without sacrificing the liberty of any individual associate." Where does Rousseau's own formulation differ from this approximation? Precisely, I think, in the introduction of that concept Rousseau has yet to announce explicitly, but which, as we have seen, motivates the escape from the state of nature: *private interest.* It is the person, the possessions, and the liberty of each associate that the pact of association must protect. But the person and possessions of each associate are his forces, and forces (including possessions) plus liberty constitute private interest. The solution, then, that will allow for supersession of the mortal contradiction of forces and obstacles is to be in the private interest of each associate, precisely as Rousseau announces at the very outset in his introductory note: "In this investigation I shall always try to unite what right permits with what interest prescribes, so that justice and utility will not be divided."

The Solution (1:6 continued)[17]

The solution to the problem posed resides in the nature of the act by which a people becomes a people (chapter 5); and this act is a contract (chapter 1). The dialectical contradiction of forces and obstacles is to be "solved" juridically.

What is a contract? It is a relation of exchange, an exchange of performances, prominent in the juridical systems of the seventeenth and eighteenth centuries and used by political philosophers outside its sphere of strict application to account for the foundation and origin of political authority. To see what is involved, we might

17. In this section and the next, I am particularly indebted to Louis Althusser, "Rousseau: The Social Contract," pp. 14–22.

imagine an ordinary contract: for example, a lease between a tenant and a landlord. The landlord agrees to provide, say, lodging and some services in return for which the tenant agrees to pay rent to abide by certain regulations stipulated by the landlord. The agreement is regarded as binding juridically on both parties, provided, of course, each party fulfills its side of the agreement. Both parties bind themselves to do what is specified in order to effect a mutually advantageous exchange; an exchange in the private interest of each party.

Schematically, then, a contract is an agreement between at least two parties—the party of the first part (*P1P*), the party of the second part (*P2P*), and so on—to facilitate an exchange in which all parties give in order that they may receive. What motivates the exchange is the advantage of each party. Or, since "advantage" is to be construed as private interest, a contract is an exchange among a number of parties (at least two) in accordance with the private interest of each. The contract between tenant and landlord may be represented as follows:

As the arrows indicate, what the *P1P* receives, the *P2P* gives; and what the *P1P* gives, the *P2P* receives. This exchange will take place, assuming the rationality of the contracting parties, only if on balance it is advantageous for each party; that is, if it is in each party's private interest.

The classical political social contract respects this form absolutely. The contract is depicted as a mutually advantageous exchange between the people, the *P1P*, and the prince, the *P2P*. Schematically:

P1P (the people)	*P2P* (the prince)
obedience ← ⟶	protection and assurance of welfare

It should be obvious that this schema is unacceptable to Rousseau:

it plainly requires the forfeiture of liberty and the reduction of the people to slavery in the sense of Book 1, chapter 4.[18]

That Rousseau is quite conscious of the originality of his use of the strict, juridical action is signaled in paragraph 5: "The clauses of this contract are so determined by the nature of the act, that the least modification would render them vain and no effect; so that, although they may never perhaps have been formally enunciated, they are everywhere the same, everywhere tacitly admitted and recognized; until, the social pact being violated, each man regains his original rights and recovers his natural liberty, while losing the conventional liberty for which he renounced it" (1:6). The social contract is to be an entirely exceptional contract: everywhere the same and everywhere tacitly admitted and recognized, if not formally enunciated.[19] It is, in short, a unique solution to the problem formulated in paragraph 4. Its uniqueness is so critical that the slightest deviation from its content amounts to a reversion to the state of nature.

The clauses of this contract, Rousseau then declares, "rightly understood, are reducible to only one—. . . the total alienation of each associate with all his rights to the whole community (*l'alienation totale de chaque associé avec tous ses droits à toute la communauté*)" (1:6). This, then, is the solution, the answer to the fundamental question of political life. But how possibly is "total alienation" of *all* rights a solution? For haven't we just been told and

18. This schema is, of course, an oversimplification. Most often, the obedience promised by the people is only partial: certain "natural rights" are retained from the state of nature. This too is unacceptable for Rousseau (and Hobbes) for reasons that must await discussion at a later stage. However nuanced, though, this literal adaptation of the juridical model remains fundamentally characteristic of the tradition.

19. Unfortunately, Rousseau's language in this passage suggests that the social contract should be regarded as the foundation of *de facto* states. That this is not what he means is evident from the corresponding passage in the first version of *The Social Contract*, the fifth chapter of Book 1: "There are a thousand ways to assemble men, but only one to unite them. For that reason I provide in this work only a method for the formation of political societies, whereas in the multitude of aggregations that now exist under this name, there are perhaps not two that have been formed in the same way, and not one formed in the way I establish. But I am investigating right and reason and not disputing facts . . ." (Pléiade edition, 3:297).

made to understand that total alienation is impossible, indeed a contradiction in terms!

Total Alienation (1:6 continued)

Our difficulty does not arise from any equivocation: the "total alienation of each associate with all his rights" includes the alienation of liberty. The individual is supposed to do precisely what it has just been claimed he cannot do, what it is contrary to his nature to do—to alienate liberty. If the total alienation of all rights is to be conceivable as a solution, it must somehow avoid the result of chapter 4: it must not reduce each associate to slavery. But to be a slave, in the sense of chapter 4, is just to obey another, to forfeit one's liberty. In giving up everything, including liberty, the individual must somehow not give up liberty. It would appear that this total alienation is indeed impossible.

But recall of whom Rousseau requires this total alienation. We are asked to imagine as entering into this contract not individuals in full possession of their liberty, but rather victims of a state of alienation, individuals separated from their liberty. Men are born free, but are everywhere in chains. The task is to recover liberty and not, strictly, to maintain it. In the state of nature, liberty is forfeited involuntarily and unconsciously through the universal opposition private interest produces. To recognize necessity (to borrow Engel's expression) will be to recover what is lost, and to be free.

Let us focus on this claim more carefully, To be free, Rousseau has told us, is to obey only oneself (1:6). To alienate one's liberty is to give it away or exchange it (1:4)—that is, for some (impossible) reason, to agree to obey another. In the state of nature become a state of universal opposition, neither is one free (except, of course, potentially) nor has one, strictly, alienated one's liberty. Rather, one's liberty is alienated; one is in a state of alienation. Everywhere man is in chains, everywhere he does not "obey only himself." But this reduction to slavery has not been consciously willed. To alienate liberty without becoming a slave one, obviously, cannot alienate liberty to another; more interestingly, Rousseau seems to be saying that the unconscious and involuntary character of alienation must also be changed. Paradoxically, a necessary condition for solving the problem of alienation is the active, willed alienation of liberty.

This is a solution inferior to the givens of the problem. It is within the world of alienated social relations that "the total aliena- tion of each associate with all his rights" takes place. It amounts to a real change in "the mode of existence" of each individual and his forces. It is a redistribution of forces necessitated by the givens of the problem. Thus the dialectical schema is completed. Not only do we have an internal opposition (of obstacles and forces) produced by alienated social relations, but the internal opposition generates its own solution, its *Aufhebung*.

This solution, again, consists in the transformation of a total (forced) alienation into a total (willed) alienation. To be sure, it is not sufficient that the alienation be willed, for a willed alienation to another would still be slavery. But it is necessary, in Rousseau's view, that alienation be willed. The problem, then, is to conceive a total alienation that is willed and that is not an alienation to another.

We know that the device through which this total willed alienation is to be conceived is a contract (1:1), a mutually advan- tageous agreement, an agreement in the private interest of each associate. Indeed, in summarizing the result of Book 1, Rousseau writes: "if the opposition of private interests has rendered neces- sary the establishment of societies, it is the agreement of these same interests that has rendered it possible" (2:1). The point is to conceive a contract of total alienation.

When we attempt to do so, however, we immediately encounter a difficulty: who are the contracting parties? Clearly, the individual is one. And it is clear, too, what the individual agrees to give: everything—himself and all his rights (including liberty). Sche- matically:

$$\frac{P1P \text{ (the individual)}}{\text{total alienation} \longrightarrow} \qquad P2P (\qquad\qquad)$$

But to whom does the individual give everything? Rousseau's first answer (1:6, paragraph 6) is "the whole community," but what, after all, is this "whole community"? Indeed, was it not the point of the social contract to create this "whole community," to *constitute* it?

Here the paradoxical character of this unique solution begins to come to surface. In any contract, the contracting parties exist prior to and "outside" the contract. The mutually advantageous exchange is effected between two *different* parties. But this schema simply cannot be made to fit here. The *P2P*, what Rousseau calls "the whole community," exists neither prior to the contract nor outside it: it is constituted by the contract. Indeed, the goal of the contract, its end, is precisely to constitute the *P2P*. Contrary to the classical schema, and the strict juridical notion of a contract, the social contract Rousseau proposes is an agreement among parties of two different orders, the one existing outside the contract, the other created by it.

Moreover, this new creation has no real existence separate from that of the individuals who constitute it. "The whole community" is just the individuals themselves in "union," working in concert, put in action "by a single motive power." Apart from the contract, the *P1P* and *P2P* are the same. Their difference is strictly *internal* to the contract; it is a difference in form, in what Rousseau calls "mode of existence."

Rousseau does not quite acknowledge the differential structure of this singular contract. He comes closest to doing so in Book 1, chapter 7: "every individual, contracting so to speak (*pour ainsi dire*) with himself, is engaged in a double relation; as a member of the sovereign towards individuals, and as a member of the State towards the sovereign" (1:7). In giving ourselves to all, we give ourselves to ourselves. It is this equivocation in Rousseau's conception of "the whole community" that makes free total alienation possible; for if we can alienate everything (consciously) without alienating it to another, we avoid slavery. This is just what is accomplished in giving ourselves to all. Paragraph 8 summarizes: "Finally, each one giving himself to all, gives himself to nobody; and as there is no associate over whom we do not acquire the same rights which we surrender to him over ourselves, we gain the equivalent of all that we lose, and more force to protect what we have" (1:6). Free total alienation is possible because "every individual, contracting so to speak with himself" becomes no one's slave but his own. And to be one's own slave is to be no slave at all; it is to obey only oneself—to be free.

We see, in other words, that Rousseau has bent the juridical concept of a contract, a concept that is not, strictly, adequate to the real content of his thought. That social contract whose clauses are reducible to "the total alienation of each associate with all his rights to the whole community" is not really a contract at all; it is the condition for the possibility of a contract, the act of constitution of the $P2P$ of a possible contract. Yet it is conceived as a contract because of the differential status of the $P1P$ and the $P2P$, a differential status Rousseau does not, and cannot, fully acknowledge.

Why must this alienation be total? The question cannot be answered finally until Rousseau's conceptual apparatus is more fully laid out. Be we can begin to get a grip on the issue now. An indication is suggested in paragraph 7: "the alienation being made without reserve, the union is as perfect as it can be, and no associate can any longer claim anything; for if any rights were left to individuals, since there would be no common superior who could judge between them and the public, each being on some point his own judge, would soon claim to be so on all; the state of nature would continue to subsist and the associate would necessarily become tyrannical or useless" (1:6). The state of nature will cease, Rousseau claims, only if the individual cedes everything. Any partial alienation, any retention of rights or liberty, is an impossible concession to the state of nature. The condition for any political power whatever is that it be absolute in principle.

This is not so much an argument as a statement of a position. As already noted, Rousseau is not yet ready to mount a full-scale defense. However, two comments are in order even here.

First, this position is strictly Hobbesian.[20] In effect, Rousseau has taken over this aspect of Hobbes's analysis of political power without qualification. The least concession to the state of nature, Rousseau learned from Hobbes, is fatal to that political association the state of nature motivates.

Second, the claim that political power be absolute in principle should not be confused with the claim that political power ought to

20. Of course, for Hobbes, each individual retains the right to preserve his own life, even in opposition to the state. This is not the place to discuss his reasons, except to point out that Rousseau thought them inconsistent. See chapter 2, "On Liberty."

be total. I will show in the next chapter that Rousseau, while adhering rigorously to the thesis that political power can only be absolute in principle, is anything but proto-totalitarian.

Since for both Hobbes and Rousseau alienation must be total, the social contract cannot be conceived as a mutually advantageous exchange in the usual way. Universal opposition cannot be ended by a simple exchange. However, if the escape from the state of nature is to be conceived through the category of private interest, this non-contract must somehow function as a contract, as a mutually advantageous exchange. This is the central theme of the concluding chapters of Book 1. Rousseau's position is unequivocal: the individual must give everything, without holding anything back, as the condition for overcoming universal opposition. Paradoxically, that total alienation in virtue of which Rousseau's contract fails to satisfy the strict, juridical schema is what allows us to conceive the individual entering into an exchange motivated by private interest.

Before directly confronting this paradox and Rousseau's resolution of it, it will be appropriate to conclude this section by focusing briefly on the differences between Rousseau's and Hobbes's contracts of total alienation. To do so is to see what a *tour de force* Rousseau's use of total alienation is.

Rousseau takes over from Hobbes: (1) his analysis of the state of nature as a state of universal opposition (though he refuses to call it a state of war); (2) his refusal of any "external" solution; and (3) his contract of total alienation. Yet Hobbes's account led to what was for Rousseau an insupportable and even scandalous result: the forfeiture of liberty. Hobbes would have individuals agree among themselves (in strict juridical contracts) to alienate everything to a third party who remains *outside* the association and who gives nothing. This third party, the prince, is constituted by the contract but remains apart from it and the contracting parties. He receives, as it were, a *donation* of power. What is totally alienated is *given* to a third party. In effect, the contracting parties collectively agree to become slaves (in Rousseau's sense) by creating a master. For Rousseau, however compelling the theses that generate this result, the result itself is plainly unacceptable.

What Rousseau does, then, is to turn the result around— through the peculiar use he makes of total alienation. Hobbes's third party becomes Rousseau's *whole community*. Sovereignty is vested in the people, that is, in the individuals in a certain form of association. Thus, in alienating their liberty, the individuals still avoid becoming slaves. In this way, Rousseau preserves Hobbes's theoretical advance, his analysis of the constituents of political life, without succumbing to his disastrous conclusions. Rousseau gives an entirely new sense to the Hobbesian account by making the individuals alienate everything *to themselves.*

The Social Contract As a Contract (1:6 continued–1:9)

If the social contract is not a contract in the strict, juridical sense, that traditional sense is not entirely inappropriate to Rousseau's thought. Rousseau's social contract is *like* a real social contract; it functions as a contract. That is, it is conceived as an exchange, motivated by the private interest of each individual associate. This is the dominant theme of the concluding chapters of Book 1.

In the first place, through this contract one's person is protected from the consequences of universal opposition. The incommodiousness of the state of nature, stressed by Hobbes, is overcome. Man, at last, can flourish: "his faculties are exercised and developed; his ideas are expanded; his sentiments are ennobled; his whole soul is exalted to such a degree that, if the abuses of this new condition did not often degrade him below that from which he had emerged, he ought to bless without ceasing the happy moment that released him from it for ever, and transformed him from a stupid and limited animal into an intelligent being and man" (1:8).

Then, with regard to property, we are told that the individual, while alienating everything, gets everything back—but in a different, more advantageous form.

> What is singular in this alienation is that in accepting the possessions (*biens*) of individuals, the community, so far from robbing them of it, only assures them of its legitimate possession, changing usurpation into true right, enjoyment into property (*proprietè*). Then the possessors being considered the depositories of the public possessions (*biens publics*), and their rights being respected by all the members of the state, and maintained by all its forces against foreigners, they have, so to speak, by a transfer advantageous to the public and still more to themselves, acquired all that they have given up. . . .[1:9]

Civil property supersedes the simple possession of the state of nature. But this is, again, only a change in form. In alienating all their property to the whole community, the individuals have gained, because that transfer to the public is, in fact, a transfer to themselves; that is, not really a *transfer* at all.

Most important by far, liberty is protected and recovered. Here Rousseau even uses the language of accounting ("balance," "compare," "gain," "acquisition") to describe the advantage: "Let us reduce this whole balance to terms easy to compare. What man loses by the social contract is his natural liberty and an unlimited right to anything which tempts him and which he is able to attain; what he gains is civil liberty and property (*proprieté*) in all that he possesses ..." (1:8). The "unlimited right" to anything which tempts us, *natural liberty*, is superseded by *civil liberty*, the right to do what the law does not proscribe. This transformation is a direct consequence of the rule of law, and is asserted to be advantageous.

But the real advantage lies elsewhere. The passage just cited continues, "Besides the preceding, we might add to the acquisitions of the civil state, *moral liberty* (*la liberté morale*), which alone renders man truly master of himself ..." (1:8). The acquisition of *moral liberty*, the recovery of the human essence, is, finally, the *raison d'être* for the social contract. Humanity was morally free in the state of nature only potentially, and the state of nature become a state of universal opposition threatened to annihilate even this potentiality. It therefore became unthinkable that the state of nature should subsist indefinitely. The possibility of the annihilation of moral freedom is what makes the social contract absolutely necessary, even from the point of view of each person's private interest. Moral liberty—or, to anticipate, *autonomy*, in the Kantian sense—is the priceless benefit acquired in this "exchange."

In sum, Rousseau unquestionably regarded the social contract—with respect to both forces (including property) and liberty (the constituents of private interest)—as overwhelmingly advantageous.

But if we give up everything, how is it conceivable that we get back everything and more? Plainly, the differential status of the contracting parties will not in itself account for the resulting advantage. Rousseau needs to appeal to additional considerations. These considerations are suggested immediately after the announcement of the single clause to which the social contract is reducible: "since each gives himself up entirely, the condition is equal for all; and the condition being equal for all, no one has any interest in rendering it onerous to others" (1:6). Total alienation is advantageous because "the condition is equal for all." Equality, then, is what allows Rousseau to consider the social contract an advantageous exchange. Equality informs and structures the will of the *P2P*. It is a mechanism of self-regulation and self-limitation,[21] through which everyone stands to gain.

This is of course a strictly formal equality. Liberty apart, individuals in the state of nature have different forces—different bodies and abilities and unequal possessions. Some will have more to give up than others; but these same persons will also have more to lose by a continuation of universal opposition.[22] The state of nature become a state of universal opposition is the great equalizer, the leveler. It renders the formal equality of total alienation advantageous to all. No one has any *interest* in rendering the situation "onerous" to others, since one would thereby render it onerous to oneself. "Equality of rights and the notion of justice that it produces," Rousseau notes further on, "are derived from the preference which each gives to himself" (2:4).

Note that the real, material equality of persons *qua* (potential) moral agents—a presupposition of Rousseau's thought—does *not* figure at all in this calculation. There is no claim introduced about the inherent and equal worth of each individual, no appeal to human "dignity." Instead, the (formal) equality of total alienation is derived strictly from a calculation of self-interest in an original position already characterized by a considerable degree of (material) inequality.

Note, finally, that this mechanism allows us to complete the schema of the juridical notion of a contract. To this point, we could identify only the following elements of that schema:

P1P (the individual)	*P2P* ("the whole community")
total alienation ⟵⟶	?

21. See Althusser, "Rousseau: The Social Contract," pp. 27-30.
22. Indeed, in the *Second Discourse*, Rousseau goes so far as to suggest that the original institution of society was a kind of swindle, foisted on the poor by those who had more to lose. This is of course a speculation about the historical origins of society, in no sense opposed to the account of the foundations of *de jure* authority reconstructed above.

It was not clear what, if anything, the *P2P* gave back. Thus, we could not conceive this (pseudo) contract as a mutually advantageous exchange, as Rousseau clearly intended. Now the mystery is cleared up. The *P2P* offers *equality* in return for total alienation; it offers a formal equality that serves as a mechanism for self-regulation and self-limitation. Schematically:

P1P (the individual)	*P2P* ("the whole community")
total alienation ←――――――→	equality

This, finally, is the structure of Rousseau's social contract.

To sum up: the formal equality of total alienation is that which allows Rousseau to envision the social contract as an exchange. Equality serves as a mechanism of self-regulation and self-limitation within the *P2P* created by the contract. It is the presence of this mechanism, finally, which makes total alienation to the *P2P* in the private interest of each individual in the state of nature. In Book 2, chapter 4, Rousseau admits this result in almost the very terms I have suggested: "equality of rights and the notion of justice that it produces are derived from the preference which each gives to himself . . ." (2:4).

The General Will (1:6–1:9)

If private interest has rendered total alienation both necessary and possible, total alienation does not leave private interest untouched. For private interest is incompatible with the equality of total alienation. Where private interest exists, universal opposition has not yet been overcome. If it is in the private interest of each individual to overcome universal opposition, *it is in his interest as well, to overcome private interest.* To put this matter another way: in the original position Rousseau describes, a perfectly rational utility maximizer would stop maximizing utility!

The consequences of the social contract for *interest* and *will* will be the main focus of succeeding chapters. For the present, it will suffice to conclude this account of Book 1 with some notice of the indications of these central themes given there.

The crucial notion in all that is to follow is, of course, the *general will (la volonté générale)*, a notion first introduced in the penultimate paragraph of Book 1, chapter 6: "If then one sets aside all that is not of the essence of the social pact, one finds it is reducible to the following terms: 'Each of us puts in common his person and his whole power (*toute sa puissance*) under the supreme direction of the general will, and we receive every member as an indivisible part of the whole' " (1:6). To see that this conclusion follows immediately from what has gone before, all we need do is reflect on the following question: how does total alienation affect the conception of rational choice, of advantage, that motivates each individual associate in the state of nature?

As has already been suggested, what brings about a change in how we conceive of rational choice is the equality of total alienation. Personal and idiosyncratic differences cease to be relevant. Each person thinks of himself as a citizen and no longer as an individual (with private wants). "The voice of duty," writes Rousseau, anticipating even Kant's *formulation* of the same idea, ". . . succeeds physical impulse, and right (*droit*) succeeds appetite. Man, who until then had regarded only himself, sees that he is forced to act on other principles, and to consult his reason before listening to his inclinations" (1:8).[23] Citizens will act, as Kant will say, "for the sake of duty." Citizens are no longer, as in the state of nature, unique bundles of wants and desires; rather, they retain individuality only as *moral* personalities—with general wants.[24] In short, citizenship is incompatible with private interest.

To act in one's advantage as a citizen is not at all to act in one's private interest. It is to aim at an entirely different sort of interest, a moral interest. This new sort of interest abstracts from individual idiosyncrasies and characteristics. Accordingly, Rousseau calls it a

23. The text of Kant's that this passage parallels most closely is the portion of part 1 of *The Foundations of the Metaphysics of Morals* where Kant, trying to identify those human actions where a good will is clearly manifest, distinguishes actions done "for the sake of duty (*aus Pflicht*)" from those done "from immediate inclination (*aus unmittelbare Neigung*)" or "with a view to self-interest (*aus selbstsuchtiger Absicht*)," even when the latter are "in accordance with duty (*pflichtmassige Handlungen*)," and concludes that "to have moral worth an action must be done for the sake of duty".

24. Although these connections are best pursued at a later point, readers familiar with Kant will again notice a striking anticipation of Kant's account of the *universality* of the moral order, and his notion of a *kingdom of ends*, governed by a harmony of rational wills. A particularly relevant text for comparison is *The Foundation of the Metaphysics of Morals*, part 2, where these notions are introduced through a succession of distinct formulations of "the categorical imperative."

general interest (intérêt générale), as distinct from the private interest (intérêt particulière) of the state of nature. And since, for Rousseau, a will is distinguished by its object, by that for which it aims, there will be two different sorts of wills corresponding to these two different sorts of interests. The will that aims at a private interest will be called a private will (volonté particulière); the will that aims at a general interest will be called a general will (volonté générale).

✗   To say that the social contract consists in submission to "the supreme direction of the general will" is to say no more than that in the equality of total alienation, private interest is replaced by general interest.

In this light, the final paragraph of Book 1, chapter 6—which introduces the notion of sovereignty and other related notions—is perfectly clear:

> From that moment, instead of the private persons of all the contracting parties, this act of association produces a moral and collective body, which is composed of as many members as the assembly has votes, and which receives from this same act its unity, its common self (moi), its life and its will. This public person, which is thus formed by the union of all the individual members, formerly took the name of city, and now takes that of republic or body politic, which is called by its members state when it is passive, sovereign when it is active, power when it is compared to similar bodies. With regard to the associates, they take collectively the name of people and are called individually citizens, as participating in the sovereign power, and subjects, as subjected to the laws of the state. [1:6]

This is the world of the P2P, the world the social contract constitutes. It is within this new world that Rousseau's theory of right and obligation is to be situated. And as is already sufficiently clear, that theory will be developed by means of this notion of a general will—the will of this public person.

To conclude this chapter, I should like to point out what already appears to be a difficulty in these distinctions (private interest / general interest; private will / general will). This difficulty is related to that already exhibited for the social contract itself: the differential status of its contracting parties. Indeed, it might even be regarded as a consequence of Rousseau's way of finessing that first difficulty, as a "displacement" of the original problem.[25]

On the one hand, private interest and general interest (and their corresponding wills) are entirely disjoint. The general interest has nothing to do with the private interest it supersedes, no more than duty has to do with impulse or calculation of self-interest. The social contract effects a complete and thoroughgoing revolution in human life, fundamentally altering the interest that motivates human behavior. Indeed, as we shall see, it is private interest that threatens to undo the world created by the social contract. This is the fundamental point of all the "practical" portions of *The Social Contract:* the accounts of government, of opinion, of manners and morals, of education and civil religion, and so on.

But on the other hand, this public person formed by total alienation of each associate is just the associates themselves in a different "mode of existence." As we have seen, the two contracting parties, in the final analysis, are the same. And so too are their wills. The general will (that aims at a general interest) is just the private will (that aims at a private interest) in a different form— *under the form of generality imposed by the equality of total alienation.* The general will is a private will compelled, by its own logic, to the requisite generality of form.

In short, the general will both is and is not a private will.

This is the same structure—of identity and non-identity—that allowed Rousseau to conceive of a social contract in which the individual alienates everything without becoming a slave. The old puzzle, supposedly resolved, has only been shifted, or "displaced." The social contract solves the fundamental problem of political philosophy by dislocating and masking the puzzlement it elicits. That puzzlement now shifts to the notions of interest and will.

In elaborating the foundation of *The Social Contract* in Book 1, chapter 6, and its surrounding texts, has Rousseau really advanced beyond his starting point? Or is *The Social Contract* a devious circle?

---

25. See Althusser, "Rousseau: The Social Contract," especially pp. 146–54. Althusser's account of *The Social Contract* is built around a number of these "displacements (décalages)" in its conceptual structure.

2

The Sovereign

The "public person" established by the social contract is just the individual associates to the contract in a different (and differential) form of association. We have seen how this differential form allows Rousseau to conceive the social contract as a solution to the fundamental problem of political philosophy. We have also seen how this differential form, obscured in Rousseau's formulation of the social contract, re-emerges in the distinction between private and general wills. This chapter examines this distinction from the point of view of Rousseau's theory of sovereignty.

The framework for the investigation is already indicated by the definitions Rousseau proposes in the final paragraph of Book 1, chapter 6: that "public person" the individuals establish, Rousseau writes, "is called by its members *state* when it is passive, *sovereign* when it is active" (1:6). To form a state by convention is to establish sovereignty, supreme authority in its "active" aspect. Insofar as the individual associates participate in the sovereign power, they are *citizens;* insofar as they are obligated by it, they are *subjects.* Thus, for Rousseau, everyone is simultaneously a citizen and a subject, a participant in the sovereign and a member of the state. These are just different aspects of the public person, aspects Rousseau calls respectively *active* and *passive.*

That an examination of sovereignty (and citizenship) is, at the same time, an examination of the general will is clear enough from what has already been said. To be a participant in the sovereign, a citizen, is to will what is in the common or general interest: to put one's person and forces "under the supreme direction of the general will." The general will holds supreme authority; it *is* sovereign. Thus, in Book 2, chapter 1, Rousseau is merely resuming the argument of the preceding book when he declares sovereignty to be "nothing but the exercise of the general will." Sovereignty is the general will in its active aspect; it is its "exercise." This "exercise of the general will," is the subject of the first six chapters of Book 2 and the first two chapters of Book 4.

In reconstructing Rousseau's account, it will be less useful to follow Rousseau's order of presentation than was the case in the last chapter. Perhaps nowhere else in *The Social Contract* is there so much insight and so little system. Rousseau himself is perfectly lucid about this disorganization. "All my ideas are connected," he remarks in exasperation, "but I could not expound them all at once" (2:5). Nor does he do the next best thing: expound them systematically. I think this lack of system accounts, at least in part, for some of the more serious failings of Rousseau scholarship, particularly the confusion about his alleged totalitarianism. We shall return to this question further on.

In any event, if one approaches the text through Kant, an ordering concept that effectively structures the argument of the opening chapters of Book 2 does suggest itself: the notion of *law*. In this light, the key text—for which all the rest is really just commentary—is the chapter on law: Book 2, chapter 6.

Law (2:6)

For Rousseau, law is the essence of sovereignty. The sovereign is, by definition, that which issues laws; laws are, by definition, that which the sovereign issues. So far, then, the claim is strictly definitional and circular.

Since sovereignty is "nothing but the exercise of the general will," and since the sovereign is that which issues laws, we can say that the general will *expresses itself* in laws. For this reason, we can also say that the activity of citizens is to legislate. To create a sovereign, then, is to create a law-making apparatus, a legislature.

To give "existence and life to the body politic," writes Rousseau, is "to give it movement and will through legislation" (2:6).

Plainly, this account will be useless unless it is possible to break out of the pattern of circular definitions. The need is to identify laws—and, therefore, acts of sovereignty—independently, to distinguish laws from other enactments that (falsely) claim authority. If criteria can be found for identifying laws, we shall have an effective test for determining whether an enactment is legitimate; whether it has sovereign authority; whether the individual is under a moral obligation to obey. In short, we shall have criteria for determining whether or not the general will is expressed. In the same way, since law is the essence of sovereignty, and since sovereignty is the active aspect of the *de jure* state, we shall also have a test for distinguishing the *de jure* state from *de facto* states.

Book 2, chapter 6, begins the elaboration of such criteria. Two necessary conditions are stipulated. As we shall see, there are circumstances—of particular relevance for a Kantian reading of Rousseau—where these conditions are both necessary and sufficient for an enactment to count as law.

The first condition is that the enactment be *general in its object*. That is, the law must always consider "subjects as a body and actions as abstract, never a man as an individual nor a particular action" (2:6). The object of the law can only be the whole community, the *P2P*. If inequalities within the *P2P* are to be sanctioned by law—or, better, if the law is to give rise to unequal treatment of the members of the whole community—these inequalities or differences of treatment cannot be specified by reference to a particular individual or action. "No function which has reference to an individual object appertains to the legislative power" (2:6).

This condition follows from the stipulation that law is the expression of the general will. The general will, by definition, is that will which aims at a general interest, the interest of the *P2P*. To make mention of any particularity is to detract from the generality of this interest and to accede thereby to private interest. The generality of the object of the law is just the generality of the interest towards which a general will aims.

Rousseau apparently intends this condition quite literally; it is to be a strictly *formal* requirement for enactments. In other words, the form of the enactment, and not its effective content, is at issue:

"The law can indeed decree that there shall be privileges, but it cannot confer them on any person by name; the law can create several classes of citizens, it can even assign the qualifications which give persons title to rank in these classes, but it cannot nominate such and such persons to be admitted to them; it can establish a royal government and a hereditary succession, but it cannot elect a king or name a royal family" (2:6). Individuals may be treated quite unequally by the law, but these individuals may not be named by the law. Opportunities for unequal treatment sanctioned by law must be independent, in their formulation, of any particularity. Operationally interpreted, this stipulation means that a law cannot name particulars or, what amounts to the same thing, *groups* of particulars.

Rousseau does not say so, but I think it obvious that this requirement should be extended so as to rule out trivial attempts to contravene it. Specifically, we ought to exclude formulations that, while not naming particulars explicitly, do so effectively through definite descriptions. The law could not, on Rousseau's condition literally interpreted, have the form "Smith shall do x." Then neither should it, presumably, have the form "All persons satisfying some description [where that description picks out Smith uniquely] shall do x." If this extension is warranted, then Rousseau's condition should read: the law cannot name particulars (or groups); nor can it be formulated in such a way that it is equivalent in meaning (sense) to a formulation that names particulars (or groups). When this condition is satisfied, the law is "general in its object."

An admissible formulation cannot name particulars (or groups) or be equivalent in sense to a formulation that does. However, an acceptable formulation can plainly be *extensionally equivalent* to these proscribed formulations, by denoting the same inequalities of treatment. One wonders, then, what the force of the restriction is. The requirement that the object of the law be general is supposed to function as a *test* on enactments. Its viability as a test depends on whether it effectively allows or proscribes enactments by exclusive attention to their formulation. By Rousseau's account, for a given class of extensionally equivalent enactments, some will be allowed (namely, those formulated properly), while others will be proscribed (those that name particulars). But can't these proscribed enactments simply be reformulated?

An example may make this objection clearer. We shall see further on that a function of this condition, in Rousseau's view, is to protect the individual (or group) from the tyranny of the majority. Rousseau would want to say that in a racially divided society, for example, with a white majority and a black minority, a majority rule enactment of the form, say, "all black people shall be killed" could not possibly have the (moral) force of law because the object is a group (of particulars) and not the whole community. The formulation "all black people" is just a shorthand expression for naming particulars. However, it becomes unclear at this point what counts as a general formulation. Suppose the legislature were to enact the measure "the majority shall be entitled to kill whatever persons displease it." This formulation would certainly satisfy Rousseau's requirement of generality. Then why couldn't the legislature just get around the proscription of "all black people shall be killed" by passing the enactment in this extensionally equivalent form?

The requirement that the object of the law be general anticipates Kant's requirement that the maxim that determines individual actions be universalizable. For Kant, each person is supposed to ask himself whether he could consistently will that everyone, regardless of particular circumstances, should act on his maxim. However, this test, too, appears to be an empty one. For with sufficient ingenuity almost any maxim can be consistently universalized. All one need do is characterize the proposed action in such a way that the maxim will allow the agent to do what he wants, while prohibiting others from doing what would render the maxim problematic if universalized.[1] In both cases, it appears that exclusive attention to form will not yield the desired distinctions of content, that the proposed tests are empty because they are purely formal. Now is not the time to decide finally on this question. Generality of object is only one condition among others, and we must determine, finally, how Rousseau's conditions work in aggregate. At this point, however, the strategy of passing judgment on enactments by focusing on their form does not appear likely to succeed.

As a second condition, the law must be general in its *source:* it must issue from the entire *P2P*, from "the whole community." All the people must legislate. One is subject only to a law one has

1. Alasdair MacIntyre, *A Short History of Ethics* (New York, 1966), pp. 197–98.

enacted. Rousseau says almost nothing in support of this requirement, but his rationale is clear enough, at least in its general
direction. Since the general will is the will of the whole community,
the laws in which the general will is expressed must issue from the
whole community. We shall see in the next section how literally
Rousseau intends this requirement.

Generality of object and generality of source are necessary
conditions for law. Were reason fully in control, were law-abidingness the citizens' exclusive motive (to use a Kantian formulation),
then I think Rousseau would regard these conditions as both
necessary and sufficient—that is, as *criteria* for identifying laws or
acts of sovereignty. Later on, Rousseau introduces further requirements which amount to necessary and sufficient conditions. But the
concern at this point in the text is not so much with the identification of laws as with the elaboration of the general character of
law as such. As we shall see, the additional conditions Rousseau
will stipulate are "practical"; their function is to impose the motive
of law-abidingness. Indeed, Rousseau's practical injunctions are
concessions to that all-too-human moral recalcitrance that prevents
the realization of the moral world order.[2] Generality of object and
generality of source will not serve to identify acts of sovereignty
because we are "taking men as they are"—with an almost insur-
mountable inclination to be unreasonable. For Rousseau, this tendency is realized in the individual's persistence in entertaining
private interests.

For now, then, the point is that while not quite *criteria* for
identifying laws ("taking men as they are"), generality of object
and generality of source are the essential conditions of lawful
enactments. "When the whole people enact concerning the whole
people, they consider only themselves; and if a relation is then
formed, it is between the entire object under one point of view and
the entire object under another point of view, without any division
at all. Then the matter on which they enact is general, as is the will
which enacts. It is this act that I call a law" (2:6).

In this light, the foundation of society by a contract, as presented in

2. This is a central theme of one of the most important Kantian interpreta-
tions of Rousseau, Ernst Cassirer's *The Question of Jean-Jacques Rousseau*.
Cassirer blames imperfect rationality, dominated by passion, for the pessimism which he sees dominating Rousseau's political thought.

Book 1, chapter 6, appears in a more adequate perspective. The social contract gives sovereignty to the whole community; or, better, it constitutes the whole community as sovereign. Sovereignty, however, is "nothing but the exercise of the general will," and the general will is expressed in laws. Thus, the sovereign created by the social contract is a legislature, a legislature consisting of all individual associates assembled together to legislate. The social contract creates or, to use a spatial rather than temporal metaphor, *underlies* every legitimate act of legislation. It is, in other words, in these acts of legislation that the social contract is empirically realized. Every act of legislation, every act of sovereignty, is an act "by which a people becomes a people." The pact of association is continually "renewed" (to resume, once more, the temporal metaphor) because it is continually presupposed. So far from being an original instance, the social contract is always an actual one, when and insofar as sovereignty exists.

In this light, too, a number of apparently unrelated and puzzling theses can be seen to follow directly from the social contract. These theses can be grouped under two headings, corresponding to the two conditions stipulated for law: generality of object and generality of source. The drawing out of these implications is the principal task of the opening chapters of Book 2. I shall consider first those implications that follow from the condition that law be general in its source.

Sovereignty Is Inalienable and Indivisible (2:1-2,3:15)

That sovereignty is inalienable and indivisible, the theme of the opening chapters of Book 2, is put forward as a direct consequence of the establishment of society by a contract. Nothing is added to the account presented in Book 1, chapter 6; the object, instead, is to lay bare the implications of that account. Rousseau's method in these opening chapters is 'analytic' or 'regressive' in the Kantian sense.

It is as members of the sovereign, as citizens, that the individual associates, though subjects of a supreme authority, "obey only themselves and remain as free as before." In the form of sovereignty, neither liberty nor sovereignty itself can be alienated. The individual cannot give up what is literally priceless: the right to determine his own destiny, to obey only himself. As Rousseau has already discussed at length (in Book 1, chapter 4), there is no way in principle to motivate such an alienation, no way to make it thinkable. Liberty is inalienable; so, therefore, is sovereignty. For the alienation of sovereignty is just the alienation of liberty in political society. To alienate sovereignty is to alienate each individual's *essential* right to determine his own destiny. It is to become a slave.

Rousseau intends this injunction to apply literally. Never, under any circumstance, can the individual relinquish the right to determine himself, and still remain free: "sovereignty, being nothing but the exercise of the general will, can never be alienated and the sovereign, which is just a collective being, can only be represented by itself; power indeed can be transmitted, but not will" (2:1). In other words, even representative institutions are proscribed. On Rousseau's account, to represent sovereignty is to alienate it. "Sovereignty cannot be represented for the same reason that it cannot be alienated; it consists essentially in the general will and the will cannot be represented" (3:15). If we regard the sovereign as a legislative *apparatus,* we can already discern an essential feature of its constitution: all decision making will be direct. Indeed, any law that is not directly legislated by the entire people is invalid; it is literally not a law. A nation that allows its legislative power to be represented is, accordingly, a nation of slaves, whence Rousseau's celebrated commentary on the English: "The English people think they are free, but are greatly mistaken. They are free only during the election of members of Parliament. As soon as they are elected, they are enslaved and count for nothing. The use which they make of their brief moments of freedom renders the loss of liberty well deserved" (3:15). Whatever the merits of Rousseau's case against representation, the issue is simply an illustration of the more basic point with which we are now sufficiently familiar. Sovereignty is the exercise of the general will; the general will is expressed in laws; laws are general in their source. This last, purely formal requirement is absolutely essential. The legislation of laws must be direct.

For this reason Rousseau would not allow the enactment of laws even by an infallible judge of the general will, imagining such a judge to be possible.

The sovereign may indeed say: "I will know what a certain man wills or at least what he says he wills"; but it cannot say, "what this man wills tomorrow, I shall also will," since it is absurd that the will should bind itself (*se donne des chaînes*) for the future, and since it is not incumbent on any will to consent to anything contrary to the welfare of the being that wills. If then the people promises simply to obey, it dissolves itself by that act, and loses its quality as a people. The moment there is a master, there is no longer a sovereign, and forthwith the body politic is destroyed. [2:1]

Even perfect representation (were it conceivable) would be slavery. This injunction is not at all prudential in inspiration. The reason it is "absurd that the will should bind itself as regards the future" is not that it is unreasonable to suppose that any individual or group would always will what is in the general interest. That such a supposition is unreasonable is true, but beside the point. For even if, as is very unlikely, there were an infallible willer, his will would bind only himself. A free individual must decide for himself. He must deliberate. He must engage in practical reasoning. He must, in short, take active responsibility for legislation. To delegate authority to representatives and then to consent—openly or tacitly—to the resulting enactment is not, for Rousseau, sufficient for taking responsibility. It is not enough to consent, nor even to participate. One must legislate; one must decide. To do less is "to renounce one's quality as a man."

For this reason, too, sovereignty is indivisible. No part of the public person can legislate for the whole. "For the same reason that sovereignty is inalienable, it is indivisible; for the will is either general, or it is not; it is either that of the body of the people, or that of only a part. In the first case, this declared will is an act of sovereignty and constitutes law. In the second, it is only a private will or an act of magistracy—it is at most a decree" (2:2).[3] To be sure, a part can *determine* the whole; indeed, for Rousseau, as we shall see, the majority typically determines the whole. But a part, no matter how large, cannot *legislate* for the whole. The footnote

3. In brief, the sovereign issues *laws*; the government issues *decrees*. The outstanding point of difference is the degree of generality of the enactment. This distinction will be discussed in connection with Rousseau's theory of government in Book 3.

Rousseau added to the passage quoted above carries this sense: "That a will be general, it is not always necessary that it be unanimous, but it is necessary that all the votes be counted; any formal exclusion destroys the generality."

That sovereignty cannot be represented follows as well from this thesis as from the preceding one. Since sovereignty is indivisible, no part—that is, no legislature where part of the sovereign represents the rest—can legislate for the whole. Since sovereignty is indivisible, legislation must be direct.

It is obvious that the indivisibility of sovereignty, already implicit in the idea of a social contract, has profound implications for the theory of government and its relation to the sovereign. Rousseau introduces this topic polemically in the concluding paragraphs of chapter 2. Its theoretical elaboration is the subject of Book 3.

It was noted earlier that the inalienability of sovereignty is just the inalienability of liberty from a different point of view: from the point of view of the whole community, the *P2P*. That liberty is indivisible is a thesis Rousseau took over from Hobbes, virtually without argument. It is because of this Hobbesian thesis that partial alienation is impossible, that the condition for the establishment of political society is that alienation be absolute in principle. In Rousseau, this claim is taken for granted: it is one of the conditions for posing the fundamental problem of political philosophy. On the other hand, the indivisibility of sovereignty is nothing more than a consequence of the stipulation that law be general in its source. Nothing Rousseau says in this regard bears in any way on the indivisibility of liberty or, what comes to the same thing, the impossibility of partial alienation.

At this point, it will be useful to draw together what has so far been established about the sovereign. Three theses have been advanced:

1. Sovereignty is inalienable.
2. Sovereignty is indivisible.
3. Sovereignty cannot be represented.

Of these, (3) is an immediate consequence of both (1) and (2). And (1) and (2) are each simply different formulations of the same thought:

4. The "end" of the social contract is to establish the assembled people as a legislature.

(1), (2), and, therefore, (3) are just elaborations of (4); and (4) is just the result of the argument in Book 1, chapter 6, with the following additions:

5. The sovereign's activity is to issue laws.
6. The law is general in its source.

Thus, the sovereign of the *de jure* state will be the assembled people, issuing laws directly.

Of these additional assertions, (5) is crucial. The sovereign is that which has authority, which issues commands by right. In the state of nature, each person is potentially—but not actually—his own sovereign. It is to recover self-determination, to actualize this potential, that the individual enters into the social contract. Then, for reasons we have discussed, the individual is bound by the general will (sovereignty being "nothing but the exercise of the general will") not as an individual personality with private interests, but as a member of the state, a moral community. The individual is a moral personality, with general interests. Accordingly, Rousseau claims, he can only be addressed generally, as a member of the moral community; for his individual personality is superseded. The sovereign addresses its subjects in laws, and to issue commands by right is necessarily to issue laws.

Virtually nothing has been said so far in defense of (6). Indeed, it will be necessary to inquire more deeply into this world of morally binding laws before even an indication of a defense of (6) will become apparent. This investigation will lead directly to the central concept of Rousseau's political thought: autonomy. Ultimately, as we shall see, very little will in fact be said in defense of this most fundamental principle. Rousseau's political philosophy, in the final analysis, will be seen to lack *foundations.* It might not be inappropriate at this point once again to hazard the suggestion that a central motivation of Kant's investigations in moral philosophy was to remedy this lack.

The Object of the Law (2:3)

The law is general both in source and object. It must will by and for the whole poeple, the *P2P.* In both cases, the requirement is interpreted formally: for an enactment to have the force of law, all individuals must actively legislate, and no individual may be named. I have tried to show how, in Rousseau's view, these conditions are both necessary and sufficient for law as such, apart from the all-too-human tendency to succumb to private interest. Rousseau's contention, in other words, is that perfectly rational agents engaging in legislation will "discover" the general will; that they will will what is in the general interest.

This position depends on the truth of an unstated and undefended presupposition: that there is a general interest with respect to any question posed to the sovereign. Sovereignty exists, if it does exist, only because its *object* exists; that is, only because a general interest exists.[4] Hence, there must be a general interest on all specific questions on which the assembled people legislate, a right answer to the question "What is to be done?"

It must be stressed that, for Rousseau, the answer to this question is *factual.* There *is* a general interest; the point is to discover it. There is no question, as in the liberal (and contemporary pluralist) tradition, of resolving conflicting social forces to produce a *fair* outcome. (Indeed, conflicting social forces are incompatible with the *de jure* state). The point, instead, is to discover a matter of fact. For Rousseau, legislation serves the ideal of truth, not justice.

Rousseau is perfectly lucid about the consequences of this presupposition. His argument in Book 2, chapter 3, that the general will "cannot err" is a trivial consequence of the existence of a general interest; for, by definition, a general will aims at a general interest. If a will is truly general, by definition it cannot err in willing the general interest.

Where the general interest is not willed, then, we should not say that it does not exist. It has simply not been discovered. The general will (because of the existence of its object) is indestructible; it always exists. But it is not always revealed: "the general will is always right (*droite*) and always tends to the public good; but it

4. This claim of course includes, but also goes beyond, the thesis that each person has an interest in preserving the social unit, the *P2P*. To construe matters this way is to remain in the realm of private interest; indeed, it is to revert back to Hobbes. If the social contract does indeed bring the individual under the reign of his "true," *general* will, it can do so only insofar as this will has an *object,* only insofar as there is a general interest on all substantive matters of legislation.

does not follow that the deliberations of the people always have the same rectitude. One always desires one's own good, but one does not always see it. The people are never corrupted, but often deceived, and it is only then that they seem to will what is evil" (2:3). The parallel with private interest drawn in this passage is instructive. There is a private interest, Rousseau believes; a right answer to the question "What is to be done?" posed, let us imagine, by an individual in the state of nature. But the individual may be deceived; he may fail to act in accordance with his true interest. He still has a private will, but he has failed to discover it. The private will, too, it might be said, it always right and cannot err, though it may be eluded. In the same way, the general will exists—discovered or not—whenever the *P2P* exists. It is indestructible and also, as Rousseau adds somewhat cryptically, "constant, unalterable and pure" (4:1).

These, then, are the principal conclusions Rousseau draws from the view of law as general in its object. We may add these results to those enumerated in the preceding section. Then it follows that sovereignty, which is "nothing but the exercise of the general will," is inalienable and indivisible, indestructible, constant, unalterable, pure and unerring.

We have seen, however, that the feasibility of drawing these conclusions rests on the presupposition that a general interest exists. It rests, in short, on that concept whose paradoxical structure was suggested at the end of the last chapter: an interest constituted by private interest, yet at the same time radically distinct from it and even threatened by it. We shall have to contend eventually with this paradoxical structure, but first it must be drawn into sharper focus and its field of operation more carefully delineated.

Autonomy

It will be well at this point to focus directly on Rousseau's special sense of liberty as autonomy.

Strictly speaking, 'autonomy' ought not to be identified with 'liberty', for Rousseau uses 'liberty' in two additional, distinct senses. There is, first of all, the *natural liberty* (*liberté naturelle*) of man in the state of nature: liberty as the absence of coercive restraint, of (deliberate) restrictions. This is the sense of liberty taken over and developed by the liberals. It has its place in the *de jure* state, albeit in modified form; for with the social contract, individual human conduct is brought under the rule of law. *Civil liberty (liberté civile)* is the right to do whatever these laws do not forbid (1:8).[5] It is what becomes of natural liberty with the establishment of the state.

There is, however, a third sense of liberty, the sense in which man is "born free." This sense is only potential in the state of nature, but becomes actual by means of the social contract. This is what Rousseau calls *moral liberty (liberté morale)* and defines as "obedience to a self-prescribed law" (1:8). I prefer to call 'moral liberty' by its Kantian name—*autonomy*.

Indeed, we already know that to be free is to obey only oneself (1:6). We know, too, that the social contract is supposed to preserve and guarantee this freedom by placing each person and his forces "under the supreme direction of the general will" (1:6). And we know, finally, that the general will is expressed in laws (2:6). It follows, through the social contract, that to be free is to legislate for oneself; that is, to obey only those laws one has oneself legislated. To be free is to be self-legislating, to be autonomous.

It is clear enough how central autonomy is to Rousseau's thought. It is that concept in which converge the three fundamental notions by means of which political right has so far been envisioned: liberty, will, and law. To be free is to be self-determining, to obey no will other than one's own. And to be self-determining is to be self-legislating, for the will is expressed in laws. It is misleading, then, as I have suggested earlier, to regard the problem of political philosophy as the reconciliation of liberty and authority; for the two are one and the same. To be free is to be self-legislating; and authority, if it exists, is self-legislated. The question is not to reconcile these two concepts, but to show how authority can be self-legislated.

This is the burden of Rousseau's discussion of the mechanism by which the general will is supposed to be discovered—the method of majority-rule voting.

5. The connection between this use of 'civil liberty' and the more current sense derived from liberal political philosophy will be considered further on, in connection with 2:4–5. For now, it should be noted how idiosyncratic Rousseau's definition is.

Voting (4:1-3)

Just as laws are essentially formal in character, the method by which they are enacted is essentially procedural. The assembled people will vote on all questions of legislation; each citizen will count equally in the determination of the outcome; and a simple numerical majority will (in most cases) decide the issue. In Book 4, chapter 2, Rousseau declares this procedure implicit in the social contract itself—a consequence, presumably, of the notion of popular sovereignty.

The connection between majority-rule voting and popular sovereignty is certainly plausible intuitively, but it will be useful to try to make the connection explicit: to reconstruct how the method of majority decision suggested itself to Rousseau.[6] Plainly, if the people must legislate for itself for an enactment to have the force of law, then the method by which this determination takes place should be one where *only* the preferences of the sovereign people are taken into account. But the sovereign, as we know, is just the ensemble of individual citizens in a certain form of association. We may conclude that the decisions of the individuals collectively must serve as the exclusive ground for the determination of the enactment. This process of legislation may be construed as a collective decision problem, as illustrated in the following flow diagram:

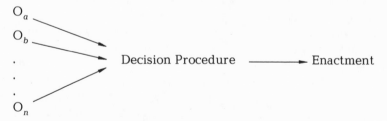

The input O_a, O_b, ... O_n represents the ordering of different possible enactments by the individuals $a, b, \ldots n$ (leaving aside, for the time being, the grounds on which the individual arrives at an

6. There are obviously many *external* motivations prompting the connection: the increasing role of majoritarian institutions in the eighteenth century, the importance of majority-rule voting in influential political theories (for example, Locke's), and so on. But I am concerned here only with motivations that are *internal* to Rousseau's conceptual framework.

ordering).[7] The decision procedure combines these orderings to produce an enactment as output. In other words, the process of legislation can be seen as the generation of an enactment through a decision procedure in which all citizen's orderings (of the enactments in contention) are aggregated.

How are we to conceive this decision procedure? All we know so far is that each citizen's ordering is to be combined in some way. But we recall that by total alienation, which is supposed to establish this procedure, "each giving himself up entirely, the conditions are equal for all" (1:6). Citizenship is inherently equal; any unequal relation, for Rousseu, is tantamount to slavery. So we may conclude from the equality of total alienation that each citizen's ordering is to count equally in the determination of the social choice. We know, in short, that we cannot assign differential weights to orderings: inputs to the decision procedure are to count equally, and there will be as many inputs as there are citizens.

We may therefore considerably restrict the range of possible decision procedures. Let n be the number of voters whose orderings are to be aggregated; this number will of course be equal to the number of citizens who collectively constitute the sovereign. Then there is a number d, where $d \leq n$, that we may define as that number which is *decisive* for an enactment according to a specified decision procedure. Where $d = n$, unanimity of all citizens is required for an enactment. Where $d = \frac{n}{2} + 1$, a simple numerical majority is decisive. There are as many possible decision procedures as there are integers between n and 1, and the range of likely candidates, for our purpose, will be that between n and $\frac{n}{2} + 1$.[8] In other words, we have to decide between unanimity, three-quarters majority-rule voting, two-thirds majority-rule voting, and so on—down to simple majority-rule voting.

7. See the appendix to this chapter.
8. Decision procedures in which a number smaller than a simple numerical majority (smaller than $n/2 + 1$) is decisive *for* an enactment are formally equivalent to procedures in which a number greater than a simple numerical majority is decisive *against* an enactment. If procedures requiring that a decisive number be greater than a simple numerical majority are weighted in favor of the status quo, as will be illustrated below, then minority rule procedures are, in the same way, weighted against the status quo. *In fact, apart from this difference, they simply are majority rule procedures.* Thus, if we do not specify whether d is decisive for or against an enactment, the only range possible is that between n and $n/2 + 1$.

How are we to decide? Intuitively, what we want is the most democratic procedure, the procedure that will best reflect the preferences of individual citizens. We might suppose that unanimity would be the best procedure; that is, we might suppose that all citizens must agree on an enactment for that enactment to become a law. This would obviously be a democratic procedure— everyone's preference would be reflected perfectly in the determination of the social choice. But, unfortunately, it is in most circumstances extremely unlikely that unanimity will be attained, and without unanimity, it would be impossible to arrive at a positive enactment. Only in the very few cases where all citizens agree could a law be made. The decision procedure then would be weighted as heavily as possible toward maintaining the status quo; indeed, a single individual could block an enactment. And the same difficulty holds, in diminishing degree as we approach simple majority-rule voting, for any decision procedure requiring that a number greater than a simple majority be decisive.

So, contrary to our initial expectation, it appears that the procedure most consonant with popular sovereignty—the procedure least biased for or against the enactment of a law—is simple majority-rule voting.

It should be stressed that Rousseau does not himself advance this argument, nor does he apply its conclusion very strictly in practice. I think it is fair to say that implicit in his account is a presumption in favor of simple majority-rule voting, for the reasons just indicated. But this presumption may, where appropriate, be overridden by a conservative bias for the status quo, requiring appropriately larger majorities.[9]

The question of elections is ultimately one where wisdom alone can balance the countervailing presumptions to determine how large a majority should count as decisive for an enactment: "With

9. Roughly, for the conservative, the status quo is at least tolerable and change is likely to be for the worse (or, at least, in most cases, to be not worth the risk). Wisdom dictating a certain caution, the presumption would be against change, except where there is overwhelming pressure for it.

The more fundamental the measure in contention, the more force would underlie the conservative argument, because where the proposed change is fundamental, the danger of going disastrously wrong is all the greater. For this reason nearly all *de facto* democracies require large majorities (and frequently other safeguards as well) for important measures, and particularly for those that bear on the constitution of the state.

regard to the proportional number of votes for declaring this [general] will, I have given the principles according to which it may be determined. The difference of a single vote destroys unanimity; but between unanimity and equality there are many unequal divisions, at each of which this number can be fixed according to the condition and needs of the body politic" (4:2). Rousseau is a majority-rule democrat, to be sure; but he is not dogmatically committed to simple majority-rule voting, except as a principle. He is willing to countenance and sometimes even to accede to conservative arguments for larger majorities.

In any event, the sovereign may now be viewed as a legislative apparatus that decides questions of legislation by majority-rule voting. This legislative apparatus, then, must somehow institutionalize individual autonomy. Yet how can it possibly do so? For is not the minority compelled by the majority against its will? Once more, we appear to find ourselves in a hopelessly paradoxical situation. Popular sovereignty requires that the minority be compelled, and yet popular sovereignty is incompatible with any compulsion.

It is this paradox that Rousseau confronts in the final paragraphs of Book 4, chapter 2: "As a result of the original contract, the votes of the greater number always obligate the other; this follows from the contract itself. But it will be asked how can a man be free and yet forced to conform to wills that are not his own. How are opponents free and yet subject to laws they have not consented to?" (4:2). This question, Rousseau replies, is "wrongly put." He then proceeds to put it right, producing what must be the most puzzling passage of *The Social Contract:*

> The citizen consents to all the laws, even to those which are passed in spite of him, and even to those which punish him when he dares to violate any of them. The constant will of all the members of the state is the general will; it is by that that they are citizens and free. When a law is proposed in the assembly of the people, what is asked of them is not exactly whether they approve the proposition or reject it, but whether it is conformable or not to the general will, which is their own. Each one in giving his vote expresses his opinion thereupon; and from the counting of the votes is drawn the declaration of

the general will. When, therefore, the opinion contrary to my own prevails, that simply shows that I was mistaken, and that what I considered to be the general will was not so. Had my private opinion carried, I should have done something other than I wished; and in that case I should not have been free. [4:2]

The original question was: how can one be free and yet be forced to conform to wills other than one's own or, what amounts to the same thing, to obey laws to which one has not consented? The answer to this question is simply that one cannot. To be free is to be autonomous; that is, to be self-determining or self-legislating. The interesting question, to which the above passage is a reply, is rather different: how are popular sovereignty and autonomy to be conceived together? Surely the minority's actions are heteronomously determined—by the majority. Haven't we then come full circle? For if the majority determines the minority, then surely the minority is forced to conform to a will other than its own or, equivalently (since the will is expressed in laws), to obey laws to which it has not consented. This is a result Rousseau must avoid at all costs if he is indeed to deduce a *de jure* state. In short, he must somehow show that the minority is autonomous while obeying the majority. This would appear to be a hopelessly impossible endeavor; yet Rousseau believes he can succeed.

The Majority Rules (4:2)

Rousseau's resolution of this paradox is indicated in the passage just cited: the minority is autonomous even when it obeys the majority because the majority decision is what it *really* wants.

This claim must be carefully distinguished from a superficially similar position with which it may be easily confused. It is not being claimed that what is right is what the majority decides. Rousseau's commitment is not to majority rule voting *per se;* he is not a majoritarian in that sense. His claim is, rather, that what is right is right independent of what anybody, including even the majority of voters, thinks, and that the majority of the assembled people, properly interrogated, will, as a contingent matter of fact, discover the right answer.[10]

It is absolutely essential that the people be properly interro-

10. This point is made by Brian Barry, *Political Argument,* p. 292.

gated. Let us recall Rousseau's account of this interrogation: "When a law is proposed in the assembly of the people, what is asked of them is not exactly whether they approve the proposition or reject it, but whether it is conformable or not to the general will, which is their own. Each one in giving his vote expresses his opinion thereupon" (4:2). The voters are to be asked their opinion as to what the general will is. They are to enter into the voting process as seekers after the truth. The vote and the surrounding deliberations in the assembly of the people are to have the character of a debate in which all participants strive collectively to discover a matter of fact: the general interest. As we shall see further on, the entire burden of Rousseau's practical political thought is to construct a voting situation that does indeed have this character. To be properly interrogated, then, is to be asked: "Is it advantageous to the state?" (4:1). When the voters address themselves to this question, Rousseau contends that the majority will discover the right answer. In other words, majority-rule voting, in the first instance a collective decision procedure, is envisioned, finally, as a method for discovering a matter of fact.

The minority, Rousseau continues, is autonomous only when it obeys the majority; for only then is it determined by the general will, which is its own. Only then does it do what it *really* wants. The minority, in Rousseau's deliberately paradoxical expression, is "forced to be free" (1:7); in being compelled by the majority, it is being compelled by itself, by its true will. Rousseau plainly delights in the paradoxical character of this result: "At Genoa we read in front of the prisons and on the irons of the galley slaves the word *Libertas*. This application of the device is becoming and just. In effect, it is only the malefactors in all states who prevent the citizen from being free. In a country where all these people are in the galleys, the most perfect liberty will be enjoyed" (4:2 n). But this is just the appearance of paradox. For given Rousseau's assumptions, the conclusion he draws follows straightforwardly and without too much difficulty. To understand, let us reconstruct Rousseau's argument for the minority's autonomy when (indeed, insofar as) it obeys the majority. This argument, we see immediately, depends on two related theses.

The first of these was already evident in the account of law as general in its object (2:6): the assertion that there exists a general interest. There must be a general interest in order for the question

"Is it advantageous to the state?" to have an answer—an answer independent logically of what anybody thinks. Only if there is a general interest on every question that comes before the assembled people can it be a matter of fact whether or not a measure is advantageous. We shall return to this issue in later chapters in connection with the practical ramifications of Rousseau's political thought. At this point, it is enough to note that nowhere in the text does Rousseau attempt a direct defense of this claim, on which his entire account rests.

The second thesis is that this general interest is discovered by majority-rule voting. Obviously, the second thesis presupposes the first: there must be a general interest, if it is to be discovered. We must provisionally concede the first thesis, then, in order to evaluate the second. Thus, in what follows, it will be taken for granted that the question "Is it advantageous to the state?" can be answered with the same objectivity as, say, "Is the sum of seven and five equal to twelve?" Conceding this objectivity, we may ask whether there is any reason to regard majority-rule voting as an infallible method for discovering this matter of fact.

Remember that Rousseau imposes very strict conditions on voting. Since the law must be general in its source, everyone must be directly involved in legislation. And since the law must be general in its object, everyone must be asked a question bearing on the generality of the object: "Is it advantageous to the state?" "Is it in the general interest?" And, finally, we must assume certain background conditions to guarantee the genuineness of the interrogation. Each voter must address himself disinterestedly, as a citizen with a general will, to the task of ascertaining the general interest. There must be no contravening private interest. As we shall see later on, the mere presence of private interests in the P2P is enough to undo the legitimacy of the enactment; to undo, in effect, the P2P itself. Rousseau is so emphatic on this point that the long passage cited above from 4:2, where Rousseau makes the argument for majority-rule voting, is followed by this rider: "This supposes, it is true, that all the marks of the general will are still in the plurality; when they cease to be so, whatever side one takes, there is no longer any liberty" (4:2). Rousseau seeks to guarantee the genuineness of the interrogation in several ways. The general strategy is to deal with private interest by suppressing it: by suppressing, concretely and materially, all partial associations that generate private interests—groups, orders, estates, classes, parties. The individual must confront the question before the assembled people directly, without any intervening mediations and contravening private interests.

The voting procedure, then, is rather like the pooling of expert opinions on some question of fact. Each individual, insofar as he is interested only as a citizen, insofar as his private will is genuinely superseded, is, for Rousseau, an expert in ascertaining the general will. Rousseau's contention is that an assembly of disinterested experts confronting a question of legislation directly, after full deliberation and debate, will arrive at the right answer. Our initial impression to the contrary, the claim is surely not implausible.

What Rousseau says in support of this position is scant and uncharacteristically obscure. It might almost be said that Rousseau just assumes the majority's ability to discover the right answer. If there is any direct defense at all, it is to be found long before the discussion of voting and elections, in an often quoted passage from Book 2, chapter 3: "There is often a great deal of difference between the will of all (*la volonté de tous*) and the general will; the latter regards only the common interest, while the other regards private interest, and is only a summation of private wills; but take away from these same wills the pluses and minuses which cancel one another, and the general will remains as the sum of the differences." What is particularly confusing about this passage is Rousseau's apparently deviant use of *private will* to stand for a will that aims mistakenly at a general interest. The point appears to be that if the assembly is properly interrogated—so that everyone does in fact aim at a general interest—the various wrong answers will somehow cancel each other out. At least, Rousseau is so understood by Brian Barry, who has offered an ingenious reconstruction of this line of argument.[11] Barry suggests that the initial implausibility of Rousseau's position is a consequence of our not being used to thinking of "right answers" in politics. Accordingly, he suggests that we replace the political context with one where we are used to thinking there are right answers. Suppose we have a group of at least competent arithmeticians before whom is set an arithmetical problem of some difficulty. If the problem is very difficult, not everyone will get the right answer, though among competent arithmeticians there will be at least a tendency towards

11. For what follows, cf. Barry, *Political Argument*, pp. 292-93.

unanimity. However, Barry suggests, "those who do go wrong are just as likely to be too high as too low in their answer; and the right answer is more likely to get a majority than any single wrong answer." This explanation is plausible and, insofar as the political case is like the arithmetical one, Rousseau's position would appear equally plausible.

Barry goes on to call attention to a theorem worked out originally by the Marquis de Condorcet in the eighteenth century in connection with juries.[12] According to this theorem, if every voter has an equal and above 50 percent chance of getting the right answer, the majority of the group will have a significantly higher probability of getting the right answer than any single member of the group. More precisely, if each member of the group is right in proportion v (verité) of the cases, and wrong in proportion e (erreur), so that $v + e = 1$, then if in a given instance h members of the group give one answer and k members another, where $h > k$, the probability that the h members are right is given by the expression:[13]

$$\frac{v^{h-k}}{v^{h-k} + e^{h-k}}$$

For example, if $v = 60$ percent and $e = 40$ percent—not an unreasonable assumption for experts in ascertaining the general will—and $h = 51$ and $k = 49$, the probability that the majority h is right is:

$$\frac{60^2}{60^2 + 40^2}$$

12. Cf. Barry, *Political Argument*, pp. 292–93. See also Brian Barry, "The Public Interest," *Proceedings of the Aristotelian Society*, supplementary volume (1964); and Duncan Black, *The Theory of Committees and Elections* (Cambridge, 1958) pp. 164–65. On Condorcet, see Gilles-Gaston Granger, *La Mathematique Sociale de Marquis de Condorcet* (Paris, 1956).

13. In accordance with Bernoulli's. Theorem, the probabilities of the different possible outcomes where $h + k$ members are reaching a decision are given by the different terms of the expansion of $(v + e)$ raised to the $h + k$ power. Thus, the probability that $h + k$ will give a right judgment is:
$$v^{h+k}$$

For $h + k - 1$, the probability of a right judgment is:
$$v^{h+k-1}$$

or approximately 69 percent. A majority of only two, in other words, has a 9 percent greater chance of being right than a single individual in a group whose members have a 60 percent chance of being right! And as the majority increases, the probability that it will be right increases exponentially.[14]

To be sure, this rather unanticipated help supports a claim slightly different from Rousseau's. For Rousseau, the majority is *certainly* right, if only it is properly interrogated. Rousseau's is, on the face of it, an unlikely claim in any event, inasmuch as the majority's being right is presented as a contingent matter of fact. It would be odd to expect certainty in contingent matters. In any case, Condorcet and Barry have supported a weaker but surely more sensible thesis: that the majority is *very probably* right,

---

and so forth. Similarly, the probability of a wrong judgment by $h + k$ would be

$$\frac{(h + k)!}{h! \; k!} \; x \; v^h e^k$$

And the probability that h members will give a wrong judgment is:

$$\frac{(h + k)!}{h! \; k!} \; x \; v^k e^h$$

It follows:

$$\frac{\text{Probability of rightness}}{\text{Probability of wrongness}} = \frac{v^h e^k}{v^k e^h}$$

Therefore, the probability that the judgment taken by h members of the voting community is right is given by the expression:

$$\frac{v^h e^k}{v^h e^k + v^k e^h} = \frac{v^{h-k}}{v^{h-k} + e^{h-k}}$$

Q.E.D. Similarly, the probability that the judgment of h members is wrong is:

$$\frac{e^{h-k}}{v^{h-k} + e^{h-k}}$$

14. If we let x stand for the probability that h is right, that is, for

$$\frac{v^{h-k}}{v^{h-k} + e^{h-k}}$$

then if v and e are constant, $h+k$ is constant,

$$\frac{dx}{dh} = 2x^2 \left(\frac{e}{v}\right)^{h-k} log \; \frac{v}{e}$$

which is positive for $v > e$, so that x increases continuously.

provided it is properly interrogated, and provided each individual has an equal and greater than 50 percent chance of being right. This additional rider is plainly compatible with Rousseau's account: the assembled people consists of citizens equally expert— *qua* moral selves—in detecting the general will.[15] The difference, then, lies just in the weakening of "certainly" to "very probably." In the former case, we have an extremely unlikely article of faith; in the latter, a powerfully corroborated position. But will Rousseau's argument work with this weakened thesis?

Let us recall the structure of the argument at this point. We know, from Book 1, that the individual cannot remain in the state of nature, for the state of nature threatens his essence, which is liberty. We know now that the liberty in question is to be understood as autonomy. We know, too, that no way out of the state of nature whose price is the forfeiture of liberty (autonomy) is possible. The necessary solution, if it exists, will be one that will allow autonomy and authority to co-exist. We have seen how this solution consists in the total alienation of each associate with all his rights to the assembled people; that is, to the individuals themselves in a different "mode of existence." The people have a will—a general will—that is expressed in laws. Since this will is the will of each individual *qua* citizen, the individual preserves his autonomy when he places himself "and his whole power under the supreme direction of the general will." The only problem, then, is to discover the general will.

In 4:2, Rousseau proposes a way to deal with this problem. We know we have discovered the general will if we know that the question "Is it advantageous for the state?" is correctly answered. For then we have discovered what each individual must want if his autonomy is to be preserved and maintained. But how can we know when we have answered this question correctly? There is plainly no way to check our opinion against the facts. The best we can hope

15. It is surely reasonable to suppose that an expert will have at least a 50 percent chance of being right, particularly when questions are posed in the form: Is it advantageous to the State? If the assembled people are only called upon to decide yes or no, they have a 50 percent chance of being right, even should they decide at random. One might, however, want to quarrel with the supposition that each citizen has an equal chance of being right. Surely differences in intellectual capacities, if nothing else, would render this supposition dubious. Strictly, all one need suppose is that the *average* chance of being right is greater than 50 percent.

to do is to hit upon a collective decision procedure, a device for pooling our opinions, that we have reason to suppose is also a general-interest-discovery procedure. Happily, the method of majority rule—for Condorcet's and Barry's reason, if not for Rousseau's—is such a procedure.

The individual in the state of nature, then, faces the following choice: he may choose to be heteronomously determined, through either the alienation of liberty in the state of nature or its forfeiture in some illegitimate convention; or he may seek to retain his autonomy, to actualize it. Since autonomy is priceless, it is obvious which choice private interest dictates. To retain his autonomy, however, he must find a way to enact laws that are general in source and bear on the general interest. The first requirement is met by the individuals deciding collectively to become equal citizens of the legislative assembly of the entire people. And the Condorcet-Barry theorem is plainly relevant for fulfilling the second requirement. The majority is more likely to be right than any single individual, and much more likely as the majority grows. (Unanimity, which would be optimally desirable, is unworkable as a general rule, for reasons already noted; and is, in any case, just the upper limit of majority rule). It is plain that the individual has no choice but to opt for majority rule.[16]

Were majority rule an infallible truth-discovery procedure, as Rousseau holds, and not just a very good one, the individual would have all the more reason to choose it. As it is, he has more than sufficient reason.

This line of argument would appear to contravene the principle established earlier that simple majority-rule voting is the best procedure, the one most compatible with popular sovereignty, because it is the least biased for or against the enactment of a law and therefore the most sensitive to the popular will. Now we see that the greater the majority, the greater the probability that the majority is right, and hence the more certainty that autonomy is maintained. But, on reflection, it is far from clear how this result affects our earlier conclusion. To be sure, large majorities are desirable, and in making social arrangements one ought to do

16. This discussion of course assumes that majority rule is a *coherent* procedure for aggregating individual judgments (about what the general interest is). This assumption is questioned in Appendix 1.

everything one can to encourage their occurence.[17] But should society require them? Apart from the conservative considerations noted above (considerations of a very different order), there does not appear to be any good reason to do so. The balance that must be drawn between these conservative considerations (insofar as Rousseau does give them credence) and the requirements of popular sovereignty would appear to be unaffected by the Condorcet-Barry theorem.

It must be repeated, finally, that this whole argument rests on the assumption that a general interest (on every question that comes before the legislature) exists. This claim is the cornerstone of Rousseau's theory of sovereignty. For only if there is a general interest can there be a general will, a true will of each individual, acknowledged or not, through which authority and liberty can coexist.

This general interest must, then, be more than a Platonic "golden lie," more than a legitimating myth. It is not enough for the citizens to *believe* there is a general interest and *aim* toward it. Aiming toward a general interest may cement social solidarity and foster a sense of citizenship, but it will not in itself guarantee autonomy. Autonomy is realized only insofar as the citizen is determined by his true will,[18] and this will can only exist if its object exists.

For Rousseau, to be sure, the general interest does play an important legitimating role—important for cementing social solidarity and fostering citizenship. But the whole enterprise cannot rest on a lie, even a universally entertained "golden lie." Alienation is no less real if it is unperceived. In short, the point is not for the people to believe themselves free, but for them to be free. Rous-

17. This point could be argued independent of Rousseau's requirement that autonomy must be preserved: if stability (and, therefore, consensus) are social goals, as has been a dominant theme in political and social thought at least since Hobbes, then large majorities (indicative of consensus) are plainly desirable.

18. In Kant's later writings in moral philosophy a parallel distinction is drawn between a person's express will (*Willkür*) and what, from a moral point of view, is his true will (*Wille*). Kant, too, stresses the social basis of *Wille*, its inconceivability outside a community of rational wills, "a kingdom of ends (*ein Reich der Zwecke*)."

seau's goal is not citizenship for citizenship's sake but for the sake of the moral life.

The theory of sovereignty requires a real, solid cornerstone: the general interest. But this cornerstone is simply assumed. In Part 2, we shall examine Rousseau's attempt to *create* this cornerstone, to fashion a general will. That attempt is indicative: if it is necessary to create the general will, it is because the existence of its object, the general interest, is deeply problematic. We shall see how problematic.

To this point, however, I have tried to give an account of the theory of sovereignty built upon this (precarious) idea. By way of concluding my account, I shall illustrate the resulting theory by focusing on its limits. This is the question Rousseau takes up in chapters 4 and 5 of Book 2: What, if anything, is left to the individual? What remains, in other words, of natural man's rights?

On Liberty (2:4-5)

What rights has the individual against the state? In principle, none at all—because of the total alienation that establishes sovereignty. In this sense, Rousseau's thought is strictly illiberal.[19] It has been suggested that Rousseau should even be seen as a precursor of totalitarian theory and practice.[20] I think this sense of the bearing of Rousseau's political thought is entirely mistaken. Rousseau's

19. By *liberalism* here, I mean the tendency in political thought that affords a central place to the principled defense of individual and minority rights against the claims of the state and broader society. It is convenient and fair to see a text like John Stuart Mill's *On Liberty* as the *locus classicus* of this tendency. As is well known, Mill attempted to delineate areas of individual life within which certain types of (coercive) interference can never be rightful.
20. See, for example, J.L. Talmon, *The Rise of Totalitarian Democracy*. To the same effect, Bertrand Russell has written: "Ever since his [Rousseau's] time, those who considered themselves reformers have been divided into two groups: those who followed him and those who followed Locke. Sometimes they cooperated, and many individuals saw no incompatibility. But gradually the incompatibility has become increasingly evident. At the present time, Hitler is an outcome of Rousseau; Roosevelt and Churchill of Locke." *A History of Western Philosophy* (New York, 1945), p. 645. Russell's claim is not quite typical. It is more common to connect Rousseau with what some liberal critics like to call "totalitarianism of the left."

position is illiberal, to be sure, but *not* because of the (allegedly proto-totalitarian) total alienation some critics inveigh against. Contrary to initial expectations, Rousseau's total alienation seems to have liberal implications.

Let us consider how Rousseau himself describes "the limits of the sovereign power," formed by the total alienation of each associate with all his rights. Book 2, chapter 4, examines this question directly:

> If the state or city is nothing but a moral person whose life consists in the union of its members, and if the most important of its cares is its own conservation, it needs a universal and compulsive force to move and dispose of each part in the manner most expedient (*convenable*) for the whole. As nature gives each man an absolute power over his limbs, the social pact gives the body politic an absolute power over all of its members; and it is this same power which, when directed by the general will, bears, as I have said, the name of sovereignty. [2:4]

When directed by the general will, the state is like an organism. And as the parts of an organism have no rights against the whole, neither have the subjects (who collectively constitute the state) any rights against it.

In principle, then, there is nothing over which the sovereign may not legislate; no domain that remains, as in classical liberal theory, inaccessible to rightful state interference. The individual has alienated in principle all right to determine himself, all individual sovereignty.[21]

To mark off an area in which state interference is inadmissible in principle, as Mill and others attempted, is to conceive the foundation of society, as Locke did, in a still partial alienation. And alienation can only be total, as we know, if the state of nature (and its threat to autonomy) is put to an end. In short, the argument against theoretical liberalism is already implicit in the thesis of total alienation.

The proto-totalitarian interpretation of Rousseau rests, entirely, on this theoretical illiberalism. Once it is granted that the

21. Of course, in doing so, as we have seen, the individual recovers his self-determination (autonomy); indeed, this total alienation is the condition for the possibility of that autonomy becoming actual.

state *can* (rightfully) do anything, then, it is argued, the state *will* (actually) do anything and everything. Totalitarianism is the alternative to liberalism.

But what are the real consequences of this theoretical illiberalism for what the liberal would want to call the individual's rights? In my view, they are not at all what those who see Rousseau as a proto-totalitarian suppose. Indeed, Rousseau's account of the *absolute* authority of the sovereign, so far from undoing all of these rights, gives them, if anything, a firmer foundation than liberal theory can provide. To restate my thesis: Rousseau's theoretical illiberalism is liberal in its consequences. The illiberal bearing of Rousseau's thought in practice has nothing to do with this theoretical illiberalism. It arises, instead, out of the theory's confrontation with the world.

It is clear enough that Rousseau does not envision very much state interference in the lives of the state's subjects. He even stresses how the social contract, far from suppressing "natural liberty," preserves and protects it with the full force of the political association (in the form of "civil liberty"). It is thus that the "simple possession" of the state of nature is turned into full-fledged and legitimated "property." The total alienation of each associate's possessions (*biens*), "so far from robbing them, only assures them lawful possession, and changes usurpation into true right, and enjoyment into ownership" (1:9). Political association actually protects what the tradition would call "natural rights." But how is this possible if the sovereign is constituted by the total alienation of each associate *with all his rights?* The answer has already been given: *the general will can proscribe or enjoin only what is in the general interest.*

In contrast to liberalism, one cannot—in principle and apart from consideration of specific cases—declare any domain out of bounds to the sovereign. But in most domains, the sovereign will not, in fact, have any interest. Rousseau writes: "It is admitted that whatever part of his own power (*puissance*), goods (*biens*) and liberty each person alienated by the social compact is only that part of the whole of which the use is important to the community, but we must also admit that the sovereign alone is the judge of this importance" (2:4). And further on, he bolsters this claim by appeal to the principle of sufficient reason: "All the services that a citizen can render to the state he owes to it as soon as the sovereign demands them; but the sovereign for his part, cannot impose on its subjects any constraint (*chaine*) which is useless to the community. It cannot even wish to do so; for by the law of reason, no less than by the law of nature, nothing is done without a cause" (2:4). These passages exhibit the two sides of Rousseau's theory of liberty. Anything may be required by the sovereign. But not very much will be. Each side is of equal importance. And each follows directly from the social contract itself.

Anything may be required, even that the individual give his life for the state. On this issue, Rousseau is explicit:

> The social treaty has as its end the preservation of the contrac-tees. Whoever wills the end also wills the means thereto, and these means are inseparable from some risks, even some losses. Whoever is willing to preserve his life at the expense of others ought also to give it up for them when necessary. Now the citizen is not the judge of the peril to which the law wills that he expose himself, and when the Prince has said to him: "It is expedient to the state that you die," he ought to die; because it is only on this condition that he has lived in security to this time, and since his life is no longer merely a gift of nature, but a conditional gift of the state. [2:5]

The argument is directed against Hobbes, for whom the individual is under no (moral) obligation to accept the sovereign's *rightful* infliction of death; for example, in punishment.[22] The discussion of the right of the state to institute capital punishment that concludes

22. In Book 1, chapter 14, of *The Leviathan*, Hobbes writes: "A covenant not to defend myself from force, by force, is always void. For, as I have showed before, no man can transfer or lay down his right to save himself from death, wounds and imprisonment, the avoiding whereof is the only end of laying down any right; and therefore the promise of not resisting force, in no covenant transferreth any right; nor is obliging. For though a man may covenant thus, *unless I do so, or so, kill me;* he cannot covenant thus, *unless I do so, or so, I will not resist you, when you come to kill me.* For man by nature chooseth the lesser evil, which is danger of death in resisting; rather than the greater, which is certain and present death in not resisting."

In short, the state is justified in taking the individual's life, but the individual is equally justified in resisting. Rather than concluding from this that the Hobbesian contract falls just short of a contract of total alienation, I prefer to follow Rousseau in concluding that Hobbes has failed to see all the consequences of a contract of total alienation.

Book 2, chapter 5, is particularly apt. Hobbes is faulted for not following the thesis of total alienation with sufficient rigor to its logical conclusion. If the condition for the formation of the sovereign is the total alienation by each associate of all his rights—of his person and forces—then even the right of self-preservation is passed on to the sovereign.

Here we see, again, how fundamentally total alienation transforms each individual's interest. From the point of view of a person in the state of nature, life, surely, is of value equal to autonomy. Indeed, it is its precondition. For this person, Hobbes's position would be appropriate and undeniable. Persons in the state of nature *do* enter into the social contract for self-preservation; but of course not only, nor even mainly, for this reason. However, with the social contract, the situation is transformed entirely. For the citizen of a *de jure* state, this conception of interest, with its underlying individualism, is overcome. The citizen has no interest, except as an integral member of the sovereign (which, of course, is his true interest). Thus, even his very life is no longer, strictly, his, as it was in the state of nature. It is, instead, "a conditional gift of the state."

But if the state can require anything, in the ordinary course of events, it will not require very much. A well-functioning state will have little reason to expose its citizens to death, nor will it have much cause to invoke capital punishment. Though capital punishment remains a prerogative of the sovereign, its frequent use, Rousseau remarks, "is always a sign of weakness or indolence in the government" (2:5). The same holds for more prosaic infringements on what liberal theory would construe as individual rights. This speculation, more than just plausible, is built into the logic of the social contract itself. Anything may in principle be required by the sovereign because of the total alienation that establishes it; but not very much will in fact be required, because of the mechanism that renders this total alienation advantageous to each associate— the equality of total alienation, and the corresponding generality of the law.

Total alienation is advantageous for each party to the social contract because the law is equal for each party and aims at the common good. Of course, the possibility exists that enactments satisfying these conditions will violate liberal principles. But the likelihood is necessarily remote. The supposed infringement would have to result from an enactment *that names no individual specifically*, and it would have to be in the *general interest.* As I have already suggested, I am skeptical about the first of these requirements; I doubt that it is really restrictive. With sufficient ingenuity, an enactment could be formulated that affects particular individuals (intentionally) without *naming* them. Such an enactment would surely violate the spirit of the requirement, but not, I think, the letter. In any case, the substantive support for liberal values (if not liberal principles) lies with the second restriction: that the enactment be in the general interest.

There is a curious parallel here with the central argument of John Stuart Mill's *On Liberty*, the classic and definitive presentation of theoretical liberalism. As will be recalled, Mill attempts to motivate a principle of liberty (that would mark off a domain in which interference is always illegitimate) precisely on the grounds that the consequences of interference in this domain are less happy (in the utilitarian sense) than those of strict non-interference.[23] This approach is not quite the same as arguing that such interference is contrary to the general or public interest; but the kinds of considerations that lend plausibility to the one lend plausibility to the other.[24] Mill argues by appeal to historical examples. It would be

23. I do not mean to suggest that this domain (in which interference is never legitimate) can be specified with precision, nor even that the underlying distinction between the public sphere (where interference is admissible in principle) and the private sphere (where it is not) can be well motivated theoretically. However, it is plain enough what kinds of things liberals want to protect from interference (above all, state interference): engaging in unconventional behavior, entertaining and advocating unpopular beliefs, and so on. For the present purposes, our rough intuitions will have to suffice. There is a distinction between liberal values and liberal principles: like Rousseau (implicitly), I am inclined to regard liberal principles, the *theory* of liberalism, as incoherent; however, like Rousseau again, I am sympathetic to what liberalism tries to formulate theoretically (liberal values).

24. In brief, the difference is that, for the utilitarian, the public interest is just the summation of *individual* utilities (one's own and others). However, where persons are integral parts of "the whole community," this kind of individualism ceases to be appropriate. It is natural, but misleading, to ask what, then, besides individual welfare figures in the determination of the public interest; by this route one is led to view the state as a supra-individual "organism," with its own corporatist interests. To be sure, Rousseau does sometimes talk as though the state were an organism; and

tedious to reproduce these reflections here. The point is every-where the same: that the public interest (however construed) is best served by respecting liberal values and never by illiberal inter-ference. To argue this way is necessarily to appeal to empirical speculations about probable outcomes of alternative policies, and one can never do so definitively or to the complete satisfaction of those who are inclined differently. Though I think Rousseau would be sympathetic to this argument, there is still the central difference: Rousseau could not concede the conclusion the liberals want to draw from these examples—that state interference can be excluded *in principle* from some specifiable domain.

It would be idle to speculate on the possible varieties of social policy arising out of this theoretical difference. As I have already suggested, I think these variations would be minimal. Insofar as this view is borne out, Rousseau would seem to have grounded lib-eral values on principles firmer than those of theoretical liberalism.

And there is more to Rousseau's theory of liberty than this theoretically motivated laissez-faire. Recall that the assembled people's task is to discover the general interest, to discover a question of fact. This process of discovery requires more than just disinterested voting. It requires deliberation and full access to information. It requires institutionalization of means adequate for each citizen to exercise his abilities in discovering the general interest to the fullest extent possible. It seems fair to suppose that liberty in this traditional sense is at least a necessary condition for the institutionalization of these background conditions for proper voting.

Again, the parallel with classic liberal doctrine is striking. In the famous second chapter of *On Liberty*, Mill argues that unlimited and unregulated freedom of inquiry is justified on utilitarian grounds because such liberty is a necessary precondition for the discovery of truth and, thereby, the promotion of happiness. Shorn of the utilitarian framework (since, for Rousseau, truth is important for realizing autonomy, not for promoting happiness), the same position could be ascribed to Rousseau. To satisfy the various

nowhere more than in the passages now being considered. However, this kind of talk is seriously misleading. The point is that the interest of the whole community is not logically reducible to the interests of individuals or collections of individuals; the public interest is not, for Rousseau, just the logical summation of individual interests.

background conditions guaranteeing that the assembly bears a general will, the citizen requires guarantees that these liberties will be protected. Thus, we have a further theoretical motivation for some of the central liberal doctrines: freedom of speech, freedom of inquiry, and the freedom—indeed, the obligation—to publish and disseminate information.

In sum, then, implicit in Rousseau's theory of sovereignty we have both an argument *against* illiberal interference and an argument *for* some central liberal values. For Rousseau, the condition for the existence of the *de jure* state is that sovereignty be absolute in principle. But, so far from inclining toward or, worse still, anticipating totalitarianism, his thesis has liberal implications.

Rousseau is not, for all that, a crypto-liberal. What prevents his being so, however, has nothing to do with the theory of sovereignty. Everything that can be done must be done, to assure that the assembly of the people votes according to a general will. This requirement amounts, as we shall see in Part 2, to the suppression of private interest by any means necessary. The implementation of the requirement accounts for the effective illiberalism in Rousseau's politics. Thus, persons are not free to form groupings of any sort that mediate between the individual and the state, nor are they free to advocate ideas to this effect. Such groupings, Rousseau thinks, bolster private interest. What will actually encourage private interest is, of course, a matter for speculation. Rousseau's warrant for advocating this or that prohibition rests ultimately on his informed intuitions about the probable outcomes of various policies. He does not advocate religious liberty (at least, on certain questions of dogma), nor freedom of assembly (except for the entire people *qua* legislature), nor the freedom to form partial associations (parties, factions, guilds, trade unions, or whatever). These prohibitions are certainly illiberal. But this illiberalism arises out of the practical implementation of a theory that in itself has, if anything, liberal implications.

Illiberalism occurs on the level of custom and opinion, while the theory of sovereignty and law inclines toward a liberal practice. But it is the level of custom and opinion that is, ultimately, the more fundamental. The sovereign should act illiberally toward individual behavior rarely, if ever, because that behavior is to be shaped and educated to require little, if any, intervention. The individual is to be educated to citizenship, to the full civic *virtue* implicit in the generality of his will. In mortal opposition to an apparently irrepressible tendency for private interest to insinuate itself, the citizen is to be formed as a bearer of the general will.[25]

Appendix   The Incoherence of Majority Rule

Majority rule is represented in the text in a flow diagram as a device for combining individual preferences for enactments (or, as we may now say, with a view toward Rousseau, individual judgments about what is in the general interest) to produce a collective decision. Collective decision making has lately been the subject of rigorous investigation by economists and others. The study of voting has been pursued along this line of investigation at least since the 1950s, principally by Kenneth Arrow, whose work appears to have many important applications to political philosophy. I should like to sketch some of Arrow's results in an attempt to assess their relevance to Rousseau's theory of sovereignty. My general view is that Arrow's demonstration of the "impossibility" of a democratic "social welfare function" undercuts Rousseau's account quite radically. However, despite the enormous advance in precision Arrow's work achieves, its critical implications, at least for Rousseau, cannot yet be established with equal precision. My suspicion, once more, is that Arrow is implicitly a profound and incisive critic of Rousseau. I cannot now establish this suspicion, but I believe I can render it plausible.

Arrow develops a conceptual apparatus for rationally reconstructing the method of majority decision, as well as other collective decision procedures that need not concern us here. It will be necessary to make at least some of this formal apparatus explicit, if

25. Sparta, for Rousseau, is the closest historical approximation to the *de jure* state, the city whose citizens are entirely absorbed in their social role. All this, needless to say, is in marked contrast to the classic liberal glorification of diversity and idiosyncracy. If Sparta is Rousseau's model, the Paris Rousseau abhorred is Mill's. Nevertheless, the direct relation between the individual and the state advocated by Rousseau is very much in the spirit of classical liberalism. But classical liberalism does not attempt to implement this theoretical exigency; nor is it aware, as Rousseau was so acutely, of the conflict between an idiosyncratic individualism and citizenship.

we are to be clear just what Arrow means by the impossibility of a social welfare function.

Arrow calls the objects of social choice *social states*. He assumes, in other words, that there exists a basic set of alternatives presented to the individual chooser. This notion is perfectly general. In the theory of consumer choice, a social state would be a commodity bundle; in the theory of the firm, a complete decision on inputs and outputs; in welfare economics, a distribution of commodities and labor requirements. In the theory of elections, a social state would be a candidate.[26] For Rousseau, a social state would be a judgment about what enactment is in the general interest. All that is required of alternative social states is that they be mutually exclusive.

Each individual is assumed to be at least minimally rational in making judgments among alternative social states; specifically, each individual is assumed to be consistent. If, for example, a person prefers chocolate ice cream to vanilla, and vanilla to strawberry, then, assuming consistency, one can infer that he prefers chocolate to strawberry and not vice versa. I will consider the justification for this requirement further on. For now, it is enough to be aware that this is the sort of requirement Arrow seeks to build into his rational reconstruction of individuals' value systems.

An individual's *value system* is to be represented by means of ordering relations for alternative (and mutually exclusive) social states. For any two social states x and y, the individual i will be said to *prefer* one to the other, or to be indifferent. The former relation will be represented by the letter P; the latter by the letter I. It is convenient to incorporate the relation P and the relation I into a single relation R, read 'is preferred or indifferent to'. Then xR_iy would be read 'x is preferred or indifferent to y by individual i', the subscript designating the individual whose value system is represented. It is obvious that all sentences involving the relations P and I may be "translated" into sentences involving just R. For example, 'xPy' may be rewritten 'xRy and not $-yRx$'; and 'xIy' may be rewritten 'xRy and yRx'. The relation R is, by stipulation, a *weak-ordering relation*; that is, a relation satisfying the logical properties of *connectedness* and *transitivity*. Thus, for all x and y, either xRy or yRx (connectedness); and for all x, y, and z, xRy and yRz imply

26. Kenneth Arrow, *Social Choice and Individual Values*, p. 11.

xRz (transitivity). Arrow, in effect, stipulates that individual value systems be representable by weak-ordering relations. How plausible is this stipulation?

That individual value systems should be represented by a connected relation is certainly unexceptionable. The stipulation simply amounts to the requirement that a choice be made among alternative social states. The requirement that the orderings be transitive is more controversial. To see its plausibility, we need only interpret an intransitive value system as a command—say, from a master to a servant. The servant is instructed to do x rather than y, y rather than z, but z rather than x. In this event, faced with a choice of x, y and z, there is no way for the servant to determine what to do. The inconsistency (intransitivity) of the master's value system renders it impossible as a command. And an inconsistent command is no command at all.[27]

We may apply this consideration immediately to Rousseau's case. If the sovereign's task is to instruct the magistrates on the assembled people's opinion about what is the general will, each citizen must at the very least have consistent judgments. Likewise, the collective judgment, formed by the method of majority decision, must produce consistent (transitive) results. Otherwise, the *public* servants or magistrates (to use Rousseau's word) would be unable to execute the sovereign's will.

Now, most generally, Arrow's aim is to construct a form device, a "social welfare function," that will aggregate individual value systems (represented by the R relation) of mutually exclusive social states "democratically." It will be useful to recall the flow diagram presented above:

27. It should be noted that the stipulated transitivity of the relation R implies the transitivity of I (indifference). To be sure, this requirement does have an air of unreality, for it supposes unlimited powers of discrimination. Between x and y, y and z, z and w, there may be no noticeable difference, so that a person is indifferent with respect to any of these pairs. Yet there may be a noticeable difference between x and w, such that the person prefers x to w or w to x. In this very plausible case, the requirement of transitivity would, of course, be violated. But however germane to the analysis of actual choice behavior, this appeal to perceptual thresholds is irrelevant to the analysis of rational choice. There are many reasons why a person's judgments may be inconsistent (intransitive), and some are no doubt cognitive. But consistency is a stipulation, not a description of how people in fact order ends. It is an ideal of reason, as it were, a value judgment, that allows the problem of political choice to be formulated.

where the input may now be represented by the R orderings of individuals $a, b, \ldots, n$, and the output is the society's R-ordering, R_s, the society's ordering of these same social states. The social welfare function, then, is a *rule* or *constitution* (to use Arrow's word) for "mapping" individual orderings (representing the value systems of the individuals who have set about making a social choice collectively) into a social ordering. Plainly, it will be possible to interpret this rule as a voting procedure.

So far we have a purely formal characterization of the problem of collective decision making. We shall need to specify a number of formal constraints on the social welfare function that will guarantee that the individual R-orderings are aggregated democratically. These constraints or conditions may be viewed as built-in value judgments. Their motivation and warrant are to reconstruct the content of those decision procedures that count as democratic. Of these procedures, majority-rule voting is obviously an important instance.

Arrow advances the following conditions, which I shall state informally:

1. *Generality* All logically possible (consistent) orderings of the alternative social states are admissible.
2. *Pareto Principle* If an alternative x is preferred to alternative y by every single individual according to his ordering, then the social ordering also ranks x above y.
3. *Independence of Irrelevant Alternatives* For any set of alternative social states, the social choice depends only on the individuals' orderings of the alternatives in that set.
4. *Non-Dictatorship* There is no individual whose preferences are automatically society's preferences independent of the preferences of all other individuals.

The first of these conditions is an admissibility condition. What it asserts, in effect, is that all logically possible (consistent) individual orderings can serve as input to the social welfare function; or, more precisely, that for any logically possible R_a, R_b, . . . , R_n for some fixed environment of alternative social states, the social welfare function defines a corresponding social ordering. Condition 1 prevents the use of any principle by which admissible sets of orderings can be selected out of the set of all logically possible orderings. It therefore has the general consequence of prohibiting the imposition of any restrictions on each individual's value system. We shall return shortly to the theoretical warrant for this sort of generality.

Conditions 2 and 4 together specify the content of what Arrow calls "consumer or popular sovereignty." They are plainly necessary conditions for any "democratic" social welfare function. Condition 2 stipulates in a very minimal way that the social ordering be responsive to the individual orderings that constitute it. It is a perfectly uncontroversial principle and a fundamental tenet of welfare economic analysis. Condition 4 guarantees some further measure of popular control over the decision procedure by prohibiting a single individual from determining the outcome.

Condition 3 has been the subject of some controversy in the literature, owing largely to some misunderstandings that need not concern us here. Properly speaking, condition 3 calls just for a fixed environment of all alternatives in contention. For such a fixed environment, it requires only that all changes in individual orderings of alternatives not in contention have no effect on the social ordering of alternatives in contention, so long as these changes have no effect on the individual orderings of alternatives in contention. For example, if a person must choose between chocolate, vanilla, and strawberry ice cream, his overwhelming desire for pistachio (an alternative not in contention) may indeed affect his ordering of the alternatives in contention (perhaps it even makes him indifferent). But once this ordering is formed, the desire for pistachio becomes irrelevant. Condition 3 does not concern how individual orderings are formed, as is often wrongly supposed. It simply stipulates how we are to treat an ordering that has been formed. It requires, in effect, that the social ordering be determined *strictly* by the individual's preferences for the social states actually in contention. Along with condition 1, then, it spells out the formulation of the problem to be investigated.

The "democratic" content of the social welfare function Arrow proposes is built in just by conditions 2 and 4. These are plainly very weak conditions. For a social welfare function to count as democratic, they would hardly be sufficient, though they are plainly necessary. However, the weaker the conditions, the more powerful the result Arrow demonstrates. For it will apply to a very wide range of decision procedures; namely, to all that satisfy these very weak and uncontroversial conditions!

What is important for our purpose is that it will apply to the method of majority decision. For the method of majority decision is just that Arrow social welfare function in which xRy holds if and only if the number of individuals for whom xR_iy is at least as great as the number of individuals for whom yR_ix. The method of majority decision is just an interpretation of the Arrow social welfare function as a voting procedure in which the numerical majority is decisive for determining the social ordering. Such an interpretation is plainly compatible with each of the four stipulated conditions.

Having formulated these quite unexceptionable conditions, Arrow goes on to demonstrate the following astounding result:

> *General Possibility Theorem:* No social welfare function satisfying conditions 1 to 4 exists.

I shall not reconstruct the proof of this theorem here, as the technical details need not concern us. What is important is to appreciate the general character of Arrow's result. Arrow's proof is an *impossibility proof:* a demonstration of the logical incompatibility of the stipulated conditions. What Arrow proposes is, in effect, a *reductio ad absurdum* argument. He assumes the existence of a social welfare function satisfying the stipulated conditions and then shows how, on this assumption, a contradiction is generated. This amounts to a demonstration of the logical incompatibility of the stipulated conditions.

It follows that an Arrow social welfare function is impossible. And since the method of majority decision is just an interpretation of the Arrow social welfare function, it follows trivially that the method of majority decision is likewise impossible.

A manifestation of this impossibility is the celebrated voting paradox. Suppose there are three voters *1, 2,* and *3* who are to choose between three alternative social states x, y, and z. Let the orderings of individuals *1*, *2*, and *3* be as follows:

1	*2*	*3*
x	y	z
y	z	x
z	x	y

Assuming the social ordering to be consistent (in accordance with Arrow's condition 1), a natural way of arriving at the social ordering would be to say that one alternative is preferred to another if a majority of the community prefers the one to the other; that is, if they would choose the first over the second, if presented with only these alternatives.[28] We can adopt a procedure of pair-wise voting between alternative social states to arrive at a social ordering. Suppose we begin by voting between alternatives x and y. In this case, *1* and *3* will vote for x against y, since x ranks higher on their orderings, while *2* will vote for y. The social choice between x and y will be x. We next compare x with the remaining alternative z, and find that while *1* prefers x to z, *2* and *3* both prefer z to x, so that the social ordering among the three alternatives in contention would be zPxPy. Now begin with a different pair of alternatives, say x and z. *1* will vote for x; while *2* and *3* will vote for z. Now pair the winner, z, against the remaining alternative y. *3* will vote for z, but *1* and *2* will both vote for y. The social ordering, determined this way, will be yPzPx. Similarly, if we begin with the remaining pair of alternatives y and z, and pair the winner against x, we will find xPyPz to be the social ordering. In short, we have a contradictory situation where every alternative is preferred to every other alternative. The method of majority decision does not, in this case, produce a transitive social ordering. This paradox is explained by the Arrow result.

We can understand the importance of Arrow's result for Rousseau's theory of sovereignty if we reflect on this example of the "incoherence" Arrow has demonstrated. In the voting paradox, every alternative is preferred to every other. In other words, when orderings are presented in "normal" form (that is, when all infor-

28. For ease of exposition, I am assuming that individuals *1*, *2*, and *3* have clear preference relations for x, y, and z. The situation would be no different if we admit indifference, or, more generally, if we reconstruct the value systems of the individuals *1*, *2*, and *3* by means of the *R*-relation.

mation about individual orderings is fed into the social welfare function), the corresponding social ordering is circular. A public servant, in this event, would be in the position of the servant depicted above, whose master presents him with an intransitive ordering of his preferences. It is literally impossible for the servant to determine what he is commanded to do. Or, what comes to the same thing, he can do anything *he* wants, since there is always a majority behind any policy he chooses to enforce.

What appears to save majority rule is the mechanism by which it operates. As we have seen, the voting procedure is capable of giving instructions to public officials, as is evident from the example of the voting paradox. There, the method of pairwise comparison of alternative social states was adopted as a natural procedure for making decisions by majority rule. No matter with what pair we began, majority-rule voting always produced an acceptable output. But the ordering, in that case, depended on the order of presentation of alternatives for pairwise comparison (in the case in point, the later the better). But this purely contingent circumstance is in blatant contravention of the ideal of popular sovereignty, according to which the preferences of the individual voters *alone* determine the social ordering. In short, voting procedures (like the one used above) that appear to contravene the impossibility Arrow demonstrates do so at the expense of the democratic content of the Arrow social welfare function.

The problem Arrow demonstrates for majority rule may thus be viewed as the following dilemma: either individual orderings are combined democratically, in which case no ordering is produced; or an ordering is produced, but it is not produced democratically. The voting procedure used above instances the latter horn of this dilemma.

The importance of this result for Rousseau is now apparent. The mechanism through which sovereignty is to be expressed is an incoherent one. Majority rule will produce social orderings, but these will not in general reflect exclusively the judgments of the individual voters. In other words, our procedure for combining "expert opinions" is faulty; the outcome is not, strictly speaking, determined by these opinions alone. The voting paradox "infects" the entire decision making apparatus. The argument for popular sovereignty rests on an incoherent foundation, almost as though one proposed to build a house on a square-circular foundation. The concept is incoherent: a house built on such foundations is impossible; it cannot exist *in principle*. Likewise, the concept of a *de jure* state, insofar as it depends on majority rule, would appear equally impossible. The deduction of that concept has apparently fallen through, unexpectedly, but decisively.

This conclusion would appear inevitable insofar as the Arrow social welfare function does indeed rationally reconstruct Rousseau's concept of majority rule. Conditions 2 and 4 specify minimally the democratic content that is plainly implicit in Rousseau's conception of sovereignty. Condition 3, I have argued, simply specifies the problem of aggregation: that the social ordering is to be determined exclusively by the preferences of the individuals for those social states in contention. And condition 1 gives the choice mechanism its generality by stipulating that all logically possible arrangements of the alternative social states (that are connected and transitive) are admissible. This condition does not strictly specify what we might on a pre-reflective level suppose to be democratic. But it does reconstruct the typical case where individual orderings are, so to speak, disjoint, where there is no *intrinsic* relation between individual orderings.

But would the individual orderings in the *de jure* state Rousseau depicts be disjoint? The suggestion is at least plausible that they would be, where private wills combined to form "the will of all"; that is, where wills took interest in alternative social states from the point of view of the atomic individual. But would individuals aiming collectively at a common interest have disjoint wills? The question does not appear to lend itself to very precise treatment. However, a finding in the literature on collective decision making does seem to bear on this question.

The result I have in mind was discovered by Duncan Black and developed by Arrow and others. Black proves that majority rule will produce a unique, transitive ordering of alternative social states, providing the set of individual orderings to be combined is "single-peaked." By "single-peakedness" is meant that the orderings to be aggregated (and these may, of course, be any logically possible, consistent orderings of the alternative social states) can be represented on a graph with the rank of preference on the ordinate and the alternatives themselves arranged on the abscissa so that each preference curve (representing the individual orderings) appears as a curve with only one peak. For example, if the alternatives x, y, and z are arranged in that order along the abscissa, and if individual *1*'s ordering of these alternatives is *xPyPz*, individual *2*'s ordering is *yPzPx*, and individual *3*'s is *zPyPx*, then, ranking the order of preference along the ordinate, we see that this set of orderings can be graphed so that each graph has only one peak:

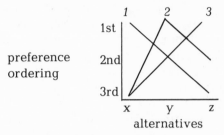

However, if individual *3*'s ordering had been, say, *zPxPy*, then, with this arrangement of alternatives on the abscissa (or any other arrangement, as can be checked by observation), at least one of the curves—in this case, individual *3*'s—would have more than one peak, in violation of Black's requirement.

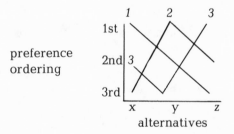

Under this assumption of single-peakedness, Black shows, first, that the method of majority decision will lead to determinate results, since there is exactly one alternative which will receive a majority over any other, provided the number of voters is odd. Then Black shows how this procedure will produce a consistent (that is, transitive) social ordering. For if the number of alternatives in consideration is finite, we may simply remove the alternative that is best (in the sense of being preferred by the majority); determine the best one among the remaining as the second best; and so on. In other words, the method of majority decision will lead to a transitive ordering of the alternative social states, provided the individual orderings to be combined according to the method of majority decision are single-peaked. As can be readily checked, the assumption of single-peakedness will rule out, among others, those arrangements of alternatives that lead to the voting paradox.

To ascertain more precisely the relevance of the Black result for the problem Arrow investigates—and, finally, for Rousseau's theory of sovereignty—we must follow Arrow's translation of the single-peakedness requirement into his own formalism. Since preference orderings are to be represented by single-peaked utility curves, then of any two alternatives one must precede the other. The relation R, a weak-ordering relation (admitting indifferences as well as preferences), will therefore not do for representing this requirement. Therefore, Arrow introduces the relation S, a strong-ordering relation, satisfying the requirements of irreflexivity, connectedness, and transitivity, respectively:

1. For all x, not xSx;
2. For all $x \neq y$, either xSy or ySx;
3. For all x, y, and z, xSy and ySz imply xSz.

The introduction of this strong-ordering relation S permits Arrow to define the concept "betweenness" B as follows:

If S is a strong-ordering relation, define $B(x,y,z)$ to mean that either xSy and ySz or zSy and ySz,

where $B(x,y,z)$ is to be read 'y is between x and z.' An immediate consequence of this definition is the following lemma:

If x, y and z are distinct, then one and only one of the following holds: $B(x,y,z)$, $B(y,x,z)$ or $B(y,z,x)$.

Arrow then formulates the Assumption of Single-Peakedness as follows:

There exists a strong-ordering relation S such that for each i, xR_iy and $B(x,y,z)$ together imply yP_iz; where $B(x,y,z)$ is the betweenness relation derived from S.

The next step is to modify condition 1 so that only individual orderings satisfying the Assumption of Single-Peakedness will be admissable. More formally, condition 1 is modified to 1′ to read:

For all sets of individual orderings satisfying the Assumption of Single-Peakedness, the corresponding social ordering R will be a weak-ordering.

Then, to show that the requirement that individual orderings be single-peaked (for some issue) is a *sufficient condition* for a social welfare function, we need to show the consistency of this modified condition 1' with the remaining conditions 2 to 4.

This is what Arrow shows. He proves that:

The method of majority decision is a social welfare function satisfying condition 1' and conditions 2 to 4 for any number of alternatives, provided only that the number of individuals is odd.

This result Arrow calls "The General Possibility Theorem for Single-Peaked Preferences." Again, the details of the proof need not concern us. Nor need we be bothered about the requirement that the number of voters be odd, as it is a formal exigency having no apparent philosophical significance.[29] The question is to evaluate Arrow's result.

The General Possibility Theorem for Single-Peaked Preferences shows that there exists a non-trivial (and non-intuitive) solution to the difficulty Arrow reveals, and that this solution involves restricting what counts as admissible preference orderings. There may indeed be other solutions: it does not appear that single-peakedness is the weakest sufficient condition for guaranteeing an acceptable social welfare function, nor is it a necessary condition. But it is so far the only solution on which there is "hard" information in the literature. And, as will be apparent shortly, it appears particularly suggestive as a reconstruction of Rousseau's notion of voting according to a general will.

Arrow has given the following interpretation of the single-peakedness requirement:

29. To examine the situation when the number of voters is not odd, suppose that there are only two voters, one of whom prefers x to y, and y to z; while the other prefers y to z and z to x. These orderings are single-peaked, if the ordering x,y,z is taken as the basic strong-ordering. The majority decision yields x indifferent to y and preferred to z; but x is indifferent and not preferred to z.

An example in which this assumption is satisfied is the party structure of prewar European parliaments, where there was a universally recognized left-right ordering of the parties. Individuals might have belonged to any of these parties; but each recognized the same arrangement, in the sense that, of two parties to the left of his own, the individual would prefer the program of the one less to the left, and similarly with parties on the right. Nothing need be specified as to the relative choice between a party to the right and a party to the left of an individual's first choice.[30]

In other words, the individuals need not have the same preferences, but they must conceive alternatives (or, more strictly, their judgments about alternatives) according to the same standard. Jerome Rothenberg has elaborated upon this point:

> The most striking fact would seem to be that all individuals order the alternatives of choice in such a way that a particular arrangement of these alternatives on a one-dimensional scale becomes particularly meaningful. This arrangement is, indeed, a geometrical projection of preference uniformities among all individuals, uniformities defined by the concept of 'betweenness'. Since it holds for all individuals, whatever their preferences, it seems reasonable to infer that, in a given community at least, the various alternatives themselves are interrelated in a way which is independent of individual orderings of these alternatives.[31]

Single-peakedness, then, is a product of cognitive agreement among voters about the arrangement of alternatives according to some standard (as defined by the "betweenness" relation).

To take a simple example (of voters or parties polarized along some ideological continuum), suppose there are three alternatives in contention: x, y, and z; and three voters: 1, 2, and 3. Let x, y, and z be different amounts of social assistance payments to the poor (say x = $500 / month; y = $200 / month; z = 0), and suppose that 1 is an advocate of the welfare state, 3 is a laissez-faire capitalist, and 2 is a "moderate." Then it is reasonable to suppose that 1's ordering will be xPyPz (since he prefers the maximum in payments and depar-

30. *Social Choice and Individual Values*, p. 26.
31. *The Measurement of Social Welfare*, p. 290.

tures from the maximum in progressively diminishing degree); 3's will be $zPyPx$ (for reasons exactly the inverse of 1's); and 2's $yPxPz$ (since he prefers some payment rather than "too much," but thinks anything is better than nothing at all). These orderings are single-peaked if x, y, z is taken as the basic strong-ordering:

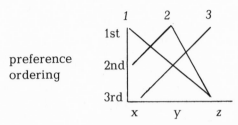

In this case, it is clear how alternative distributions are to be perceived. There is cognitive agreement. And so, in virtue of the General Possibility Theorem for Single-Peaked Preferences, the method of majority decision will produce a consistent ordering (in this case; $yPxPz$). Thus the problem Arrow reveals for the general case is solved when there is agreement about a perception of some qualitative dimension along which alternative social states may be ordered.

For there to be good reason to hold that some set of individual orderings will be single-peaked, there must be at least a presumption that voters will agree on common standards to bring the range of alternatives into line. What militates against the realization of that state of affairs is what Rothenberg calls the "multi-aspect" character of social states. A social state typically has innumerable dimensions; and, in the general case, there is no reason to suppose that any one dimension will be adopted universally as the basis for individual valuations. Where ideological polarization is intense, as in pre-war European parliaments, this multi-aspect character of social states takes on diminished importance.

Single-peakedness is likely, then, even when value systems are antagonistic toward one another, provided that these antagonisms take direct issue with one another; that is, that there are common standards against which antagonistic interests are compared (and which are of sufficient importance to render the different value systems comparable). Reflecting on this case of ideological polarization (particularly with respect to questions of distribution of benefits), Rothenberg specifies the following conditions under which the requirement of single-peakedness is likely to be fulfilled:

> (1) the "concern [of the individuals of the group] about equitable distributions is so strong that it outweighs their concern for the idiosyncratic character of their own wants; (2) the principles by which they judge equity are shared by groups of varying sizes," and individuals (including oneself) are treated in these principles as conventional ciphers with standardized wants rather than as unique creatures with idiosyncratic wants; (3) "a single method for classifying benefits and their recipients, and the relative degrees of nearness of these recipients to one another, comes to be employed by the adherents of all the various points of view."[32]

More generally, there must be reason to suppose: (a) at the very least, that there is a consensus on standards for judging alternatives; and (b) that these common standards are regarded by each voter as sufficiently important to rule out the private adoption of idiosyncratic standards. The case of intense ideological polarization satisfies these requirements fairly well. What of the consensus on ends existing in the sovereign legislative assembly created by the social contract?

There is a definite plausibility in the suggestion that the vote in Rousseau's assembly will be single-peaked. For what the general will requires is precisely the subordination of individual and idiosyncratic wants to a higher will that has its source in the collective voting community. The kind of consensus on ends enjoined by Rousseau will clearly outweigh each individual's concern for his own wants. But will it also create a presumption in favor of common principles for judging alternatives? If so, then a Black social welfare function would adequately reconstruct Rousseau's concept of majority rule, and Rousseau will have thereby avoided the general difficulty demonstrated by Arrow.

It does not appear possible to draw many conclusions on this point, however. Though Rousseau plainly anticipates a tendency toward unanimity, and so, *a fortiori,* toward the common perception

32. Rothenberg, *Measurement of Social Welfare,* p 297. Rothenberg is here quoting from chap. 10 of a forthcoming book of his own, *The Theory of Economic and Political Decision-Making as a Single System.*

of standards, there is no real expectation that unanimity will be achieved; indeed, quite the contrary. And neither does the Rousseauean consensus on ends appear to create any special presumption for expecting the requisite perceptual or cognitive agreement. In short, there is no special reason, beyond the tendency toward unanimity, to suppose that the requirement of single-peakedness will be realized.

Thus, the question must finally be left undecided and perhaps undecidable. Rousseau's conception of majority rule is apparently less general than that for which the Arrow social welfare function serves as a rational reconstruction. But it is not quite clear whether it is sufficiently less general to escape the Arrow result. I have tried to suggest that, although there is some ground for supposing it is, there is no decisive reason for supposing so.

We are left, finally, with only our intuitions. To repeat the suggestion I advanced at the outset, now in the light of Black's result, it seems to me that the apparent impotence of the general will for inducing cognitive agreement (beyond the tendency toward unanimity) suggests that (Black notwithstanding) Rousseau's account is in fact undone by Arrow's.

II
Theory and Practice

Introduction

When in the later chapters of Books 2 and 4, and throughout nearly all of Book 3, Rousseau turns from a strictly theoretical account of political right and obligation to more mundane, practical reflections on government, opinion, and manners and morals (*moeurs*), the text does not merely join together material on different and relatively independent subjects: what is involved in these chapters is a shift in focus absolutely essential for the completion of the theoretical account undertaken earlier. For if the intention is "to establish some just and certain rule of administration in civil affairs," "taking men as they are," then we cannot finally ignore the real world of human life.

The phrase "taking men as they are (*tels qu'ils sont*)" is misleading, since, for Rousseau, men are not "as they are." That is, they are not as they are essentially, and, therefore, as they *ought* to be. Essentially, man is free; in fact, he is everywhere in chains. Essentially, man is an autonomous moral agent, a "self-legislating member of a kingdom of ends" (to use Kant's expression). In fact, man is a rational egoist, directed by private interest, a slave of passion, of *amour propre*. In short, practical reason ought to determine human life and does so essentially, but not actually. When Rousseau proposes to begin from a conception of "men as they are," his appeal is to a conception of human essence and not to a description of human reality. We are to begin from a conception of man as he ought to be, as he really is.

Where the general will does not direct human life, man is not autonomously determined and is not, therefore, what he really is—an autonomous moral agent. Earlier I described this condition anachronistically as alienation. It would be possible to depict this alienation as an instance of the most fundamental opposition running throughout Rousseau's work, and indeed throughout western thought: the opposition between appearance *(paraître)* and reality *(être)*.[1] For now it is enough to note how this opposition—manifested here as a separation of man from his essence—threatens, if uncorrected, to undermine the justificatory project. A theory of right and obligation generated out of a conception of how individuals ought to be (and are not in fact) would be useless and incomplete. It must become practical; it must legislate practical measures for putting appearance into harmony with reality. In other words, the theory must, finally, impose itself upon the real world of human life if it is successfully to establish political right and obligation, "taking men as they are."

As has already been suggested, this theoretical exigency centers on the opposition *private interest / general interest* and on the corresponding opposition *private will / general will*. It will be in point, then, to reflect once more on these oppositions apart from their practical effects, before tracing their career through the practical portions of *The Social Contract.*

Interest

The pact of association described in Book 1, chapter 6, "produces a moral and collective body, which is composed of as many members as the assembly has votes, and which receives from this same act its unity, its common self *(moi)*, its life and its will" (1:6). This "moral and collective body," the *P2P* of the social contract, is conceived as a person, albeit a collective one. It is said, like a person, to have a will: a will that aims at the interest of this collectivity. The will of this person is the general will; its interest, the general interest.

The general will is characterized in two apparently different ways: with reference to its *bearer*, and with reference to its *object*.

1. See Jean Starobinski, *J.-J. Rousseau: la transparence et l'obstacle*, chap. 1, especially pp. 33–34.

Thus, it is depicted as the will of the collectivity, the *P2P*; and it is, at the same time, that will which aims at the interest of the *P2P*, the general interest. The "moral and collective body" constituted by the pact of association is, as we have seen, just each individual contractee in a certain "form of association." This form of association is just that arrangement of forces that makes a general will possible: "the total alienation to the whole community of each associate with all his rights" (1:6). Thus, the bearer of the general will, strictly speaking, is not the collectivity but the individual when and insofar as he aims at the general interest. Of course, the existence of the collectivity is a necessary condition for an individual's bearing a general will; it is the good of this collectivity for which the individual aims. But the collectivity itself has a will only in a manner of speaking. Strictly, through the method of majority decision, it discovers, according to Rousseau, what the general will of each individual is. In the final analysis, the bearer of the general will, like the bearer of a private will, is the individual, the *P1P*.

The intelligibility of this account is obviously bound up with the problem of the differential status of the parties to the social contract. The will of the *P2P* is that will of the *P1P* that aims at the interest of the *P2P*—that is, at the interest of the *P1P qua* citizen. In this way, the original problem of differential status is displaced: from the sovereign (the *P2P*) to the will of the sovereign and, finally, to the interest of that will.[2] Thus, the whole drama of *The Social Contract* comes to center on the intelligibility of this notion of the general interest. It is this, finally, that calls for a 'deduction': a demonstration of the concept's coherence and possible application. Such a deduction is the only hope of making sense of that "moral and collective person" that is the "solution" to the "fundamental problem" posed in Book 1, chapter 6. And to achieve this deduction, Rousseau must finally descend from the realm of abstract principle and come to terms with the world of appearance. Should appearance prove recalcitrant, then it must be reformed.

General interest is distinguished from private interest, where by "private interest" is meant the object of a private will. To establish bearings for the investigation to follow, it will be well to reflect briefly on this notion, *private interest*.

The notion of private interest is common enough in the eight-

2. Cf. Louis Althusser, "Rousseau: The Social Contract."

eenth century and finds its definitive expression in the classical economists. The "economic man" of classic political economy values alternative social states according to his direct consumption of satisfactions, according to his advantage. Adam Smith's celebrated description in *The Wealth of Nations* may be cited in this regard: "It is not from the benevolence of the butcher, the brewer, or the baker that we expect our dinner, but from their regard to their own interest. We address ourselves not to their humanity but to their self-love, and never talk to them of our own necessities but of their advantages. Nobody but a beggar chooses to depend chiefly upon the benevolence of his fellow-citizens."[3] *The Second Discourse* effectively recounts the development of this species of egoism (*amour propre*). Of course the point here is not, as it is in the work of classical economists, to found a starting point for the description of economic behavior; the point is, instead, to motivate the account Rousseau offers in Book 1, chapter 6, of that critical conjuncture that culminates in the social contract. However, the description of human nature is essentially the same.

Private interest, then, is the object of the will of man in civil society. It is the outcome of the confrontation of each person's innate self-love (*amour de soi*) with the social relations of the state of nature. Private interest is the historical product of self-love in civil society; it is the societal deformation or corruption of what would be the object of interest of natural man. Thus, private interest, far from being "natural," is in Rousseau's account a corruption of nature. It is nonetheless universal,[4] and this universality is what must be overcome if men are ever to become "what they are."

As has already been intimated, when we attempt to envision private interest in opposition to general interest, we face apparently insoluble difficulties. This problem is evident in the way in which the notion *general interest* was introduced.

We have seen how the general interest is what all private interests have in common at that critical moment that culminates in the social contract. At that moment, the general interest is the

3. Adam Smith, *The Wealth of Nations* (New York, 1937), p. 14.
4. Unlike the classical economists, Rousseau does not regard egoism as human nature. Rather, it is explicitly conceived as a historical product, a consequence of antagonistic social relations.

common denominator of each person's will because of the "total alienation" that suppresses private interest—in the private interest of each associate. The private interest thus "contains" the general interest, and each private will is the "bearer" of the general will. Therefore, so long as any interest at all exists, the general will exists and always will exist, whether it is actually manifested through collective decision procedures, or eluded.

Of course, for reasons that have been discussed, the general will may well not be manifested. Indeed, it is even possible, and consistent with Rousseau's position, that in actual societies it has always been eluded: perhaps the general will, though it has always existed and always will exist, has never been manifested! Why? We needn't search far for an answer. Private interest, Rousseau tells us on nearly every page of *The Social Contract*, prevents its realization. The great antagonist of the general interest, its negation, what threatens its realization—is private interest. It is because private interest exists that the general will—though "indestructable, constant, unalterable, pure and always right"—is systematically eluded. And so, once again, we are apparently in plain contradiction: private interest contains the general will; yet these notions are, at the same time, opposites, threats to one another's realization, obstacles.

This is the contradiction Rousseau must somehow resolve. To do so, he shifts attention from the *object* of the will to the will's *bearer*. In so doing, he effectively shifts the focus from pure theory to the real world where this theory is supposed to have a possible application.

The Bearer(s) of the Will

How does Rousseau conceive the bearer of a private will (a will that aims at a private interest) and of a general will (a will that aims at a general interest)? We should first note some peculiarities of his usage that shape his "political ontology."

On the one hand, private interest is the interest of the person in the state of nature. It is interest untouched by the social contract. This is plainly the primary model of attribution: the bearer of private interest is the individual in the state of nature. On the other hand, private interest is also, for Rousseau, the interest of social groups. These groups may be partial associations—religious formations, guilds, trade associations, unions, parties, classes—or they may be the entire social collectivity. In Rousseau's account, when individuals vote according to private wills, the result of the vote will be a simple combination of private wills (*la volonté de tous*), the will of all, and not a general will. It is even conceivable that this will of all will be unanimous, as it would be where the private interests of all persons happened to coincide on the point in contention.[5] The resulting directive, we are told, has nothing to do with the general will, except, perhaps, accidentally: it is simply the revelation of the private interest of each member of the collectivity.

Private wills, then, are borne by both individuals and groups (including even the entire collectivity regarded as a social group, and not as a moral and collective 'person'). However, the attribution to the individual in the state of nature is primary—an important difference from Rousseau's model of attribution of general wills. Of course, Rousseau also attributes general wills to both individuals and the collectivity. The individual bears a general will when he votes in the assembly of the people as a citizen, when he expresses his opinion on the question "What ought we—citizens— to do?" The result of this collective truth-discovery procedure is the general will, and the resulting directive is the general interest. Once again, the general will of the collectivity is just the general interest of each citizen, of each component part of the sovereign. But the primary model of attribution is different, since, for the general will, the collectivity is primary. If Rousseau's picture of the bearer of a private will is the person in the state of nature, the bearer of the general will is the social collectivity, the *P2P*.

Strictly speaking, the difference is at most one of imagery. There is no logical difference in calling the private will the will of the *P1P* of the social contract and the general will the will of the *P2P*, because, in the final analysis, the *P1P* and *P2P* are the same. But the imagery has consequences: particularly for Rousseau's way of dealing with social groups. The only social group that can bear a general will, in Rousseau's account, is the *P2P* itself. A partial association can never bear a general will. From a moral point of view, the will of any group other than the *P2P* is, for this reason, construed on the model of the private will of the individual still in a state of nature. In the moral universe created by the social contract,

5. This would be the Rousseauean analogue to the welfare economic concept of Pareto optimality; see the appendix to chap. 2, above pp. 80-95.

partial associations no longer figure. Rousseau's political ontology is to consist of individuals (*qua* citizens and *qua* subjects) and the state. There will be no social groups countenanced other than the state, and none outside it. The theory simply cannot allow such groups. Where they do exist, they are construed as recalcitrant vestiges of the pre-moral, pre-political universe that culminates in the social contract; and they are treated accordingly.

It is important to realize that the interest of these groups that bear private wills is private only in the sense that it is not general, only in the sense that the bearer of the will is not the *P2P*. We are not dealing here *in fact* with the wills of private persons in the state of nature. Yet in calling these wills private, in using the same name for the wills of both entities, we are forced to regard the will of collectivities other than "the whole community" *as if* they were the wills of isolated individuals in the state of nature. It is at this point that the imagery of Rousseau's model of attribution takes its toll. Social groups—*qua* bearers of wills—are assimilated theoretically to private individuals in the state of nature. In terms of the traditional, philosophical opposition appearance / reality—where what appears to be the case, what is evident to the senses, is often a pale and even inverted reflection of a deeper reality—social groups exist on the order of appearance, but they do not, on the order of reality, *really* exist.

If the theory is to have a possible application, then, appearance must be drawn into line with reality. It will not be enough to declare partial associations or social groups unreal. Indeed, if it is necessary to theorize these formations away, it is only because in some deeply recalcitrant sense, they are there.

There is only one way to proceed: appearance must be re-formed. If private interests—the interests of social groups and, above all, of classes—cannot exist in the *de jure* state, then, since they do exist, the theory must enjoin their suppression. What is not countenanced in theory must be vigorously suppressed in practice. This is the burden of the less theoretical portions of *The Social Contract.*

Yet this move from theory to practice is bound, finally, to fail. For the fundamental reality—the real constituents of any sound political ontology—are and can only be the social groups, particularly the social classes, whose existence Rousseau would deny in theory and suppress in practice. The opposition private interest / general interest serves only to mystify this intractable situation.

The Social Contract stands, then, as a kind of fictional account of the relationship between these two illusory and mystifying notions: private interest and general interest. This account is and can only be ideological: in concealing the reality of social classes, it serves, in the final analysis, only to further particular class interests. This is what I should like to try to show in what follows. In centering on the institutional features Rousseau would build into the de jure state, we shall see the outlines of the ideological gesture that underlies his political thought. It will be convenient to begin with a particularly striking and elaborated instance: the theory of government presented in The Social Contract, Book 3.

3

On Government

Introduction (3:1)

Undoubtedly, the most striking aspect of Rousseau's treatment of government in Book 3 is the sharp distinction he draws between sovereignty and government. This distinction consists roughly in the difference between the legislative and executive functions. What is involved, however, is plainly not a theory of the separation of powers as developed in Montesquieu's *The Spirit of the Laws* and taken over, most notably, in the United States constitution. Indeed, Rousseau's argument for the indivisibility of sovereignty in Book 2, chapter 2, is often taken to be an express rebuttal of Montesquieu.[1] Whether or not Rousseau explicitly attacks Montesquieu's theory, it is clear he does not himself hold it. The difference between the legislative and executive functions, for Rousseau, is a difference not *within* the sovereign but between the sovereign and something else *not* sovereign. From a moral point of view, the difference is qualitative. The sovereign *bears* the general will and is the source of moral

1. The extent of Rousseau's very substantial debt to Montesquieu is discussed by Robert Derathé in *Jean-Jacques Rousseau et la science politique de son temps*, pp. 48–52. Following A. Cobban, Derathé goes on to argue (pp. 280 ff.) that Rousseau's target in this chapter is not Montesquieu's theory of the separation of powers but the theory of 'parts' of sovereignty set forth by Grotius and developed by Pufendorf.

obligation. The government simply *executes* the will of the sovereign. What right to command the government enjoys, it enjoys strictly because of its relation to the sovereign. From the point of view of a theory of obligation, the sovereign is the essential category; the government is entirely secondary and derivative.

Government is nonetheless essential for the sovereign: it is a condition for the sovereign's very existence. Rousseau's argument around this point is interesting and problematic. It will be instructive to follow his exposition carefully.

The opening chapter of Book 3 makes the distinction between the sovereign and the government explicit by appeal to the causes of a free action:

> Every free action has two causes which concur to produce it; the moral one, viz., the will which determines the act; the other, physical, viz., the power which executes it. When I walk towards an object, I must first will to go to it; in the second place, my feet must carry me to it. Should a paralytic wish to run, or an agile man not wish to do so, both will remain where they are. The body politic has the same motive powers in it, likewise, force and will are distinguished, the latter under the name of *legislative power*, the former under the name of *executive power*. Nothing is or ought to be done in it without their cooperation. [3:1]

The legislative power resides in the assembled people and results in laws. These laws, we have seen, have the form of generality in both source and object. The task of government is to make these directives actual, to interpret them, to effect their application to particulars. Rousseau expresses this difference when he distinguishes the enactments of the sovereign from the enactments of the government. The former are laws and have the form of generality; the latter are *decrees* and have the form of particularity.

Since these functions are distinct, the sovereign cannot be its own executive, however much it may require an executive power for its own functioning. Rousseau continues: "the executive power cannot belong to the generality as legislative or sovereign, because that power consists only in particular acts, which are not within the province of the law, nor consequently within that of the sovereign, all the acts of which must be laws" (3:1). In other words, the institution of sovereignty necessarily implies the institution of a governmental apparatus distinct from it to execute the sovereign's will.

Government as such is defined by its function, which is, in the first instance, to *execute* the sovereign's will. Government serves that function, in Rousseau's account, by serving as an *intermediary* between the subjects and the sovereign. This is indeed the definition of government Rousseau proposes: "What then is the government? An intermediate body established between the subjects and the sovereign for their mutual correspondence, charged with the execution of the laws, and with the maintenance of liberty both civil and political" (3:1). At this point, a host of difficulties seem to swarm into what had appeared to be an unproblematic notion. How are we to conceive of this intermediate body? Between what and what is it intermediary? What is its membership? What is its relation to the bodies it mediates between?

These questions become troubling when we realize that the "sovereign" and the "state" are the same entity under different aspects, as are "citizen" (member of the sovereign) and "subject" (member of the state). The problem becomes particularly vexing when we realize that, with popular sovereignty, the members of the government must be equally members of the sovereign. The governmental apparatus is distinct from the sovereign conceptually, yet its membership is drawn from the same source.[2] A member of the government is, at the same time, a member of the sovereign and a subject; and his function is to serve as an intermediary between the sovereign and the state. Apparently, he is to serve as an intermediary between himself and himself.

Just before propounding the above definition of government, Rousseau draws a parallel between this "intermediate body" and the point of contact between body and soul: "The public force, then, requires an appropriate agent to concentrate it and put it to work according to the directions of the general will, to serve as a means of communication between the state and the sovereign, to effect in some manner in the public person what the union of soul and body

2. All members of the government are members of the sovereign, but not all members of the sovereign need be members of the government. The situation where all members of the sovereign are members of the government Rousseau calls *democracy*. As we shall see further on, he does not look upon this form of governmental apparatus with particular favor, not at least for large states.

effects in a man. This is in the state the reason for government, improperly confounded with the sovereign of which it is only the minister" (3:1).

At this point, one might suppose Rousseau to have in mind those "animal spirits" that, according to Descartes and his successors, effect the "substantial union" in human beings of the two (logically independent) substances mind (thinking substance) and matter (extended substance).[3] Mind is essentially not extended; it has no spatial dimension. Matter, on the other hand, is extended substance: extension is its essential trait, its defining characteristic. How, then, can something that does not have spatial dimension be in contact with something that does? More important for our purposes, how can volitions, a species of mental event, be effective in the material world? How can volitions issue in actions? To conceive this apparent impossibility, Descartes supposed the existence of "animal spirits," which provide what amounts to a pictorial solution (or non-solution) to the mind-body problem. To theorize the point of contact between extended and non-extended substance, Descartes imagines the existence of minute "metaphysical cones," concentrated in the pineal gland, verging on non-extension at their apex and spreading down to a surface of determinate extension at their base. Pictorially, they touch spacelessness (mind) at one end and extension (matter) at the other. They are neither one nor the other, but somehow—impossibly—a little of both, and therefore a point of contact between the two.

In the Cartesian case, the problem of the relation of mind and body is dissipated—not solved—if we allow ourselves to be carried away by the imagery the supposed solution suggests. If mind and matter can meet in the animal spirits, a single entity, why can they not meet elsewhere, without the mediation of animal spirits? The Cartesian "solution" is really just the Cartesian problem represented pictorially. This sort of move may make some people more comfortable with the problem in the sense that what appeared (psychologically) impossible—that something non-extended could be in contact with something extended—is made to appear more plausible. Instead of crass bodies and ethereal minds, we simply

3. See *Discourse on Method*, part 5. Descartes' most extended discussion of "animal spirits" is to be found in *The Passions of the Soul* (1649). In that text, as is well known, Descartes declares the highest concentration of "animal spirits" to be lodged in the pineal gland (Article 31).

imagine minute, metaphysical entities where contact appears less jarring. Needless to say, however, doing so has not advanced the real problem—of conceiving the interaction of substances that are by definition logically independent—an inch toward a genuine solution.

There is a similar element of deception (or self-deception) in Rousseau's use of government. It is the notion of government that allows us to consider the effectivity of the sovereign's will without having to face the problematic character, discussed in chapter 1, of the relation between the sovereign and the individual. We are told to think of government as something that translates a moral cause into a physical one, that allows for the effectivity of the general will, for its determination of individual action. Execution of the sovereign's will by the government is the alternative—the sole moral alternative—to the determination of individual action by the private wills of egocentric individuals and social groups. Yet for this function to be fulfilled as it is conceived, the government must itself be without a will. It must be pictured as a non-substantial point of contact between essentially different entities: the contracting parties of the social contract. To make us see things this way is the point of alluding to "the union of soul and body" in man. But we already know that what is really at issue is something quite contrary, even the inversion of what we are asked to picture. Government is in fact a "substantial" institution in society. Indeed, it is even a partial association of a certain sort—one formed to execute the enactments of the assembled people. And the two terms it is supposed to mediate are, in reality, two different aspects or "forms" (to use Rousseau's word) of the same entity. Instead of a "something" somehow "mediating" between two aspects of the same thing, we are asked to imagine a "nothing" (analogous to the Cartesian "animal spirits") mediating between two "somethings."

Functioning precisely to mask the real difficulty (of which Rousseau is apparently unaware), the problem of conceiving a "contract" between parties of differential theoretical status, we are asked to imagine a false problem (on analogy to the Cartesian problem of the relation of mind and body), for which government furnishes a neat and ready-made solution. We shall see further on that Rousseau, even if he is unaware of what it masks, is not unaware of the paradoxical character of his description of government. His awareness is indicated by his account of the *will* of governments and of the measures he would introduce to counteract or neutralize the threat posed by the will of governments to the expression of the general will.

It should be stressed that the institution of government has nothing to do with a social contract in the sense of Book 1, chapter 6. There what was at issue was the establishment of civil society. The election of a government is an entirely different matter, one Rousseau does not wish to conceive in contractarian terms. On this issue he is unequivocal: "Those who pretend that the act by which a people submits to its chiefs is in no way a contract are quite right. It is absolutely nothing but a commission, an employment in which, as simple officers of the sovereign, they exercise in its name the power of which it has made them depositories, and which it can limit, modify and take back as it pleases. . . ." (3:1). The government has authority by *commission*. When it commands rightfully it does so in the name of the sovereign, not in its own name. Its authority is "authorized" (Hobbes) by the sovereign, and it holds this authority in "trust" (Locke).

Since government plays a role secondary to sovereignty in establishing obligation, the *vocabulary* in which it is discussed should reflect this difference. Accordingly, Rousseau introduces definitions: "The members of this body (the government) are called magistrates or *kings*, that is *governors*; and the body as a whole bears the name of *Prince*" (3:1). This vocabulary is somewhat idiosyncratic and might be misleading. As later chapters make entirely clear, there is no exclusive commitment to monarchical forms of government implicit in it. The identification of "magistrates" and "kings" suggests that, by "king (*roi*)" Rousseau has in mind the etymological sense—*rex*, or ruler. Similarly, it is evident that "prince" in this context does not necessarily refer to a single person, still less to any particular office. Rather, it has a collective and neutral sense. The prince is the individual or group of individuals who actually perform the governmental function. The institutional organization of these individuals can be quite varied, as Rousseau makes clear throughout Book 3.

Incorporating these reflections, Rousseau, by way of summary, offers the following extended definition of government: "I therefore call *government* or supreme administration the legitimate exercise of the executive power; and Prince or magistrate the man or body charged with that administration" '(3:1).

The Geometrical Formula for Government (3:1 continued)

Book 3, chapter 1, concludes with an extended mathematical account purporting to fix, with more precision than before, the correct relationship between sovereignty and government. This text is interesting but obscure, particularly inasmuch as the sense of some of Rousseau's terms has changed considerably since the eighteenth century. Still, these few paragraphs merit careful scrutiny for the light they cast on Rousseau's conception of government.

Since the intention, for most of Book 3, will be to study different *forms* of government, Rousseau wants a general definition that will draw attention to the "relations" of "intermediate forces" that are found in government.

It is in the government that are found the intermediate forces, the relations (*les rapports*) of which constitute the relation of the whole to the whole, or of the sovereign to the state. This last relation can be represented by that of the extremes of a continued proportion (*une proportion continuè*), of which the mean proportional (*la moyenne proportionnelle*) is the government. The government receives from the sovereign the commands which it gives to the people; and in order that the state may be in stable equilibrium (*dans un bon èquilibre*), it is necessary, everything being balanced (*tout compensè*), that there should be equality between the product or the power (*le produit ou la puissance*) of the government taken by itself, and the product or power of the citizens who are sovereign on the one hand and subjects on the other. [3:1]

In this passage, Rousseau shifts from a non-technical, non-mathematical use of "relation" to a technical sense not current today. To discover Rousseau's thought, then, we have to investigate the precise significance his terminology had for him.

One says that four numbers of terms A, B, C, and D form a proportion when the relation of A to B is equal to that of C to D. The terms A and D are called the *extremes*, B and C are the *means*. In a given relation A / B, A is the *antecedent*; B is the *consequent*. In Rousseau's time, a *continued proportion* (*proportion continuè*) was defined as a proportion where the consequent term of the first relation and the antecedent term of the second relation are equal. That is to say, the two means are equal: $A / B = B / C$.[4] When this is the case, the proportion, in effect, consists of only three terms: A, B, and C. Since, for any proportion, the product of the extremes is equal to the product of the means, $B^2 = A \times C$. One then calls B the *mean proportional* (*la moyenne proportionnelle*) between A and C.

Rousseau proposes to let A stand for the sovereign (the individuals collectively, regarded as citizens), B for the government, and C for the state (the individuals collectively, regarded as subjects). This background explains what is meant at the end of the passage quoted above, where Rousseau declares: "it is necessary, everything being balanced, that there should be equality between the product or power of the government taken by itself, and the product or power of the citizens, who are sovereign on the one hand and subjects on the other." It should be noted that *product* here is used in a technical sense, while *power* is not.

In the next paragraph, Rousseau points to some of the advantages of this formulation. First, it underscores the necessity of government for the exercise of sovereignty over the state. Rousseau's way of bringing out this necessity is rather odd: he appeals to the unalterability of the three terms as a condition for the existence of the continued proportion: "one could not alter any of the three terms without at once destroying the proportion. If the sovereign wishes to govern, or if the magistrate wishes to legislate, or if the subjects refuse to obey, disorder succeeds order, force and will no longer act in concert, and the state, dissolved, thus falls into despotism or anarchy" (3:1). Further, having already established that government is to be regarded as the mean proportional between the sovereign and the state, and pointing out that "there is but one mean proportional between each relation," Rousseau concludes that "there is only one good government possible in a state": an apparently striking conclusion, but one already implicit in Rousseau's mathematical language. Indeed, this last claim is just a more literary translation of what has already been asserted.

4. More generally, $A / B = B / C = C / D$ and so on. However, this generalization need not concern us, as we have only three terms in contention: the sovereign, the government, and the state.

Having put forward this mathematical account, Rousseau offers a brief illustration destined to bring out yet further consequences. Consider, he says, the relation that exists between the sovereign and the number of individuals comprising the sovereign. Considered as members of the sovereign, the citizens must be regarded collectively, as a single body. As subjects, however, each person remains an individual, absolutely subject to the general will. Therefore, in our continued proportion, A = the number of citizens and B = unity. More generally, if there are n citizens, $A / C = n / 1$. Each person, then, is only $1 / n$th part of the sovereign, although absolutely subject to it. Rousseau remarks: "The subject, then, always remaining a unity, the proportional power of the sovereign (*le rapport du Souverain*) increases in the ratio of the number of the citizens. From which it follows that the more the state is enlarged, the more liberty is diminished" (3:1). This last phrase deserves comment. The point is obviously not that the size of the sovereign modifies the rights of the individual in any libertarian sense. All political communities, no matter what size, are, in Rousseau's view, founded on the total alienation of *all* the rights of each person. Nor can the claim be that "moral liberty" (autonomy) is diminished as the state grows. Any *de jure* state preserves autonomy absolutely. The point simply is that the larger the sovereign, the less weight each individual citizen carries in the determination of the social choice. In this last sentence, then, Rousseau is using *liberty* in what is, for him, a deviant sense.

At this point, Rousseau directs his discussion toward what will emerge as the central theme of Book 3: the relativity of forms of government. The discussion around this point is replete with technical notions, borrowed from eighteenth-century mathematics, that have subsequently passed out of usage. For example, the paragraph following the claim that liberty diminishes with the size of the sovereign reads: "When I say that the proportional power (*le rapport*) increases, I mean that it is farther removed from equality. Therefore, the greater the ratio (*le rapport*) in the geometrical sense, the less is the ratio (*rapport*) in the common acceptation; in the former, the ratio considered according to quantity is measured by the exponent (*l'esposant*), and in the other, considered according to identity, it is estimated by similarity" (3:1). The point of this passage is simply to recall the difference between the technical sense of the word *relation* (*rapport*) and the ordinary language sense. The claim is that the two senses are effectively in inverse relation to one another. What renders this point obscure for contemporary readers is that the term *exponent* (*exposant*) had another sense in the eighteenth century, in addition to the sense it now has. An exponent of a geometric ratio (*raison*) would today be called a *quotient*; it is the result of the division of the consequent of the ratio by its antecedent.

Further on, Rousseau speaks of another unfamiliar term: *double ratio* (*double rapport*). "It follows from this double ratio that the continued proportion between the sovereign, the Prince, and the people is not an arbitrary idea, but a necessary consequence of the nature of the body politic" (3:1). Given two equal relations, A/B and C/D, the double ratio is defined as $(A \times C)/(B \times D)$. Now in the case at hand, we have a continued proportion with only three terms—A, B, and C, corresponding to the sovereign, the government, and the state, respectively. The double ratio, therefore, is the relation $(A \times B)/(B \times C)$. However, one of the extremes of the proportion, C, is fixed in value, being always equal to 1. The double ratio is therefore equal to $(A \times B)/B$ or A. Now, obviously, when A varies, the relation A/B varies as well. So if that relation is to remain constant, as the requirement of a continued proportion demands, B must vary directly with A. "It follows ... that one of the extremes, viz. the people as subject, being fixed and represented by unity, whenever the double ratio increases or diminishes, the single ratio increases or diminishes similarly, and consequently *the middle term is changed*" (3:1, italics mine). In other words, the larger the body politic, the stronger must the government be: "The government should be relatively stronger in proportion as the people are more numerous" (3:1).

Further, since $A \times C = B^2$, and since $C = 1$, $B = \sqrt{A}$. But here our mathematical illustration is getting out of hand, and Rousseau must finally call a halt:

> If for the sake of turning this system to ridicule, it should be said that, in order to find this mean proportional and form the body of the government, it is, according to me, only necessary to take the square root of the number of the people, I should answer that I take that number here only as an example: that the ratios of which I speak are not measured only by the number of the combination of multitudes of causes; that more-

over, if for the purpose of expressing myself in fewer words, I borrow for a moment geometrical terms, I am nevertheless aware that geometrical precision has no place in moral quantities. [3:1]

In other words, we do not have a mathematical demonstration after all. We have instead a use of mathematical language with a view to a more concise and forceful presentation than would otherwise be feasible. That these technical terms may, finally, prove misleading is less important than what they allow Rousseau to express: the relativity of forms of government. Rousseau draws this conclusion explicitly: "There is no unique and absolute constitution of government, but there may be as many governments different in nature as there are states different in size" (3:1).

These conclusions do not follow mathematically, but mathematical language, in Rousseau's view, helps to draw them out. It may be questioned whether he is correct. Rousseau has an indisputable tendency to shift from technical to non-technical senses of terms, not always with sufficient warning for the reader. And the resulting obscurity—from a contemporary point of view—is intensified by changes from Rousseau's time to ours in the meaning of the technical terms used (though, of course, these changes are not his fault).

Nevertheless, as we have seen, two clear and important theses do emerge. These may be restated as follows:

1. The form of government, unlike that of sovereignty, which is everywhere the same, varies.
2. Among the factors affecting the relativity of governmental forms, the size of the sovereign is particularly crucial; the larger the size, the stronger the government.

Rousseau does not say much here about what other factors may also be involved; though we may assume that, as an admirer of Montesquieu, he did consider such other factors as population, climate, and so on. We shall return to this problem shortly, as we take up the question of the varieties of governmental forms.

The Varieties of Government (3:1 continued–3:3)

We have seen how the possibility of conceiving government as an intermediate body between the sovereign and the state rests on the possibility of conceiving government as a morally insubstantial entity; that is, as an institution in and of society somehow posing no threat, by its existence as an intermediate body, to the realization of the general will. And we have seen further how the feasibility of this conception rests on the government itself having no will. Government must somehow be neutral with respect to willing, serving as a simple point of contact (and transmission) between the terms it connects.

However, as Rousseau immediately concedes, this situation is impossible. Government is an institution. It is a determinate grouping within the body politic. Moreover, it is necessarily so, if it is to function as a government: "in order that the body of the government may have an existence, a real life, to distinguish it from the body of the state; in order that all its members may be able to act in concert and fulfill the object for which it is instituted, a particular personality (*un moi particulier*) is necessary to it, a sensibility common to its members, a force, *a will of its own* tending to its preservation" (3:1, italics mine). For government to exist, then, it must have a will; yet if it is to function as a government—as an intermediate point of contact between the sovereign and the state—it cannot have a will. This is the paradox that the extended discussion of varieties of government in Book 3 attempts to resolve.

In the concluding paragraphs of chapter 1, Rousseau seems intent on drawing this paradox as sharply as possible. He goes so far as to picture government as a miniature state, a complex structure including "assemblies, councils, a power of deliberating and resolving, rights, titles and privileges," with its own internal divisions and conflicts. These miniature states, like all social groupings, have interests. And there is no reason to suppose any intrinsic relationship between these interests and the general interest.[5] The interests of governments, like those of all social groups, are private interests.

However, viewed genetically, these are of a sort rather different from the private interests of other social groups. The

5. Of course these interests may coincide. And it might even be argued that they will typically coincide: that what is good for the government is good for the state and vice versa. When this is the case, however, it is so as a contingent matter of fact. The coincidence of interests, whenever it exists, is accidental. The government's interest and the general interest are essentially disjoint.

private interests of other groupings are depicted as pre-moral vestiges of the state of nature, of the time prior to the total alienation of each associate with all his rights. Government, on the other hand, does not antedate the institution of sovereignty. Quite the contrary: it is derived from sovereignty—both logically and (in terms of the temporal metaphor of the social contract) chronologically. Thus, unlike other social groups, government does not threaten the general will because it "holds something back." Instead, what threatens the general will, in this case, is precisely what allows the general will to be exercised: the institutional organization of at least some citizens for the purpose of carrying out the sovereign's enactments. This is the crux: that government is and can only be an institution. As such, it cannot be morally neutral. For an institution, Rousseau seems to think, in anticipation of later theories of bureaucracy and institutional organization, wills its own preservation and its own internal development.

It might be argued that since government is necessary for the exercise of sovereignty, whatever strengthens government is in the general interest and whatever undermines government is a threat to the general interest. In this way, one might conclude that the internal interest of government as an institution does indeed bear an intrinsic relation to the general interest. However, to argue this way is to miss the point of the problem. The government actually in power is committed not to the existence, preservation, and strengthening of government *as such,* but to its own self-interest and development. To a certain extent, it does have an interest in, say, promoting the ideal of obedience to government generally, as a way of promoting obedience to itself. But its self-interest far exceeds these general requirements (requirements that do, arguably, bear an intrinsic relation to the general interest). As a social group, institutionally organized, the government must to some extent regard itself as distinct from the sovereign. Indeed, as Rousseau warns, the government threatens constantly to set itself up as an alternative sovereign, with disastrous consequences for the body politic: "If the prince should chance to have a private will (*volonté particulière*) more active than that of the sovereign, and if, to enforce obedience to this private will, it should employ the public force which is in its hands, in such a manner that there would be, so to speak, two sovereigns, the one in right and the other in fact; the social union would immediately disappear, and the body politic would be dissolved" (3:1). In short, the existence of government, though absolutely essential for the realization of the general will, constantly threatens that realization.

Rousseau summarizes the problem: "The difficulties lie in the method of ordering within the whole, this subordinate whole, in such a way that it will in no way change the general constitution in affirming its own; that its private force, destined for its own preservation, may always be kept distinct from the public force destined for the preservation of the state; and that, in a word, it may always be ready to sacrifice the government to the people, and not the people to the government" (3:1). His formulation in the sixth of the *Letters Written from the Mountain* is even more forceful: "The government as an integral part of the body politic participates in the general will that constitutes it. But as a body itself, it has its own will. These two wills are sometimes in agreement (*s'accordent*) and sometimes in disagreement (*se combattent*). It is from the combined effect of this cooperation (*concours*) and conflict that the play (*le jeu*) of the entire machine results."[6] The whole problem of government, then, is bound up with the problem of the will. The task is to discover forms of government that will neutralize the threat the will of the government poses, while at the same time allowing the government to function *as an institution* for executing the sovereign's enactments.

The point of introducing the geometrical formula for government was to show that there is no unique solution to the problem. Governments will differ for different states, "so as to accord with the accidental and particular relations by which the state itself is modified." We already know that one of these "accidental and particular relations" is the size of the body politic. This thesis will figure prominently in what is to follow.

Chapter 1 of Book 3 poses the question of the varieties of governmental forms as a theoretical consequence of the distinction between sovereignty and government. In chapter 2, Rousseau goes on to investigate the principle (*principe*) which "constitutes the different forms of government."

Thus, if there is no unique governmental form that is right for all states, there is nevertheless a principle that determines the appropriate governmental form. Apparently, what Rousseau wants

6. *Oeuvres complètes* (Pléiade edition), 3:808.

is something like a *law* in the scientific sense that had become prevalent by the eighteenth century: a constant relation between phenomenal variables. Then the "principle" or "general cause (*la cause générale*)" that constitutes the different forms of government will be whatever makes this constant relation intelligible, whatever accounts for it.

However, in this case, the variables in question—sovereign and state on the one hand, government on the other—are not very likely candidates for (scientific) laws. For sovereignty, though observable in principle, may never in fact have been observed. What then is to count as evidence for the principle Rousseau seeks to discover? We must be very careful here. The intention is to account *not* for observable differences in existing, *de facto* states, but for differences in the governmental forms of *de jure* states of which none may ever have existed! This is certainly a curious situation for one who has imported the notion of principle or cause in the scientific sense. It is obvious, at the very least, that we cannot investigate the question in the usual way, by careful attention to the evidence. Rousseau announced in *The Second Discourse* that it was essential to begin by "laying the facts aside."[7] That procedure is in force here.[8] For all *de jure* states, the principle of sovereignty, announced in the terms of the social contract, is everywhere the same. Accidental and particular factors determine the appropriate form of government. And the "principle" determining these modifications is to be investigated: diversity is to be conceived

7. Cole's translation, p. 161.
8. Rousseau's concern throughout *The Social Contract* is the investigation of political right (political philosophy), not the description of political fact (political science). For reasons that are not altogether clear, Rousseau regarded the former study as a prerequisite to any useful application of the latter. It is worth recalling what Rousseau says on this theme in Book 5 of *Emile*, particularly in view of the overwhelming influence of Montesquieu's attempt at descriptive political science in his own account of governmental forms: "The science of politics is and probably always will be unknown. . . . In modern times the only man who could have created this vast and useless science was the illustrious Montesquieu. But he was not concerned with the principle of political law; he was content to deal with the positive laws of settled governments; and nothing could be more different than these two branches of study. Yet he who would judge wisely in matters of actual government is forced to combine the two: he must know what ought to be in order to judge what is" (Barbara Foxley, trans. [London: Everyman's Library, 1911], pp. 421–22).

through a unifying principle, just as scientific laws make apparently different and unrelated phenomena intelligible through the discovery of a "general cause." But how is this investigation to proceed with the facts laid aside, of necessity, as irrelevant?

It can proceed only by further reflection on the nature of government and its relation to the sovereign and the state. Specifically, Rousseau will get at the principle he is looking for by developing the analogy, already proposed in chapter 1, between the government and the state: that the government is indeed "on a small scale what the body politic which includes it is on a large scale."

For this reason, Rousseau proposes that the prince be distinguished from the government in the way that, earlier, the state was distinguished from the sovereign. That is, the prince is to the government as passive is to active, as unity is to collectivity.[9] We can therefore substitute "prince" and "government" for "state" and "sovereign," respectively, in the geometrical formula of Book 3, chapter 1. As a member of the prince, the individual magistrate will then count as one; as members of the government, the magistrates will be considered collectively. Thus, the larger the number of magistrates, the greater the ratio of government to prince, and, Rousseau continues, the more force must be disposed internally— on its own members—and the less deployed on the people at large. Rousseau concludes that the larger the government (that is, the greater the number of magistrates), the weaker it is, the less force it is able to exercise externally, in executing the sovereign's enactments.

This seems a rather perverse way of putting the very unlikely claim that the efficiency of governments varies inversely with size. The claim could, of course, be tested empirically. Large governmental apparatuses may sometimes (perhaps even typically) be unwieldy and inefficient. But it is by no means the case that efficiency increases with diminished size, particularly where governmental functions are complex. What Rousseau seems to have had in mind is the exercise of force for keeping the members of the government, the magistrates, in line. Such force, he maintains,

9. "The entire body (of magistrates, etc.), considered in terms of the men who compose it is called *prince* and considered in terms of its action is called *government." Emile*, bk. 5 (Pléiade edition), 4:844.

would necessarily be deflected in a large government from the general maintenance of order and would therefore diminish the government's strength. Hence the cryptic assertion put forward in the third paragraph of chapter 2: "the total force of the government, being always that of the state, does not vary." Rousseau seems to have been led to this result by the supposition that the repressive state apparatus—the "force" of the state at the government's disposal (the police, the army, and so on)—is a force exterior to the government and independent of it. Then the relative efficiency or strength of government has to do solely with the relative efficiency of the government in deploying this force, externally. If it must use this force on itself, its efficiency is naturally diminished. But why suppose this force need be used internally at all? And, especially, why in direct proportion to the number of magistrates? Surely, it would be the exception—certainly not the rule—if an external, repressive force were needed to insure order and obedience *within* the government to the government's own edicts.

Nevertheless, this claim is an important constituent of the principle Rousseau will offer to account for the variety of governmental forms. It will shape a good part of the argument of Book 3.

To explain the claim that the strength of government varies inversely with size—Rousseau calls it a "maxim"—he asks us to distinguish three wills the magistrate might entertain. As an individual, he has a private will that "tends only to his personal advantage"; as a member of the government, he shares in "the common will of the magistrates, which has reference solely to the advantage of the Prince, and which may be called a corporate will"; and as a citizen, he participates in "the will of the people, or the sovereign will," that is, in the general will. The corporate will, Rousseau goes on, is general in relation to the government and private (*particulière*) in relation to the state.[10] The sovereign, or

10. Therefore, the existence of a corporate will does not really contradict the claim that all wills are either private or general. The corporate will is a private will entertained by several persons (when the government consists of more than one member) in their capacities as magistrates. The private wills of all social groups are of this sort. However, as we have seen, government is the only intermediate body Rousseau can countenance. That its will is problematic has already been discussed: it must *not* have a will if it is to function strictly as an executive; yet it cannot avoid having a will if it is to execute.

general, will is, on the other hand, "general both in relation to the state considered as a whole, and in relation to the government considered as part of the whole."

The practical problem is to make the general will dominant: "In a perfect [system of] legislation, the private or individual will should be inoperative; the corporate will proper to the government quite subordinate: and consequently, the general will or sovereign always dominant, and the sole rule of all the rest" (3:2). The creation of this last condition is the goal of all of Rousseau's practical measures. Of these, the institution of the correct form of government is an important part. The task is to find a form that, in the peculiar and accidental circumstances of the territory and population in question, allows the corporate will to remain "quite subordinate" to the general will.

Rousseau's way of posing the problem seems peculiarly inept. According to the natural order, he tells us, a will is more or less active according to its "concentration": "Thus the general will is always the weakest, the corporate will has the second rank, and the private will, the first of all; so that in the government each member is, firstly, himself, next a magistrate and then a citizen—*a gradation directly opposed to that which the social order requires*" (3:2, italics mine). Taken literally, the meaning here is that no will can ever in principle be stronger than a private will, for no will can possibly be more "concentrated." Again taken literally, this passage attributes the general will only to the community as a whole, specifically to the sovereign; and not to each individual *qua* citizen, *qua* member of the sovereign. The obvious consequence, then, is that the general will can never be dominant; that, therefore, a state founded on legitimate authority can never exist. We know, however, that this literal reading cannot be maintained, that it is inconsistent with the main thrust of *The Social Contract*. Specifically, the general will, properly speaking, is entertained by each individual citizen, and by the sovereign (the set of all citizens) only in a manner of speaking. The question of differential "concentration" cannot arise: all wills are entertained exclusively by individuals. The only sense in which a will is shared is the sense in which more than one individual aims at the same object, whether that object be some group or corporate interest or the general interest. Then the several individuals in question might be said to entertain the *same* will, not because they share in some finite magnitude that is somehow weakened by being "divided" among several individuals, but because the will is defined by its object.

Nevertheless, there are at least two points to be salvaged from this passage. The first is incontrovertible: that the institution of a form of government that does not threaten the general will goes against nature. Government is an artificial, human product. In this domain, Rousseau stresses, the natural inclination is "directly opposed to what the social order requires." The institution of government is an art, requiring extraordinary insight on the part of the lawgiver. The second point is the now familiar claim that a government is strong in inverse proportion to its size. The obvious measure indicated by the text is to "concentrate" the corporate will by diminishing the number of magistrates—a hopeless measure, nonetheless, since the prince can never consist of fewer members than one and can therefore never be "stronger," as defined here, than a private will. In any event, this, once again, is that keystone of "the principle that constitutes the different forms of government," the same point already defended a few paragraphs above by substitution into the mathematical account of Book 3, chapter 1. Rousseau is as insistent on this point as he is incapable of providing an adequate argument for it. One suspects that the difficulty lies in its blatant falseness.

The second constituent of Rousseau's principle is already suggested in chapter 1: that the larger the state, the stronger the government should be; that is, the more powerful should be the repressive force. This was one of the points of the geometrical formula for government. However ingenious that argument, though, it can hardly be taken as conclusive. Neither can the following argument from the same chapter: "Now the less the private wills correspond with the general will, that is manners and morals (*moeurs*) with laws, the more should the repressive force be increased. The government, then, in order to be effective, should be relatively stronger in portion as the people are more numerous" (3:1). We shall take up the issue of manners and morals in the next chapter. For now, it is clear enough that the first sentence is unobjectionable. In more contemporary terms, what is asserted is that the greater the degree of social cohesion, the less repressive force is required to maintain order. However, it is not at all clear how the second sentence follows from the first. It would do so only on the assumption that correspondence of customs with laws varies inversely with the size of states. This, again, seems a very unlikely empirical claim. At any rate, there is no argument offered on its behalf.

To sum up, two aspects of "a principle which constitutes the different forms of government" have been put forward:

1. The strength of government varies inversely with its size; that is, with the number of magistrates comprising the prince.
2. The need for strong government varies inversely with the size of the body politic.

From these two claims, the following principle is deduced:

3. The state and the government should vary inversely in size.

Here is Rousseau's statement of the conclusion:

> I have just shown that the government is weakened in proportion to the number of magistrates, and I have before demonstrated that the more numerous the people is, the more ought the repressive force to be increased. From which it follows that the ratio between the magistrates and the government ought to vary inversely as the ratio between the subjects and the sovereign; that is, the more the state is enlarged, the more should the government contract; so that the number of chiefs should diminish in proportion as the number of people is increased. [3:2]

It should be stressed that (1) and (2) are not put forward as descriptions of how things are, but as reflections on how things ought to be. As I have tried to show, these reflections are faulty in a number of respects: they are based on almost certainly false empirical assumptions; they depend on a misleading analogy between the government and the state; and they follow from a strange and extremely idiosyncratic conception of governmental strength. These reservations will have to be borne in mind in evaluating what is built on the principle (3) that follows from (1) and (2).

Finally, it is important to realize that, in Rousseau's view, these considerations need to be balanced by considerations pulling in the opposite direction. For Rousseau, it is "incontestable" that govern-

ment is "weakened in proportion to the multiplication of its magistrates" and that "the more numerous the people, the more ought
the repressive force to be increased" (3:2). Yet it does not follow
necessarily that, in all cases, the smallest government—at the limit,
government by a single magistrate—is best. For such government,
Rousseau cautions, threatens the general will. Rousseau's expression of this caution is awkward in that here—as earlier in the
chapter—he speaks as though the general will can only be attributed to the community as a whole and not, as is strictly correct,
to persons. Still, the reservation that concludes chapter 2 is very
much in point:

> I speak here only of the relative force of the government, and
> not of its rectitude. For, on the contrary, the more numerous
> the magistracy is, the more does the corporate will approach
> the general will; whereas under a single magistrate, this same
> corporate will, as I have said, is only a private will. Thus, what
> is lost on one side can be gained on the other, and the art of the
> lawgiver[11] consists in knowing how to fix the point where the
> force and the will of the government, always in reciprocal
> proportion, are combined in the ratio most advantageous to the
> state. [3:2]

In other words, increased efficiency may be accomplished by a
serious threat to sovereignty, because where the government has
few members the corporate will (of the government) is likely to
become confounded with the private will(s) of the magistrate(s).
This point—apart from its misleading account of the attribution of
the general will—is essentially a psychological one. In fact, there
are really two claims asserted:

1. The temptation to give in to one's private will, at the expense
   of one's general will, is particularly acute when one is in a
   situation—as is the magistrate—to make one's private will
   effective; that is, to attain one's private interest.
2. The fewer the magistrates—that is, the greater the difference
   between the magistrates and the people—the more likely are
   the magistrates to succumb to this temptation.

11. For a discussion of Rousseau's notion of "the lawgiver," see my account
of 2:7 in chapter 4 below.

This last situation is precisely the one where the state is large and the government small. In view of Rousseau's evident liking for mathematical expression, at least in the opening chapters of Book 3, one feels justified in attributing to him the following claim:

> 2'. The tendency to succumb to the temptation of a magistrate to substitute his private will for the general will is in direct proportion to the size of the state, and in inverse proportion to the size of the government.
>
> In short, the claim is that power corrupts; and more specifically, that the power of magistrates—necessarily greater as the prince is smaller and the state larger—threatens the sovereignty of the general will.

Rousseau has, then, concocted the following dilemma: on the one hand, the larger the state, the greater the need for strong government; and, therefore, the smaller the government should be. On the other hand, the larger the state, the more likely that government will distance itself from the people and will therefore deviate from and undermine the general will; thus, the larger the state, the larger the government should be. The problem is to balance these relative advantages and disadvantages, taking account of the "accidental and particular" circumstances of the state. The assumption is that a "golden mean" can always be found, that the dilemma can always be resolved.

The rigorous distinction of sovereignty from government is a radical departure from traditional political theory, and this difference pervades Rousseau's entire discussion of government. Still, Rousseau takes over from traditional political theory the classification of government into three categories: democracy, aristocracy, and monarchy. These categories are ideal types: conceptual divisions useful for organizing a host of actual or potential data. As we might anticipate, the principle underlying this classificatory scheme is the size of the magistracy. That is, what determines whether a government is a democracy, an aristocracy, or a monarchy is the number of people actually engaged in administration, relative to the size of the population of the state.

The three ideal types are defined explicitly in Book 3, chapter 3. Where the executive power rests in the whole people, or very nearly so—or, as Rousseau puts it, "when there are more citizens who are magistrates than simple individual citizens" (3:3)—the form of government is called *democracy*. When the government is confined to a (relatively) small number of citizens, such that "there are more ordinary citizens than magistrates" (3:3), the form of government is called *aristocracy*. And, finally, when the whole government is concentrated "in the hands of a single magistrate from whom all the rest derive their power" (3:3), the form of government is called *monarchy*. A number of comments are in order.

First, the distinction Rousseau draws between the sovereign and the government gives these definitions a rather idiosyncratic cast. Rousseau's theory of sovereignty is patently democratic, even majoritarian. But this theory does not commit him to defending a democratic form of government in the sense just defined. For democratic government to be defensible, given Rousseau's definition, it would have to be the case that circumstances favor a magistracy consisting of more than half the population of the state. Our expectation is that such circumstances are highly unlikely; and, as we shall see shortly, Rousseau agrees. There is a sense, then, in which Rousseau is not a democrat at all, but in fact is, if anything, more sympathetic to monarchy. We shall return to this point. For now, it is enough to note two things: that to be anti-democratic in Rousseau's sense is hardly to be anti-democratic in any relevant contemporary sense; and that these definitions are exceedingly tendentious. One would have to be almost a lunatic to advocate democracy in Rousseau's sense; and, for large states (given other assumptions, some of which have already been made explicit), monarchy emerges as almost the only feasible solution to the problem of government.

Second, it should be noted that Rousseau conspicuously omits a traditional form of government: the republican form. He does so because he considers every legitimate government, whatever its form, to be republican. "I . . . call any state a republic which is governed by laws, under whatever form of administration it may be; for then only does the public interest predominate and the commonwealth count for something (*et la chose publique est quelque chose*). Every legitimate form of government is republican" (2:6). It has been claimed that this is an entirely new definition, as in a certain sense it is.[12] However, what is really new, again, is the distinction between the sovereign and the government. For Montesquieu, a republic was any form of government where the people, or some significant body of the people, are sovereign; for Rousseau, no form of government can be legitimate where the people are not sovereign. Any *de jure* state, for Rousseau, is a republic in Montesquieu's sense. However, what, from Rousseau's point of view, Montesquieu cannot see—precisely because he fails to distinguish the sovereign from the government—is the compatibility of many forms of government, even monarchy, with popular sovereignty. In other words, what is new here is not the definition of *republic*, but the application of a traditional definition—traditional at least since Montesquieu—to a radically new theory of government.

Third, the government, unlike the sovereign, is divisible. "Mixed government" is possible, that is, a government in which different governmental functions are organized differently—involving, for example, monarchical, aristocratic, and democratic elements all at the same time. Rousseau discusses "mixed government" in Book 3, chapter 7. In chapter 3, he is only concerned to establish its possibility.

Finally, as Rousseau is to discuss at length in Book 3, chapter 8, and as has already been suggested, there is no single, best form of government. Still, a tentative conclusion does follow: "If, in the different states, the number of the supreme magistrates should be in inverse ratio to that of the citizens, it follows that, in general, democratic government is suitable to small states, aristocracy to those of moderate size, and monarchy to large ones" (3:3). However, Rousseau cautions, a "multitude of circumstances" may "furnish exceptions."

Democracy (3:4)

To repeat: by democracy, Rousseau means any form of government where a majority of citizens are magistrates. At the limit, the entire citizenry is coextensive with the magistracy in a democracy. Rousseau, then, does *not* mean by democracy what many classical and contemporary theorists mean: a state where the people are

12. See Paul Bastid, "Rousseau et la theorie des formes de gouvernement," p. 319.

sovereign. As we know, in his definition popular sovereignty is a necessary condition for any *de jure* state—democratic, aristocratic, monarchical, or mixed. Still less does Rousseau mean by democracy representative government. As is well known, he finds representative government incompatible with individual autonomy: sovereignty cannot be represented (see Book 3, chapter 15). In a democracy, in Rousseau's sense, the people are *both* sovereign *and* executive.

The democratic solution is most suitable for one aspect of Rousseau's dilemma: the reconciliation of the corporate interests of the government (and the private interests of the magistrates) with the general interest. Moreover, as Rousseau tells us, "he that makes the law knows better than any one how it should be interpreted" (3:4). For these reasons, democracy would seem to be the best form of government; Rousseau is, however, quick to point out the mistake in this assumption. The very size of democratic government renders it generally incapable of governing. A democratic government, in Rousseau's expression, is "a government without a government."

These are the reasons why a pure democracy, strictly speaking, never has existed and likely never will exist. It is too impractical; it will not really function as a government. Also, it is unwise and dangerous: unwise to expect or want people to "remain in perpetual assembly to attend to public affairs" (3:4) (the very time required would be an unacceptable burden, for people then would be unable to devote themselves to other pursuits); and dangerous to divert public attention away from questions of legislation towards questions of execution (since execution involves attention to particulars, private interest would almost certainly reimpose itself). There is no greater evil, Rousseau insists, "than the influence of private interests on public affairs" (3:4); it far outweighs the evils of "the abuse of the laws by the government" which may, as we have seen, be a consequence of small government.

Still, under certain conditions, democratic government—or some approximation to it—is, if not desirable, at least feasible. First, as we have already been told, the state must be very small; indeed, so small, Rousseau comments, that all citizens would know one another and could be easily assembled. Second, there would have to be, in Rousseau's expression, "great simplicity of manners (*moeurs*)," to prevent a multiplicity of affairs and thorny discussions. There would need to be a substantial measure of equality in "rank and fortune" in order to insure equality in "rights and authority." And finally, Rousseau adds, there would have to be "little or no luxury, for luxury is either the effect of wealth or renders it necessary," thereby corrupting both rich and poor (3:4). For this reason, Rousseau continues, alluding to Montesquieu, "a famous author has assigned virtue as the principle of a republic."[13]

For Montesquieu, as we have seen, a republic is something like Rousseau's sense of a democracy; it is any system of popular sovereignty and government. Lacking Rousseau's distinction between sovereignty and government, Montesquieu failed to appreciate to what extent virtue is the principle of all *de jure* states. The citizens of a democracy, however, would need be exceptional. As Rousseau concludes: "If there were a nation of gods, it would be governed democratically. So perfect a government is unsuited to men" (3:4). So perfect a government is not really a government at all. Democracy is feasible only where virtue is so well established that there is really no need for government. As Rousseau wrote some paragraphs earlier: "A people which would never abuse the government would likewise never abuse its independence; a people which always governed well would not need to be governed" (3:4).

We should note the warning Rousseau gives in the penultimate paragraph of chapter 4. He claims that democratic government (or any reasonable approximation to it) is inherently unstable; that it is inclined to civil war and internal strife. It is curious that this argument should be produced by Rousseau himself. It is precisely this argument that is often invoked today *against* theories of a Rousseauean inspiration, theories enjoining a high degree of popular participation in collective decision making.[14] However, there really is no deep inconsistency. What Rousseau opposes is a democratic executive, not a legislative apparatus with the very highest possible degree of popular participation. And his principal argu-

13. See *L'Esprit des lois* 3.3.5.2.
14. The anti-participationist argument has its roots in Hobbes, but today finds its chief support in sociological writers. Joseph Schumpeter's *Capitalism, Socialism and Democracy* (New York, 1942) is the fountainhead for much of this literature. Almost any recent piece of writing on democracy will furnish examples of the contemporary anti-participationist argument. See, for example, G. A. Almond and S. Verba, *The Civic Culture* (Boston,

ment against a democratic executive is precisely that it diverts energy and attention away from the legislative process. The resulting internal agitation and civil strife is seen as a consequence, not of a high degree of politicization, as contemporary anti-democrats would have it, but of corruption of the sovereign through diversion of its proper energies.

Although, as a careful student of Hobbes, Rousseau cannot but be aware of the danger to order inherent in a high degree of popular participation—whether executive or legislative—the motto that concludes chapter 4, with special reference to a democratic executive, could be taken as a motto for *The Social Contract* generally: *Malo periculosam libertatem quam quietum servitum* (I prefer dangerous freedom to quiet servitude).

Aristocracy (3:5)

By aristocracy is meant, strictly, that form of government where the number of magistrates is greater than one but smaller than half the number of citizens. Within this broad definition—formulated, again, in terms of the size of the magistracy relative to the size of the citizenry—the understanding is that the minority who rule will be elite in some sense. This understanding is suggested even by the literal meaning of the term: *aristo-cracy*—rule by the best. Especially in view of the preceding account of democracy's impracticality and imprudence, it might appear that aristocracy is the preferred form of government. "In a word, it is the best and most natural order that the wisest should govern the multitude, when we are sure that they will govern it for its advantage and not their own" (3:5). Here, too, Rousseau is careful not to be too categorical in his praise. Its appropriateness depends on the circumstances of the state, particularly its size. Aristocracy is the form of government suitable in general for moderately sized states: "a state must not be so small, nor a people so simple and upright (*droit*), that the execution of the laws should follow immediately upon the public

1965), S. M. Lipset, *Political Man* (London, 1960), H. B. Mayo, *Introduction to Democratic Theory* (Oxford, 1960), L. W. Milbrath, *Political Participation* (Chicago, 1965), and W. H. Morris Jones, "In Defense of Apathy," *Political Studies* 2 (1954): 25–37. For a critical review of this literature and a brilliant defense of participatory theory (along Rousseauean lines), see Carole Pateman, *Participation and Democratic Theory*.

will, as in a good democracy. Nor again must a nation be so large that the chiefs, who are dispersed in order to govern it, can set up as sovereign, each in his own department, and begin by making themselves independent so as at last to become masters" (3:5).

There are, according to Rousseau, three types of aristocratic government—natural, elective, and hereditary. Of these, the second is plainly best: it is based, at least in principle, on merit rather than wealth or inherited privilege. For that very reason, hereditary aristocracy, on Rousseau's view, is "the worst of all governments"; it allows for the installation of rulers without regard to "probity, intelligence, or experience" (3:5). Natural aristocracy—wherein the population spontaneously accedes to the natural authority of, say, priests or elders—is possible only in relatively simple communities.

Unlike democracy, aristocracy does not require—in fact, is likely to be incompatible with—any substantial equality of wealth or position. What is required, instead, is satisfaction with one's lot; or, as Rousseau would have it, "moderation among the rich and contentment among the poor." The point is not that the wealthy should govern; merit, not riches, ought to be the grounds for membership in the elite. What Rousseau wants to stress is rather the need for a general acceptance of unequal distribution of power. Contentment with one's lot is the "virtue" of a state governed aristocratically.

In short, aristocracy is characterized by moderation. It is the mean between rule by the majority and rule by a single magistrate. As such, it is most fitted for states of moderate size, characterized by a moderate, but not glaring, inequality in the distribution of wealth and privilege.

Recall, however, that what is meant by aristocracy is not that system where the wisest *legislate* for the rest, but only that where they *execute* the sovereign people's enactments. As citizens, all individuals count equally. Thus, aristocracy is, for Rousseau, compatible with popular sovereignty and individual autonomy. Were it not, no *de jure* state could have this form of government. It is significant that Rousseau's discussion of aristocracy is prefaced with a reiteration of the distinction between the sovereign and the government. "Although the government can regulate its internal policy as it pleases, it can never speak to the people except in the name of the sovereign, that is, in the name of the people themselves. *This must never be forgotten"* (3:5, italics mine).

Monarchy (3:6)

By monarchy is meant that form of government where the executive power is "concentrated in the hands of a ... person ... a real
man, who alone has a right to dispose of it according to the laws"
(3:6). This definition is very close to Montesquieu's, according to
which, in a monarchy, the monarch alone governs, but in conform-
ity to fixed and established laws—in contradistinction to despotism, where also there is only one ruler, but his rule is lawless,
determined only by his will and caprice. The difference between
Montesquieu's conception and Rousseau's is just the difference in
formulation that grows out of Rousseau's distinction between the
sovereign and the government. In a monarchy, for Rousseau, the
prince is not a body (*corps*) but an individual, who alone has the
right to dispose of the executive power according to the laws
enacted by the sovereign. On this condition, rule by a single
monarch is republican in the sense established in Book 2, chapter 6.

Rousseau's discussion of monarchy is unfortunately sometimes
careless of this distinction—at least in terminology. At one point,
he even goes so far as to oppose monarchical government to
republican government. In reading this text, it is important to be
wary of such lapses.

It has been suggested, no doubt correctly, that the moderate
and indeed almost approving tone with which Rousseau discusses
monarchy here is in large part due to his fear of censorship and to
an acute personal sense of living and writing under a monarchical
regime.[15] There is nonetheless a fairly evident anti-monarchical
strain running through even these relatively moderate remarks;
and in some of Rousseau's other writings, anti-monarchism is far
more pronounced.

As has already been indicated, the great advantage of monarchy, for Rousseau, is its "concentration," and consequently its
strength. As the monarch need not exercise any coercive force
internally, the full strength of the repressive state apparatus can be
easily and efficiently applied to the proper task of governing the
state: "all the springs of the machine are in the same hand,
everything works for the same end; there are no opposite move-
ments that counteract one another, and no kind of constitution can

15. See Ronald Grimsley's introduction to the Oxford edition of *Du Contrat
Social* (1972), p. 40.

be imagined in which a more considerable action is produced with less effort. Archimedes, quietly seated on the shore, and launching without difficulty a large vessel, represents to me a skillful monarch, governing from his cabinet his vast states, setting everything in motion, while he appears motionless" (3:6). However, if there is no government that is stronger and more vigorous, there is also none in which the general will is more threatened. "Everything works for the same end, it is true; but this end is not the public welfare, and the very power of the administration turns continually to the prejudice of the state" (3:6). In other words, there is a tendency for monarchy to degenerate into despotism in the sense defined by Montesquieu.

Monarchy is, in effect, the only feasible form of government for large states, where the need for strong government is greatest; yet it is the form of government most threatening to the legitimacy of the state.[16] There is an inevitable tendency, Rousseau thinks, for kings to wish to become absolute, that is, to wish to become sovereigns. The problem is that the private interest of the king—an interest that the king is very often in a position to realize—is typically opposed, and sometimes even diametrically opposed, to the general interest. Only in somewhat atypical circumstances, Rousseau argues, would it be the king's principal private interest even to please the people or to attempt to gain their favor. In general, the private interest of the king is for the people to be weak and submissive. This, Rousseau tells us, was the advice Samuel gave to the Hebrews and the thesis Machiavelli demonstrated— ostensibly on behalf of the Medicis he served; actually, Rousseau contends, for the people and liberty.[17]

16. One could well construe these remarks as a veiled argument for the *illegitimacy* of existing states in Rousseau's time (and, by extension, in our own). I have suggested above that Rousseau's theory of sovereignty, far from accounting for the legitimacy of *de facto* states, as is sometimes claimed, in fact constitutes a critical principle through which the legitimacy of these states (past and present) can be attacked. According to the reading proposed above, the description of governmental forms in Book 3—whatever its apparent connection to *de facto* states—corroborates the view I have set forth in earlier chapters.

17. For Rousseau's admiration of Machiavelli as a defender of liberty, see Paolo M. Cucchi, "Rousseau, lecteur de Machiavel," in *Rousseau et son temps*, ed. M. Launay (Paris, 1968), pp. 17-35. Cucchi's argument is summarized in Grimsley, Introduction to *Du Contrat Social*, pp. 73-77.

To be sure, this difficulty is not essential to the monarchical system. The monarch, like any other citizen, could in principle submit to the general will and thereby overcome private interest. Rousseau's point is just that it is more difficult for a monarch to do so than for any other citizen; indeed, that it is so difficult as to make the degeneration of the system—from monarchy in the republican sense to despotism, from legitimate to illegitimate government—virtually inevitable. This danger is all the more acute the larger the state, where the monarch—however sound his intentions—is necessarily the more remote from his subjects.

There are other defects of monarchy. Among these, Rousseau cites the tendency to attract "petty mischief-makers, petty knaves, and petty intriguers" with "petty talents" to high government posts, while less concentrated governmental forms tend more to fill government posts with "enlightened and capable men." This problem, too, becomes acute in large states, where the monarch must rely on subordinate officials to administer his vast territories. Another difficulty is the problem of succession. "Elections leave dangerous intervals," Rousseau maintains, where internal strife, intrigue, and corruption are almost inevitable. If succession is hereditary, the problem is even worse. There is no guarantee that the most competent will rule, and every reason to expect the contrary. Moreover, there is the risk of having "children, monsters and imbeciles" for kings.

Of course, there is the occasional good king under whose governance the state flourishes. But the occasional appearance of such monarchs, Rousseau cautions, is small compensation for the defects of the monarchical system: "if according to Plato, a king by nature is so rare a personage, how many times will nature and fortune conspire to crown him? And if the royal education necessarily corrupts those who receive it, what should we expect from a succession of men trained to rule? It is then voluntary self-deception to confuse royal government with that of a good king. To see what this government is in itself, we must consider it under limited or wicked princes; for such will come to the throne, or the throne will make them such" (3:6).

In short, monarchy may be the strongest form of government; and it may, for that reason, be the only form possible—given Rousseau's principle for constituting the different forms of government—for large states. But it is a form almost certain to result in the corruption of the state.

Mixed Government (3:7)

The possibility of mixed government—that is, of government where elements of different ideal types are to some degree present—has already been established in Book 3, chapter 3, by appeal to the divisibility of the governmental function. In Book 3, chapter 7, Rousseau goes on to consider this possibility expressly. The problem of mixed government had much occupied Rousseau's predecessors, for example, Aristotle, for whom the republican form was a kind of composite of oligarchy and democracy. Rousseau's treatment of mixed government is brief and unhistorical. He says nothing terribly new in theory, but, in view of the historical importance of the notion of mixed government, he cannot ignore the subject.

The idea of mixed government is important, too, in that any pure instance of democracy, aristocracy, or monarchy is exceedingly improbable: "Properly speaking, there is no simple government. A single chief must have subordinate magistrates; a popular government must have a chief. Thus, in the partition of the executive power, there is always a gradation from the greater number to the less, with this difference, that sometimes the majority depends on the minority, and sometimes the minority on the majority" (3:7). Some sort of mixed government is almost inevitable. From a theoretical point of view, it may be most important to clarify the component elements of any possible mixture; but in practice, one would have to attend, finally, to mixed government itself.

Again, the relative merit of mixed as opposed to (relatively) simple government, a question much debated by Rousseau's predecessors, is too indeterminate to answer in general. Everything depends on the circumstances of the state, chief among these being its size. However, since the relative strength of government must be taken into account for determining whether a governmental form is better or worse, it can be determined *a priori* that no mixed government will be as strong as monarchy; for monarchy is, by definition, the most concentrated and therefore the strongest governmental form. For the same reason, no mixed government will be as weak as democracy. However, as has been amply attested, strength is not the sole virtue of a government; nor is weakness, necessarily, a fault.

The Wealth of Nations (3:8)

For Rousseau, size is not the only factor that ought to affect the question of governmental form; another is prosperity. As might be expected from an eighteenth-century writer, prosperity is conceived as agricultural, not manufacturing, wealth. Accordingly, the fertility of the soil and the nature of the climate take on the character of independent variables in determining the form of government; at least to the extent that for certain climates and certain natural conditions, certain forms of government can be shown in general to be more desirable than others, and other forms can be shown to be entirely inappropriate. Hence the title of Book 3, chapter 8: "that every form of government is not fit for every country."

This line of investigation had already been pursued by Montesquieu in Books 14 to 18 of *The Spirit of the Laws*. In this chapter, Rousseau acknowledges his debt to Montesquieu, claiming that he seeks only to reconfirm Montesquieu's results. The chapter begins with an assertion clearly dependent on Montesquieu's celebrated thesis to the effect that despotism flourishes in hot climates, barbarism in cold ones. Rousseau begins, "Liberty, not being a fruit of all climates, is not within the reach of all peoples."

Rousseau's argument appears burdened throughout this chapter with the principle that the size of the government should be inversely proportional to the size of the state, with reference here to wastefulness in taxation. Governments, he points out, only consume; they never produce. They exist solely on revenue extracted through taxation. In prosperous countries, the burden of taxation will be relatively light; in poor countries, typically, it will be severe. But it is not the amount of revenue raised through taxation that is significant; rather, it is the rapidity of circulation—that is, the efficiency in returning to the public (in the form of useful services) revenue extracted from the public—that renders taxation more or less burdensome. At this point Rousseau reintroduces the question of the size of governments. He says, in effect, that a system of taxation is wasteful in proportion to the distance taxes must travel in order "to return to the hands from which they have come." And distance is construed—even more peculiarly—in terms of the relative difference in size between the population of the state and the prince. Thus Rousseau concludes that "the more the distance between the people and the government is increased, the more onerous do the tributes become; therefore, in a democracy the people are least encumbered; in an aristocracy, they are more so; and in a monarchy they bear the greatest weight. Monarchy, then, is suited only to wealthy nations, aristocracy to states moderate both in wealth and size; democracy to small and poor states" (3:8). In other words, the size of the government relative to the state determines the onerousness of taxation, and tolerance for taxation varies directly with the wealth of the nation. Only rich states can tolerate monarchy (where the size of the government is smallest relative to the size of the state); and, more generally, the poorer the state, the larger must the government be. At the limit, poor states must be democracies. Two comments are appropriate.

First, this argument does not, in itself, suggest that rich states *ought* to be monarchies, but only that they *can* support monarchies. That rich states ought to support monarchies is intimated further on in chapter 8, for reasons even more tenuous than those offered thus far.

Second, the plausibility of this argument depends strictly on the peculiar interpretation Rousseau gives to both *wastefulness* and, especially, *distance.* With regard to *distance,* the argument plainly rests on confounding *distance* in a sense that would suggest wastefulness with *distance* in the sense of *difference* in size between the prince and the state. There seems to be no good reason for confounding these senses; nor is the conclusion that follows established. The wastefulness of government is clearly independent of the size of the magistracy. And, if anything, the larger the magistracy, the more reasonable it is to expect wastefulness in the ordinary sense—the more will revenue be deflected to internal government operations. But Rousseau has not adequately shown what wastefulness in either sense has to do with the appropriate form of government. We can only conclude that here, as elsewhere, Rousseau's attempt to link the size and form of government has not succeeded.

There are two other substantive theses advanced in this chapter. The first of these is that insofar as natural conditions determine the wealth of nations—and they will to a very great extent where agricultural wealth is at issue—nature provides important guidelines to the citizenry in its choice of a form of government. Or, in Montesquieuean terms, government must be adapted to the nature of the climate. This claim is advanced in the following passage, which also introduces the final substantive thesis of the chapter.

> Unfruitful and barren places, where the product does not repay the labor, ought to remain uncultivated and deserted or should be peopled only by savages; places where men's toil yields only bare necessities ought to be inhabited by barbarous peoples; in them any polity would be an impossibility. Places where the excess of the produce over the labor is moderate are suitable for free nations; those in which abundant and fertile soil yields much produce for little labor are willing to be governed monarchically, in order that the superfluity of the subjects may be consumed by the luxuries of the prince; *for it is better that this excess should be absorbed by the government than dissipated by private persons.* [3:8, italics mine]

The claim, then, is not just that a rich nation can suffer a monarchy, but that it *ought* to do so—that the wastefulness of monarchy, because of the distance between the prince and the state, is beneficial, because it is better that the economic surplus of wealthy nations be absorbed or even wasted by the prince than that it be consumed by private persons. We have already encountered Rousseau's abhorrence of private luxury: it corrupts the individual and leads, almost inevitably, to private interest. Luxury, in short, threatens sovereignty. The citizens of a just state must be Spartans, not Parisian courtiers.[18]

What is curious is not the injunction to remove the temptation of private luxury but the insistence that the economic surplus must be consumed. However, this insistence is curious only in light of the still-standard view that emerged late in the eighteenth century among the British political economists—largely in response to the growing importance of manufacturing wealth—that, rather than being consumed in the form of luxuries, economic surplus ought, so

18. See Judith Shklar, *Men and Citizens,* chap. 1.

far as possible, to be reinvested in such a way as to expand productivity and thereby increase the wealth of the state. For Rousseau, in a pre-industrial, eighteenth-century frame of reference, wealth is agricultural. Then, indeed, given the prevailing level of technology, the product of labor would have to be consumed within a relatively short time, and investment in anything other than manpower would be practically useless. Given the prevailing social organization of agricultural production—small peasant holdings—even investment in manpower would be exceptional. Thus, if we conceive the wealth of nations as Rousseau and his contemporaries did, the assumption that surplus must be consumed becomes plausible. If surplus must be consumed, and if it is beneficial to the state that it not be consumed privately, a feasible solution is to have an exceedingly wasteful form of government— monarchy.

The theses set forth in this chapter, Rousseau acknowledges, are not categorical laws, true come what may; and still less are they empirical generalizations (although Montesquieu's work, on which this chapter is based, is largely empirical). Rousseau's theses are 'tendential' laws, arrived at through reflection on the nature of government and its relation to the size and prosperity of the state. As such, these laws constitute presumptions for which countervailing conditions are conceivable.

> We should always distinguish general laws from the particular causes which may modify their effects. If the whole south should be covered with republics and the whole north with despotic states, it would not be less true that, through the influence of climate, despotism is suitable to warm countries, barbarism to cold countries, and a good polity to intermediate regions. I see, however, that while the principle is admitted, its application may be disputed; it will be said that some cold countries are very fertile, while some southern ones very unfruitful. But this is a difficulty only for those who do not examine the matter in all its relations. [3:8]

The rest of chapter 8 is taken up not with a sketch of the "relations" that might modify the application of these general tendential laws, but with a further reflection on the Montesquieuean thesis that despotism flourishes in warm climates. We need not regret the lack of such an account, inasmuch as the general law it is supposed to modify is plainly unsound.

At this point, it will be useful to draw together the conclusions Rousseau has so far reached. It should be noted, again, that none of these conclusions have been established by sound argument. The question is, in effect, what tendential laws can provide guidance in the choice of a form of government? Rousseau's answers are as follows:

1. Democratic government, though best a priori (for preventing the corporate will of the government from compromising the general will), is always impractical. If it is ever feasible, it can be so only in small and poor states.
2. Aristocratic government *ought* to be instituted in states of moderate size and moderate prosperity. This is a kind of golden mean between pure democracy and strong monarchical government.
3. Large and wealthy states *ought* to be governed by monarchy, despite the inherent danger of despotism, because they require strong and wasteful government.

Again, these results hold only relatively; they are tendential laws. And insofar as simple governments—democracy, aristocracy, and monarchy—are ideal types, they probably cannot be instituted in pure form. Strictly speaking, then, what Rousseau has done is to set forth principles suggesting guidelines for selecting the elements that *ought*—in the particular circumstances of the state—*to be dominant in mixed governments*.

The Sign of a Good Government (3:9)

If there are no hard and fast rules for selecting the proper form of government, there is nevertheless a clear sign by which one can determine whether a state is well governed, as Rousseau specifies:

> For my part, I am always astonished that people fail to recognize a sign so simple, or that they have the bad faith not to agree about it. What is the end (*la fin*) of the political association? It is the preservation and prosperity of its members. And

what is the surest sign that they are preserved and prosperous? *It is their number and population.* . . . All other things being equal, the government under which, without external aids, without naturalizations, and without colonies, the citizens increase and multiply most, is infallibly the best. That under which a people diminishes and decays is the worst. [3:9, italics mine]

There are really two assertions here: first, that the end (*la fin*) of political association is "the preservation and prosperity of its members"; and, second, that increase in population is the surest sign of prosperity, as decrease in population is the surest sign of its absence. As the second assertion is by far the less problematic, I shall begin with it.

That the population of a prosperous country will increase and that of an impoverished country decrease is contradicted by experience. However, it is not an unreasonable speculation, given the social organization and technological and medical level of eighteenth-century Europe. Unlike more universal but less incisive indicators, population figures are in principle measurable. Perhaps immeasurability is the reason Rousseau adamantly rejects happiness as a criterion of prosperity. Other quantifiable indicators, such as measurements of economic growth, are plainly beyond the reach of eighteenth-century economic technique. The second assertion, then, is incorrect as it stands; but, given the specific circumstances for which it was introduced, it is not unreasonable. Inasmuch as the aim is to find quantifiable indicators for prosperity, Rousseau's suggestion does not seem indefensible.

More problematic from a theoretical point of view is the assertion that the end of political association is "the preservation and prosperity of its members." This statement would appear to contradict one of the central tenets of *The Social Contract*, formulated explicitly in Book 1, chapter 6: that the end of political association is the actualization of a potential for individual moral autonomy, a potential systematically thwarted in that state of alienation Rousseau calls the state of nature. It might be possible to construe *preservation* in terms compatible with this central text (Rousseau does speak in Book 1, chapter 6, of the state of nature threatening the human race), but the expression "preservation and prosperity" leaves this account inadmissible or, at best, disingenuous. It might appear, then, that Rousseau has forsaken his own rigorous formulation of the fundamental problem of political philosophy for a Lockean account of society as a kind of joint stock company in which each associate pools his resources with a view to attaining a higher level of prosperity.

I would suggest that, as the text stands, it is inconsistent with the formulation of Book 1, chapter 6, but that it is possible to "correct" Rousseau in such a way as to preserve some of what he has in mind, while maintaining the consistency of the whole work. First, instead of talking about the end of political association, it will be better to talk about the end of government. It will be recalled that the actualization of each individual's potential for moral autonomy is a condition for any just state, no matter what its form of government, and regardless whether it is well or poorly governed. The function of government is to execute, within the body politic, that will of each citizen which is the general will. Government, then, is that institution which allows the individual to realize his moral autonomy in political society. Strictly speaking, this is its end.

Where this end is substantially realized, where the modalities of execution are in harmony with the natural and human circumstances of the state, the state is well governed. And a well-governed state, one might speculate, will be a state whose subjects efficiently realize their individual *and* collective goals. For this reason, it is likely, other things being equal, that a well-governed state will prosper, and its collective wealth increase. This claim is a long way from Rousseau's formulation suggesting that "the preservation and prosperity of its members" is the "end of political association," but it is perhaps not too far from Rousseau's actual intention.

Thus, prosperity is the by-product of good government. It is what some philosophers would call a natural sign. And, for reasons that we have discussed and dismissed, Rousseau takes changes in population as indicators of changes in prosperity and is enabled thereby to say that the surest sign of good government is an increasingly populous state.

Decline and Fall (3:10–15)

The central point of the preceding reflections on the nature of government and the varieties of governmental forms has been the absolute dependence of the government on the sovereign. It is only through this dependence that a government rules legitimately. This dependence is, however, always tenuous. As a substantive institution in society, a partial association established by the social contract (which proscribes all other partial associations), the government has a will of its own that constantly threatens the sovereignty of the general will. In this opposition, which the proper choice of a governmental form can mitigate but cannot cause to disappear, lies the seed of the degeneration of government and the decline and fall of the state. This theme was central in the work of many of Rousseau's predecessors, among them Aristotle, Bodin, Pufendorf, Hobbes, and Locke, and especially among the Latin authors Seneca and Tacitus.[19] It is introduced by Rousseau in the opening paragraph of Book 3, chapter 10:

> As the private will acts incessantly against the general will, so the government makes a continual effort against the sovereignty. The more this effort is increased, the more is the constitution altered; and as there is here no other corporate will which, by resisting that of the prince, may produce equilibrium with it, it must happen sooner or later that the prince finally opposes the sovereign and breaks the social treaty. *Therein is the inherent and inevitable vice which, from the birth of the body politic, tends without intermission to destroy it, just as old age and death destroy the human body.* [3:10, italics mine]

There is, in short, inherent in the inevitable tension between the corporate will of the prince and the general will an inevitable tendency to degenerate.

One way for government to degenerate is through contraction: the natural tendency of executive power to become increasingly concentrated in fewer hands. Contraction makes more likely the dissolution of the state, that is, the end of the rule of autonomously legislated law, and therefore the rupture of the social contract. This

19. This tradition has been acknowledged by a number of recent writers on Rousseau, chief among them being C.W. Hendel in *Jean-Jacques Rousseau, Moralist*, 2:210, and Bertrand de Jouvenel in a number of articles (see "Rousseau the Pessimistic Evolutionist," pp. 93–96; and "Essai sur la politique de Rousseau," in his edition of *Du Contrat Social* [Geneva, 1947], pp. 18–38).

dissolution can occur if the prince is not governing in accordance with law, or if he actually usurps the sovereign authority. Then, plainly, the social contract is dissolved: the associates to that contract regain their natural liberty and obey the prince, if at all, out of compulsion or prudence, rather than right. The same process occurs when a number of magistrates effectively usurp that power which ought to be exercised by them collectively in accordance with law.

Rousseau calls the abuse of government, whatever its form, *anarchy*.[20] And corresponding to each of the ideal types of governmental form is a degenerate form: democracy degenerates into *ochlocracy* (literally, mob-rule), aristocracy into *oligarchy*, and monarchy into *tyranny*.[21]

The tendency toward the dissolution of the state is universal and, in the final analysis, irresistible. "If Sparta and Rome have perished," laments Rousseau, "what states can hope to endure forever?" (3:10). There is no reason, in short, to suppose a *de jure* state will fare better than these historical approximations to it.

An analogy with human life and death is well taken. The state, like the human body, begins to die from the moment of its birth. In each case, life may be prolonged but not preserved indefinitely. The prolongation of life is particularly in point so far as the state is concerned, for, unlike the human body, a work of nature, the state

20. See Grimsley, Introduction to *Du Contrat Social*, p. 183, n. 2: "Rousseau uses the word 'anarchy' to describe illegal governments, not (as today) absence of government."

21. Rousseau proceeds to nuance this definition:

In the vulgar sense a tyrant is a king who governs with violence and without regard to justice and laws. In the strict sense, a tyrant is a private person who arrogates to himself the royal authority without having a right to it. It is thus that the Greeks understood the word tyrant; they bestowed it indifferently on good and bad princes whose authority was not legitimate. Thus *tyrant* and *usurper* are two words perfectly synonymous.

To give different names to different things, I call the usurper of royal authority a *tyrant* and the usurper of the sovereign power a *despot*. The tyrant is he who contrary to the laws, takes upon himself to govern according to the laws; the despot is he who sets himself above the laws themselves. Thus the tyrant cannot be a despot, but the despot is always a tyrant. [3:10]

This distinction had already been made, in effect, by Aristotle in Book 4, section 10, of *The Politics*.

is a product of human *art*. Mankind can effectively prolong the life of the state by giving it the best practicable constitution. To persist with this analogy, the legislative power is the heart of the state, the executive its brain. The brain may be paralyzed, Rousseau writes, and the individual still live, but when the heart ceases its functions, the organism dies. To prolong the life of the state, then, one must pay special heed to its vital principle—the legislative power.

Accordingly, Rousseau advises periodic popular assemblies. He insists that even in relatively large states, such assemblies are not a utopian dream. Ancient Rome, with four hundred thousand citizens bearing arms, and an estimated population of four million (excluding subjects, foreigners, women, children, and slaves), held frequent assemblies. "Few weeks passed without the Roman people being assembled, even several times" (3:12).

It is best, Rousseau continues, that these popular assemblies meet on dates fixed by law, "which nothing can abrogate or prorogue" (3:13). In this way, the people cannot be prevented from meeting except by blatant usurpation. Rousseau suggests that the frequency of these popular assemblies should be in direct proportion to the strength of the government. For, besides legislation, the intention is to force both magistrates and citizens to become aware of the absolute dependence of the prince upon the sovereign. Thus, when popular assemblies meet, the executive power is suspended, only to be re-established or, if necessary, reconstituted later.

Obviously, this stricture does require a rather severe limitation on the size of states. In Book 3, chapter 13, Rousseau suggests that the ideal state would be no larger than a single city. In the next chapter, he concludes, "After very careful consideration I do not see that it is possible henceforward for the sovereign to preserve among us the exercise of its rights unless the state is very small" (3:14). When it is not feasible for a state to be very small or to be confined to a single city, Rousseau suggests that there be no fixed capital and, therefore, no tendency to concentrate sovereign power. Most importantly, if civic virtue is to flourish, the countryside must not be subordinated to the towns, as was already the rule in Rousseau's day. It is well known that Rousseau's vision of the good life is more rural than urban; urban life is at the root of the artificiality and pretence he despises.

In the final analysis, it is the civic virtue and simple patriotism of the population that sustains the state. Proper psychological and moral attitudes are indispensable. The surest road to the degeneration of government and the dissolution of the state is for patriotism to decline in favor of the pursuit of private interests. Rousseau argues against representative government, as we have already seen, on the grounds that sovereignty cannot be represented. In Book 3, chapter 15, where this claim is made explicit, he asserts that the predominance of private interest and a general decline in civic virtue are responsible for the institution of representative government: "So soon as the service of the state ceases to be the principal business of the citizens, and they prefer to render aid with their purses rather than their persons, the state is already near ruin. Is it necessary to march to battle, they pay troops and remain at home; is it necessary to go to the council, they elect deputies, and remain at home. As a result of indolence and wealth, they at length have soldiers to enslave their country and representatives to sell it" (3:15). To elect representatives is to succumb to indolence and the desire for private gain. This theory apparently underlies Rousseau's celebrated estimation of the English: "The English nation thinks that it is free, but it is greatly mistaken, for it is so only during the election of members of Parliament; as soon as they are elected, it is enslaved and counts for nothing. The use which it makes of the brief moments of freedom renders the loss of liberty well-deserved" (3:15). Rousseau is adamant: people should do for themselves—absolutely, in legislation; as far as possible, in government. In the end, the pro-monarchical implications of the opening chapters of Book 3 are more than counterbalanced. The personal involvement of the citizens in all political functions is a condition for the enjoyment and exercise of freedom, the object of the social contract.

The Institution of Government (3:16–17)

In the concluding chapters of Book 3, Rousseau turns to the question of the establishment of government. In opposition to some of his predecessors,[22] Rousseau categorically rejects the view that government is instituted by a "pact of submission," a second social contract following the "pact of association" by which "a people becomes a people." According to the view Rousseau attacks, this

22. Particularly Jurieu and Pufendorf. See J. W. Gough, *The Social Contract*, pp. 122 ff. and Grimsley, Introduction to *Du Contrat Social*, pp. 34–35.

second contract is made between the people (constituted by the first contract) and the government. However, such a contract is inconceivable, given Rousseau's idea of popular sovereignty and the nature of government: the government is just a part of the sovereign people, called together to execute its will. That the sovereign should acknowledge a part of itself as a party to a pact of submission with the whole, and moreover that it should regard that part of itself as its master, is "absurd and contradictory." Again, to institute a government by contracting with particular persons is a particular act of a sort that cannot be an act of the sovereign, for reasons discussed in Book 2. And if the alleged pact of submission cannot in principle be an act of the sovereign, then it cannot be conceived as lawful. Finally, the contractees in this proposed contract would be "under the law of nature alone," without guarantee that reciprocal commitments would be honored or enforced. This situation, Rousseau maintains, "is in every way repugnant to the civil state." The Rousseauean contract, as we have seen, renders the problem of guarantees—a problem that plagued Hobbes, among others—theoretically superfluous. To hypothesize the institution of government by contract is to restore this problem in full vigor. As Rousseau points out, the pact of submission has a form analogous to the following agreement: "I will give you all my goods (biens) on condition that you restore to me what you please" (3:16). There is and can only be a pact of association, a social contract in the strict sense. "No public contract can be conceived which would not be a violation of this first" (3:6).

The real act of institution actually consists of two independent acts. The first is an act of law in the strict sense: "the sovereign determines that there shall be a governing body established in such or such a form" (3:17). The second is not an act of law, but a particular act: "the people nominate the chiefs who will be entrusted with the established government" (3:17). This second act, given Rousseau's formulation of the function of government as the executor of the sovereign's enactments, is, strictly speaking, already an act of government. Here, of course, we see a problem: how are we to conceive of an act of government prior to the institution of government?

The answer is that, in some sense, the people, who are so far only citizens, must, at least for the purpose of nominating magistrates, somehow become magistrates, too. "Here, however, is disclosed one of those astonishing properties of the body politic, by which it reconciles operations apparently contradictory; for this is effected by a sudden conversion of sovereignty into democracy in such a manner that, without any perceptible change, and merely by a new relation of all to all, the citizens, having become magistrates, pass from general acts to particular acts, and from the law to the execution of it" (3:17). That is, the nomination of magistrates is effected by the sovereign's spontaneous conversion—for that purpose—into a democratic prince. In this sense, democracy is the most natural form of government; it is that form which arises without conscious contrivance. But, as such, its tenure is brief and its powers limited to the execution of the sovereign's enactment determining the form of government.

This account has a disconcertingly ad hoc character. Still, Rousseau insists, the process of conversion on which it depends is not in the least fanciful or speculative. It occurs each day, he contends, in the English parliament, where the lower chamber "resolves itself into Grand Committee in order to discuss business better, and thus becomes a simple commission instead of the sovereign court that it was a moment before" (3:17). In any case, there is no description of the mechanism of this conversion, nor any account of its possibility. It is simply asserted as "an astonishing property of the body politic." That is, it is asserted in order to conceive the institution of government in a manner consistent with the principles established elsewhere in *The Social Contract,* as Rousseau virtually acknowledges in the concluding sentence of this chapter: "It is impossible to institute the government in any other way that is legitimate without renouncing the principles heretofore established."

A Final Warning (3:18)

From a theoretical point of view, any government, regardless of its form, is strictly dependent on the sovereign both for its institution and for its maintenance in power. Even where the form of government involves hereditary succession (which Rousseau does not recommend), the people may always introduce whatever changes they please, whenever they please. Practically, however, it is dangerous to interfere with government. To do so, Rousseau cautions, is to incite civil disorder that can threaten the very existence of the state. Thus, for prudential reasons, it is unwise to modify the government significantly except when it is plainly incompatible with the public good.

Rousseau concludes with a warning to be wary of carrying through, on a practical level, the theoretical implications of his theory of government. Governments should be brought to heel delicately, and in such a way as to incite the least possible instability. Above all, modifications of government, and especially of the form of government, should be carried out lawfully, by an act of the sovereign. Revolution is in order only where popular sovereignty is usurped.[23] Then, from a moral point of view, anything is permitted against *de facto* authorities. In a *de jure* state, however, where sovereignty exists, the recourse to revolution is inappropriate and indeed irrelevant.

To facilitate the lawful change of government where necessary, and to further instill in all a sense of the government's dependence on the sovereign, Rousseau suggests that the regular popular assemblies always be opened with two questions:

> The first: "Whether it pleases the sovereign to preserve the present form of government."

> The second: "Whether it pleases the people to leave the administration to those presently entrusted with it". [3:18]

It is important that these questions be institutionalized, in order to mitigate, as far as possible, the unsettling consequences that may follow from their being asked—and answered.

Rousseau concludes this long account of government, then, with the warning that one should proceed with infinite caution against government, but understanding that the composition of the government and its form, like all laws—indeed, like the social contract itself[24]—are always subject to revocation.

23. I have suggested earlier that this state of affairs, at least according to Rousseau's interpretation, may prevail everywhere.
24. Rousseau's text is as follows: "Grotius even thinks that each man can renounce the state of which he is a member, and regain his natural liberty and his possessions (*biens*) by leaving the country. Now it would be absurd if all the citizens combined should be unable to do what each of them can do separately" (3:18).

The social contract, it will be recalled, consists in the total alienation of each individual and all his rights. This alienation precludes the possibility of each individual's deciding whether or not, in a given case, to obey the

Appendix 1   Extra-Governmental Institutions

The Tribuneship (4:5)   Drawing on the historical examples of Rome and Sparta, Rousseau cites the need for extra-governmental, magisterial institutions, called *tribunals*. In Book 4, Rousseau discusses two tribunal institutions: the *censorship*, which will be taken up in another context; and the *tribuneship*, strictly speaking. In ancient Rome, the tribuneship was a corporate representation of the popular mass of the citizenry, of the plebians. Elected in relatively egalitarian, tribal assemblies, the tribunes formed a secondary and parallel executive agency, functioning to protect their constituency from the oppression of the Roman aristocracy.

Thus, like government the tribuneship is an intermediary institution; indeed, a parallel government:

> When an exact proportion cannot be established among the constituent parts of the state, or when indestructible causes are incessantly changing their relations, a special magistracy is instituted, which is not incorporated with the others, but which replaces each term in its true relation, forming a middle term between the prince and the people, or between the prince and the sovereign, or if necessary between both at once. This body, which I shall call the tribuneship, is the guardian (*conservateur*) of the laws and the legislative power. [4:5]

As the defender of the laws, the tribuneship is "more sacred and more venerated . . . than the prince that executes them and the sovereign that enacts them" (4:5). Rousseau resorts here to sheer hyperbole, but the need to protect and defend the institutions of the state and government is thereby underscored.

That a tribuneship can function without usurping executive power is proved, for Rousseau, by the historical example of Rome. Still, the danger is always present. In the final analysis, the only

---

law. It is irrelevant whether or not a particular enactment is in the individual's private interest. However, the individual is free—in principle—to decide that it is not in his interest to remain a part of the sovereign (though this decision would never be rational, even in a strictly instrumental sense); and so to leave the state. This is the sense of Rousseau's concluding note: "Of course no one should leave in order to evade his duty and relieve himself from serving his country at a moment when it needs him. Flight in that case would be criminal and punishable; it would no longer be retirement, but desertion" (3:18 n).

defense is the vigilance of the citizenry and the extent of their moral development.

Historically, the greater danger is that the executive power will usurp the tribuneship. For Rousseau, this was the principal cause of the decline of both Sparta and Rome. To guard against such an eventuality, Rousseau proposes a number of guidelines. First, like government, the tribuneship is stronger when its members are fewer. Accordingly, the way to strengthen the tribuneship against the government is to reduce its size. Second, to safeguard both the institution and the state it protects, it is best that the tribuneship not be a permanent body but periodically remain suspended. Since the tribuneship is extra-legislative and extra-governmental, no injury will befall the state if it is temporarily removed from the political scene. Rousseau suggests that the intervals during which it is suspended be fixed and determined by law in order to protect it further from manipulation by interests bent on dominating the state.

Protected by the vigilance of the citizenry, "the tribuneship, wisely moderated, is the strongest support of a good constitution." "This was very clearly seen in Rome," Rousseau notes, "when those proud patricians, who always despised the people as a whole, were forced to bow before a simple officer of the people, who had neither auspices nor jurisdiction" (4:15).

The Dictatorship (4:6) In the same vein, Rousseau notes that extraordinary circumstances may arise from time to time in which it is expedient to suspend the laws of the state and the normal executive apparatus. It is impossible to anticipate all contingencies. "A thousand cases may arise for which the legislator has not provided, and to perceive that everything cannot be foreseen is a very needful kind of foresight" (4:6). The *dictatorship* is the institutional means Rousseau proposes to deal with such emergencies.

Rousseau suggests that the people provide one or a number of magistrates with the power to suspend the laws when it is in the general interest to do so, and to govern dictatorially. This act is not, Rousseau insists, an alienation of sovereignty. On the contrary, what the general will demands above all is that the state not perish. It is legitimate to legislate means for the suspension of other legislation under extraordinary circumstances:

if the danger is such that the formal apparatus of law is an obstacle to our security, a supreme head is named, who may silence all the laws, and suspend for a moment the sovereign authority. In such a case, the general will is not doubtful, and it is clear that the primary intention of the people is that the state should not perish. *In this way the suspension of the legislative power does not involve its abolition; the magistrate who silences it can make it speak; he dominates it without having power to represent it; he can do everything but make laws.* [4:6, italics mine]

The dictatorship does not replace the sovereign authority; it suspends it for the sole purpose of protecting it. The people do not agree to have the dictatorship *represent* them, nor does the dictatorship *usurp* their authority. The people remain sovereign; the dictatorship acts *for them* and *in their name.*

Obviously, the sovereign would resort to this expedient only in the gravest of circumstances. And obviously, too, the danger that the dictatorship will usurp the sovereign's authority is very great. Again, a high level of public morality is the only defense in the final analysis. But institutional safeguards will still be useful. Rousseau concludes:

in whatever way this important commission may be conferred, it is important to fix its duration at a very short term which can never be prolonged. In the crises which cause it to be established, the state is soon destroyed or saved; and the urgent need having passed away, the dictatorship becomes tyrannical or useless. In Rome the dictators held office for six months only, and the majority abdicated before the end of this term. Had the term been longer, they would perhaps have been tempted to prolong it still further, as the Decemvirs did their term of one year. The dictator had time only to provide for the necessity which led to his election; he had no time to think of other projects. [4:5]

The danger that the dictatorship will devolve into tyranny is extremely great. But dictatorship is not itself tyranny. It is a desperate expedient of sovereignty.

Appendix 2 Roman Institutions (4:4)

The long discussion of the Roman *comitia,* or assemblies, appears at first to be out of place in *The Social Contract.* In fact, this digression into Roman history illustrates several of Rousseau's most central theses, and the chapter, if not essential to Rousseau's argument, is at least in line with it and corroborative of it.

What is of moment here is less the historical veracity of Rousseau's account of Rome than the image of a just and powerful state, of stable institutions and virtuous citizens. Even the name of that city, Rousseau tells us, and the name of its first legislator, invoke the idea of force joined with law. "The name of *Rome* which is supposed to be derived from Romulus is Greek and means *force;* the name of *Numa* is also Greek and means *law.* What likelihood is there that the first two kings of that city should have borne at the outset names so clearly related to what they did" (4:4).[24] The Romans were "the freest and most powerful nation in the world" (4:4), and theirs is probably the only historical state Rousseau believed legitimate. However, we cannot be certain how seriously to take the claim that the Roman *comitia* were genuine popular assemblies and therefore sovereign in Rousseau's sense. With the exception of the chapters on the tribuneship, dictatorship, and censorship, Rousseau draws few lessons from the historical experience of Rome. Rome is for him less a model to be described in order to draw out principles of political right than an illustration of certain of these principles. It is not ultimately important, then, if this illustrative city is little like the historical Rome.

It is interesting to point out that in arguing for the *de jure* character of the Roman state, Rousseau appeals to the generality of the *source* of enactments, but is silent on the other condition for legitimate legislation—generality of the object. He writes: "No law received sanction, no magistrate was elected, except in the *comitia;* and as there was no citizen who was not enrolled in a *curia,* in a *centuria,* or in a tribe, it follows that no citizen was excluded from

24. In fact, *Rome* etymologically has nothing to do with the Greek *rômê,* nor does *Numa* derive from *nomos.* This point, and other challenges to the historical accuracy of Rousseau's account of Roman institutions, can be found in Jean Cousin, "J.-J. Rousseau interprète des institutions romaines dans le *Contrat Social,* pp. 13–34. On the significance of Rome (and Sparta) for Rousseau, see Judith Shklar, *Men and Citizens: A Study of Rousseau's Social Theory.*

the right of voting, and that the Roman people were truly sovereign *de jure* and *de facto*" (4:4). This claim is asserted in the midst
of a long account of the division of the Roman people into classes;
and, as the whole burden of Rousseau's investigation of political
institutions bears witness, a society divided in this way does not
presuppose a general interest. It is significant that Rousseau is
never fully explicit on this point, and that he is here inclined to
denegate the problem.

In any event, the central focus of the discussion of Rome lies
elsewhere. It is the virtue of the Roman citizen that Rousseau wants
to stress. In his account, the greatness of Rome—and the durability
of its institutions—rests almost entirely on the virtue of its citizens.
It was in *moeurs*, in manners and morals, that the Romans distinguished themselves among the nations of the world. This is of
course a thesis central to Rousseau's argument: the sort of "law" on
which all the others rest is that which "is graven neither on marble
nor on brass, but in the hearts of the citizens" (2:12). What is
especially interesting here is how Rousseau conceives the superi-
ority of Roman manners and morals to be an effect of the domination of the countryside over the towns, of rural over urban values:

> From this distinction between the urban and rural tribes
> resulted an effect worthy of notice, because there is no other
> instance of it, and because Rome owed to it both the preserva-
> tion of her manners (*moeurs*) and the increase of her empire. It
> might be supposed that the urban tribes soon arrogated to
> themselves the power and the honors, and were ready to
> disparage the rural tribes. It was quite the reverse. We know
> the taste of the old Romans for a country life. This taste they
> derived from their wise founder, who united with liberty rural
> and military works, and relegated, so to speak, to the towns
> arts, trade, intrigue, fortune and slavery. [4:4]

As the Roman ruling class remained essentially rural, rural values
enjoyed the greatest prestige and set the general moral tone:
"every eminent man that Rome had being a dweller in the fields
and a tiller of the soil, it was customary to seek only there for the
defenders of the Republic. This condition, being that of the wor-
thiest patricians, was honored by everyone; the simple and la-
borious life of the villagers was preferred to the lax and indolent
life of the town-dwellers of Rome; and many who would have been

only wretched proletarians in the city became, as laborers in the fields, respected citizens" (4:4). For Rousseau, the city is the source of corruption, the well-spring of private interest. In effectively subjugating the town to the countryside, the Romans, in Rousseau's account—alone among the nations of the world—were able to mitigate this corrupting tendency and to instill thereby the virtues of citizenship among the population. Accordingly, also, in Rousseau's view, the decline of Rome is to be explained by the decline in the size and influence of the rural tribes.

In the final analysis, then, the strength of Rome rested in the simplicity and virtue of its people, in "their disinterestedness, their taste for agriculture, their contempt for commerce and the ardent pursuit of gain" (4:4). This simplicity of manners allowed their wise institutions to function properly.

Rome illustrates for Rousseau at least three essential features of a *de jure* state: popular assemblies; resilient and wise institutions adapted to extraordinary circumstances (the dictatorship) and to preserving and maintaining good manners and morals (the tribuneship, the censorship); and, above all, that simplicity of manners Rousseau believed essential for overcoming private interest. This last point is a dominant motif of *The Social Contract*, as we shall see in the next chapter.

4

The Formation of the Sovereign

We have seen that a necessary and sufficient condition for an enactment of the sovereign—that is, for an obligatory enactment, a law—is that it be general both in its source and in its object. We have also seen how private interest threatens this generality. Rousseau's principal strategy for mitigating the threat is educating or socializing the population away from private interest and toward the values of citizenship. For the just state to exist, it is not enough that the sovereign be constituted; it must also be educated. In other words, society must be arranged in such a way as to produce moral agents, self-legislating members of a commonwealth of ends. Rousseau discusses a number of social arrangements conducive to this goal, among which are the institution of the most fundamental laws of the state, the prevailing customs or manners (*moeurs*), and the state's educational and religious apparatuses. These institutions work together to educate the body politic and thereby promote the sovereignty of the general will.

The Legislator (2:7-11)

The associates that come together in the social contract are a "blind multitude, which often knows not what it wishes because it rarely knows what is good for it" (2:7). By definition, each citizen desires what is good but, unless morally educated, will be ill-equipped to discern it. In Rousseau's words, "the general will is always right, but the judgment that guides it is not always enlightened" (2:6). This is particularly the case for mankind emerging from the state of nature. How can the fundamental laws of the state possibly be enacted by those whose moral and intellectual capacities have developed only in the state of nature? And the state of nature must be transcended, as I have argued, precisely because it threatens the development of these capacities!

In the concluding paragraph of Book 2, chapter 6, a text we have discussed at length in chapter 2, Rousseau places this problem in sharp focus: "It [the general will] must be made to see objects as they are, sometimes as they ought to appear; it must be shown the good path that it is seeking, and guarded from the seduction of private interests; it must be made to observe closely times and places, and to balance the attraction of immediate and sensible advantages against the danger of remote and concealed evils" (2:6). In other words, the body politic requires enlightenment. Without it, there can be no social harmony and, ultimately, no state. But from where does such enlightenment come? It certainly does not come, one must realize, from *within* the body politic, for the body politic that emerges from the state of nature is still a "blind multitude." Apparently, the only hope is for an external intervention, a transcendent solution.

In formulating this problem, I have followed Rousseau in depicting the social contract as an event in time: once society is formed, but before mankind has advanced morally by living in political society, there is apparently no way to find within the community the necessary wisdom to legislate the fundamental laws of the state. Apart from this temporal interpretation of the social contract, the establishment of institutions that will encourage the moral education of the citizenry requires a wisdom that transcends innate moral capacities. Not everyone, according to Rousseau, is an expert in the *art* of constructing political institutions appropriate to a given territory and population. The actual creation of political institutions requires a *guide*, possessed of a special skill and a special wisdom. The bearer of this wisdom is the *legislator*.

The legislator, in this special sense, is not concerned with the enactment of legislation, in the ordinary sense, which is the province of the collective citizenry. Rather, the legislator is that extraordinary person who establishes the most fundamental laws according to which the state is to be governed. He must not do so by force, for then he would be a mere despot. Rather, the legislator persuades. His natural authority is decisive. The uncharacteristically emotive tone of Rousseau's description of the legislator in the opening paragraph of Book 2, chapter 7, is particularly telling:

> In order to discover the rules of association that are most suitable to nations, a superior intelligence would be necessary who could see all the passions of men without experiencing any of them; who would have no affinity with our nature and yet know it profoundly; whose happiness would not depend on us, and who would nevertheless be quite willing to interest himself in ours; and lastly, one who, storing up for himself with the progress of time a far-off glory in the future could labor in one age and enjoy in another. *Gods would be necessary to give laws to men.* [2:7, italics mine]

The figure of the legislator is of Platonic inspiration and had fired the imagination of many of Rousseau's predecessors.[1] For Rousseau, the historic function of the legislator is the launching of mankind decisively out of nature and into fully human, moral society.

This task consists in nothing less than the total transformation of human nature, the substitution of "a social and moral existence for the independent and physical existence which we have all received from nature" (2:7). The creation of this form of character is a work of human art, of contrivance, and not of nature, which supplies only the capacity. To actualize this capacity successfully is a work of genius.

1. Cf. *The Statesman.* Among the predecessors of Rousseau in whose thinking this idea played a prominent role are Machiavelli, Spinoza, and Montesquieu. It is significant that the legislator apparently does not appear in the writings of Hobbes or Locke. There is an extended discussion of Rousseau's relationship to classical conceptions of the legislator in R.D. Masters, *The Political Philosophy of Rousseau*, pp. 359 ff. See also C.J. Friedrich, "Law and Dictatorship in the *Contrat Social,*" pp. 77–79.

As if to emphasize the peculiar and extraordinary role of the legislator, Rousseau insists that he occupies no status, strictly speaking, in the state. He is neither magistrate nor sovereign. "The position, which constitutes the republic, does not enter into its constitution. It is a special and superior function, having nothing in common with the human domain; for, if he who rules men ought not to control legislation, he who controls legislation ought not to rule men. Otherwise his laws, being ministers of his passions, would often serve only to perpetuate his acts of injustice; he would never to able to prevent private views from corrupting the sacredness of his work" (2:7). That the legislator ought not to be confused with the sovereign follows directly from the analysis of sovereignty in the opening chapters of Book 2. To corroborate this conclusion, Rousseau alludes to the historic example of Rome. "Rome," he writes, "at her most glorious epoch, saw all the crimes of tyranny spring up in her bosom, and saw herself on the verge of destruction, through uniting in the same hands legislative authority and sovereign power" (2:7). That the legislator ought not to be confused with the government is only a little problematic. Rousseau appears to advocate this distinction largely on prudential grounds. It is in this vein that he discusses Lycurgus's abdicating his royalty before giving laws to Sparta, and the practice of many modern republics, including Rousseau's own Geneva, in calling upon foreigners to draft their laws.[2] More straightforwardly, if government has the function of executing laws, it cannot, at the same time, be their author, without that dangerous abuse of power Rousseau discusses amply in Book 3.

Seen in this light, the legislator's position appears highly paradoxical. On the one hand, his task requires superhuman powers; on the other, he has no authority. Indeed, for reasons we have discussed, it is crucial that the legislator have no defined legal status and that he be unable to compel compliance through the use or threat of force. In addition, it would be foolish to suppose the

2. Rousseau was himself called upon to draft constitutions for Corsica and Poland. The texts *Projet de constitution pour la Corse* and *Considérations sur le gouvernement de Pologne,* accompanied by useful introductory material, may be found either in volume 2 of *The Political Writings of Jean-Jacques Rousseau,* ed. C.E. Vaughan, or in volume 3 of the *Oeuvres complètes de Jean-Jacques Rousseau* (Pléiade edition).

legislator able to persuade the "blind multitude" by argument. The point is to create laws conducive to the development of capacities for deliberation and practical reason, to create a citizenry that can be persuaded by argument. Obviously, this ability cannot be presupposed.

The only recourse is for the legislator to somehow succeed in invoking divine authority in order to "compel without violence and persuade without convincing": "It is this which in all ages has forced the founders of nations to resort to the intervention of heaven, and to give the gods the credit for their own wisdom, in order that the peoples, subjected to the laws of the state as to those of nature, and recognizing the same power in the formation of man and in that of the city, might obey willingly and bear submissively the yoke of the public welfare" (2:7). The way out of the paradoxical situation of the legislator is to appeal to that "sublime reason which soars beyond the reach of common men" and reduces them to submission. Ultimately, the authority of the legislator rests on a kind of "golden lie," a theme we shall take up when discussing the celebrated chapter in Book 4 on civil religion.

When, because of the "great soul" of the founder, this appeal is well executed, the resulting institutions are durable. In this regard Rousseau praises the founders of Jewish and Islamic law: "The Jewish law, which still endures, and that of the child of Ishmael, which for ten centuries has ruled half the world, still bear witness today to the great men who dictated them; and while proud philosophy or blind party spirit sees in them nothing but fortunate imposters, true politics admires in their systems the great and powerful genius which presides over durable institutions" (2:7). In the origin of nations, religion is the instrument of politics.

The wisdom of the legislator consists in framing laws appropriate to the people. The impression is overwhelming that, in Rousseau's view, all but the most backward peoples in Europe are by his time already too corrupt to be saved by even the wisest legislator. Rousseau does not say this explicitly in *The Social Contract*, but instead reminds the reader of Plato's refusal to legislate for the Arcadians and Cyrenians, "knowing that these two peoples were rich and could not tolerate equality" (2:7).

In forming just and durable institutions, timing is of crucial importance. The nation must be neither too young nor too old and set in its ways to benefit from the legislator. It is to a failure in timing that Rousseau attributes Peter the Great's lack of success in legislating for the Russians. The celebrated passage making this assertion, a passage which has struck many as prophetic, deserves to be quoted at length.

> The Russians will never be really civilized (*policés*), because they have been civilized too early. Peter had an imitative genius; he had not the true genius that creates and produces something from nothing. Some of the things he did were good, but the majority were ill-timed. He saw that his people were barbarous, but he did not see that they were unripe for civilization. He wished to civilize them, when it was only necessary to discipline them. He wished to produce at once Germans and Englishmen, when he should have begun by making Russians; he prevented his subjects from ever becoming what they might have been, by persuading them that they were what they were not. It is in this way that a French tutor trains his pupil to shine for a moment in childhood, and then to be forever a nonentity. The Russian empire will desire to subjugate Europe, and it will itself be subjugated. The Tartars, its subjects or neighbors, will become its masters and ours. This revolution appears to me inevitable. All the kings of Europe are working in concert to accelerate it. [2:8]

Among the factors the legislator must consider is the size of the state. As we know, a related question is discussed at length in Book 3, the problem of the choice of a form of government relative to the size of the state. The essential point here is that the state must be neither so large as to be ungovernable—or governable in such a way as to encourage the usurpation of the sovereign power by the magistrates—nor so small as to fail to be self-sufficient. Of these limits, Rousseau views the latter as the most important. A state that is not independent will tend necessarily in one of two directions, each of which will hasten its fall. Either it will be "swallowed up" by another state, or it will embark on wars of conquest. Rousseau is particularly scornful of the latter eventuality. Wars of conquest, he asserts, inevitably upset the political equilibrium and threaten the general will.

There is at least one rough indication that may aid the legislator in determining the proper size of the state: the state should be large enough in arable territory to sustain its population. That its own territory be sufficient for its agricultural needs is the condition, for Rousseau, of a state's independence. Since the satisfaction of this condition depends on a number of factors—the fertility and quality of the soil, the nature of its produce, the climate, the temperament and industriousness of the population—it is impossible to express the relationship between territory and population with mathematical precision. It must be noted, nonetheless, that, like so much of what Rousseau says in Book 3 on the size of the state, this account of self-sufficiency or independence, however reasonable for eighteenth-century European conditions, cannot help but strike a contemporary reader as hopelessly anachronistic.

Finally, at the moment of legislation, abundance and peace are absolutely essential. For this is the moment when "the body is least capable of resistance and most easy to destroy" (2:7). Should war, famine, or sedition occur at this critical period, the chance of establishing stable and durable institutions is virtually nonexistent.

In summary, only some peoples are adapted for legislation, and even then, only at the correct moment in their history. Rousseau concludes:

> What people, then, is adapted for legislation? That which is already united by some original union, interest or convention, but has not yet borne the real yoke of the laws; that which has neither customs nor superstitions firmly rooted; that which has no fear of being overwhelmed by a sudden invasion, but without entering into the quarrels of its neighbors can single-handedly resist each of them, or aid one in repelling another, that in which every member can be known by all, and in which there is no necessity to lay on a man a greater burden than a man can bear; that which can subsist without other nations and without which every other nation can subsist; that which is neither rich nor poor, and is self-sufficing; lastly, that which combines the stability of an old nation with the docility of a new one. [2:10]

In short, there is a fair chance of establishing durable state institutions in a small population, evidencing a relatively high degree of cultural coherence *and* malleability, economic and military self-sufficiency, and equality. Moreover, this population must be relatively uncorrupted by luxury, with its debilitating influence on the capacity to act for the general interest. Obviously, the outlook is bleak. With a touch of irony and a profound pessimism, Rousseau concludes: "There is still one country in Europe capable of legislation. It is the island of Corsica" (2:10).[3]

Self-sufficiency is not the only value the legislator should seek to maximize. He should also always bear in mind the two fundamental principles on which the state is based—liberty and equality. Since our concern here is with the legislator, this is not the place to resume what I have already said about liberty, nor to anticipate what I shall have to say about equality. For now, a number of comments must suffice.

First, when Rousseau talks of liberty in this text (Book 2, chapter 11), he means *civil liberty:* the freedom to do what the law does not proscribe. The legislator should seek to avoid any infringement on civil liberty. Rousseau does not elaborate an argument apart from the following fragment of a sentence: "any individual dependence (*dépendance particulière*) is so much force withdrawn from the body of the state" (2:11). Still, the unelaborated argument can be easily enough reconstructed. The aim of the social contract is to create the conditions for individual moral autonomy. The *de jure* state is that in which the individual, in obeying the sovereign, obeys only himself. To infringe civil liberty is to establish extra-legislative restraints on individual activity. That is where civil liberty is infringed, some actions are determined neither by the individual in isolation nor by the sovereign (the individual in concert). These actions, then, are heteronomously determined, determined by another. In that sense, "force" is "withdrawn" from the individual or, what comes to the same thing where legitimate political institutions exist, from "the body of the state."

3. This passage continues: "The valor and constancy which that brave nation has exhibited in recovering and defending its freedom would well deserve that some wise man should teach it how to preserve it. I have some presentiment that this small island will one day astonish Europe." Later readers have seen in this passage another prophetic reference, this time to Napoleon.

In other words, to say "any individual dependence is so much force withdrawn from the body of the state" is, I think, just an obscure way of saying that any infringement of civil liberty is an attack on moral autonomy. And, needless to say, the protection of autonomy is a categorical requirement of any system of legislation.

Second, Rousseau's position is plainly not egalitarian. He emphatically does not advocate equal distribution of power or wealth, but rather, a limit on unequal distribution.

> With regard to equality, we must not understand by this word that the degrees of power and wealth should be absolutely the same; but that, as to power, it should fall short of all violence, and never be exercised except by virtue of rank and of the laws; while, as to wealth, no citizen should be rich enough to be able to buy another, and none poor enough to be forced to sell himself, which supposes, on the part of the great, moderation in property and influence (*credit*), and on the part of ordinary citizens, moderation of avarice and covetousness. [2:11]

The function of these limits is strictly to suppress private interest. There is no conception of equality—whether of rights or of wealth—as a good in itself.[4] Equality is introduced, instead, for the purpose of guaranteeing liberty. Equality is strictly a means for promoting civil liberty and moral autonomy.

Finally, since each population and territory has peculiar and idiosyncratic characteristics, there is no single constitution that is proper for all states. No constitution is best in itself, but only for those for whom it is intended. This, to repeat, is why legislation is an art. "What renders the constitution of a state really solid and durable is the observance of expedience in such a way that natural relations and the laws always coincide, the latter only serving as it were to secure, support, and rectify the former" (2:11). That is, equality is a regulative principle in the Kantian sense: an ideal toward which the legislator ought to strive, constrained only by his sense of the particular characteristics of those for whom he legislates. It is not clear whether Rousseau regards (civil) liberty as a

4. Thus, Rousseau does not even advocate equality of opportunity, and talks, in this passage, of inequalities of power in virtue of "rank." In Book 3, chapter 5, he allows—albeit disapprovingly—government by hereditary aristocracy. This is all evidence of a striking inegalitarianism, even by conventional liberal standards.

regulative principle as well. The argument I have reconstructed above suggests that it ought to be viewed categorically, that civil liberty ought to be maintained absolutely. But in discussing the art of the legislator, Rousseau does seem to waver from this conclusion toward the more sensible but less rigorous view that civil liberty, too, is a goal rather than an absolute requirement of legislation.

Opinion and Manners and Morals

In the final chapter of Book 2, Rousseau proposes a classificatory scheme for laws corresponding to the complex nature of the individual's position in the state. There are first of all *political* laws that pertain to the relation of "the whole to the whole or of the sovereign to the state" (2:12). Then there are *civil* laws that pertain to the relations between members of the state or between a member of the state and the political body as a whole. And, finally, there are *criminal* laws that determine "the relationship between the individual man and the law; viz. that of punishable disobedience" (2:12). Criminal law, Rousseau notes, is not so much a different kind of law as the sanction of the others.

A fourth type is added as the condition for the efficacy of all the rest:

> To these three kinds of laws is added a fourth, the most important of all, which is graven neither on marble nor on brass, but in the hearts of the citizens; *a law which creates the real constitution of the state,* which acquires new strength daily, which when other laws grow old or pass away, revives them or supplies their place, preserves a people in the spirit of their institutions, *and imperceptibly substitutes the force of habit for that of authority. I speak of manners (moeurs), customs (coutumes), and above all of opinion (opinion)*—a part unknown to our politicians *but one on which the success of all the rest depends;* a part with which the great legislator is occupied in secret while he appears to confine himself to particular regulations, that are merely the arching of the cult, of which the manners, slow to develop, form at length, the immovable keystone. [2:12, italics mine]

It is obvious that this fourth sort of law is not really a law at all, but something of an entirely different order. If it is less fundamental than law from the point of view of a theory of obligation, it is no less important for the establishment and support of the *de jure* state.

Rousseau in *The Social Contract* says almost nothing directly of opinion, or of *moeurs* or *coutumes*—what I shall henceforward call *manners and morals*. His concern there, he says, is just the investigation of political laws, particularly as they "constitute the form of government" (2:12). A good deal, however, can be gleaned from Rousseau's other writings, even where the subject is not explicitly political right.[5]

If there is little in *The Social Contract* that bears directly on opinion and manners and morals, there is no lack of material with an indirect bearing. The thrust of many of the less theoretical portions of the text is concerned precisely with the control and reform of opinion and with the shaping of manners and morals, because the character of opinion and manners and morals is crucial for overcoming private interest, for shaping individual wills into general wills, and, ultimately, for substituting "force of habit" for "authority."[6] It is in this domain—more even than in the domain of laws, strictly speaking—that the struggle must be waged. It will be decided here, finally, whether the population will remain a "blind multitude" or be transformed into a citizenry. Here, above all, is where the sovereign is to be formed.

To reformulate this point: we can say that the possibility of a *de jure* state depends on the character of each associate's will. If that will cannot be educated to generality, the *de jure* state cannot exist. The point, then, is to educate that will to generality, to arrange social institutions to that end.

The Social Contract presupposes what amounts to a causal account of the formation of the individual's will. The first cause is the one that has been discussed at length in the chapters on the legislator: the laws. The aim of the legislator is to establish by law institutions that will foster the moral development of the individual toward citizenship. However, no institutions can have this effect directly. We need, then, to take account of mediating causes.

5. Of particular interest is the *Letter to D'Alembert.* See Rousseau, *Politics and the Arts: Letter to M. D'Alembert on the Theater*, trans. with notes and introduction by Allan Bloom (Glencoe, Ill., 1960); see particularly chapter 8, "The Law and Morals," pp. 65–74.
6. Rousseau's use of *authority* in this context is misleading. What he means, apparently, is that a properly educated sovereign will obey laws automatically without external coercion.

It is not clear to what extent Rousseau conceives this process as a causal chain. It is at least plausible that he has something like the following in mind:[7]

laws ⟶ opinion ⟶ manners and morals ⟶ individual's will

Rousseau does apparently conceive the individual's will as determined immediately, if not exclusively, by the prevailing manners and morals. And it is quite certain that he regards manners and morals as shaped, in very large measure, by opinion. He says so explicitly in the *Letter to D'Alembert:* "Where then can the government take hold over manners and morals (*moeurs*)? I reply that it is through public opinion. If our habits (*habitudes*) are born from our own sentiments in isolation, they are born from the opinions of others in society. When we do not live in ourselves, but in others, it is their judgments that determine everything. Nothing seems good nor desirable to individuals except insofar as the public has so judged, and the only happiness that most men know is to be esteemed happy."[8]

However, opinion is not the exclusive determinant of manners and morals. There is also, Rousseau tells us in the same *Letter to D'Alembert,* law itself and "the appeal of pleasure." While law does operate on opinion, it is clear that opinion is shaped at least to some extent by other factors as well. With these considerations in mind, I should like to suggest the following pictorial representation as an improvement over the one suggested above:

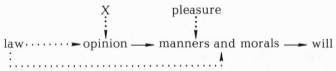

The broken lines in this picture indicate relatively less important causes; the unbroken lines represent dominant causes. The X above *opinion* indicates those factors, not clearly specified by Rousseau, that shape public opinion. These are to some extent established or at least sanctioned by law, but are largely extra-legal. It is impossible, on the basis of what Rousseau tells us, to establish clearly what causes are dominant in producing public opinion.

7. See L. Althusser, "Rousseau: The Social Contract," p. 156. For consistency of exposition, I have modified Althusser's terminology somewhat.
8. *Oeuvres choisies de Jean-Jacques Rousseau* (Paris: Garnier, 1962), p. 176.

Everything, then, depends on the character and efficacy of these causes. Where they work together to produce citizens, to educate the sovereign, the *de jure* state can exist. Where they do not, it is unattainable.

The key point in this complex chain of causes is the domain of public opinion, in part because opinion is the overwhelmingly dominant factor shaping manners and morals and, thereby, determining the character of the individual's will.[9] The chief reason for centering on opinion, however, is that intervention here is always possible. To be sure, the work of the legislator might be regarded as a kind of external intervention into the legislative process with the intention of establishing institutions conducive to moral education. But this procedure, by its very nature, can occur only at a certain point early in the historical existence of the state. Moreover, this intervention can hardly be contrived. The appearance of the legislator is an extraordinary phenomenon. His work is a work of genius that cannot be anticipated, except roughly—in the way Rousseau himself attempts. To intervene directly at the level of manners and morals is scarcely more feasible. By Rousseau's account, these can be reformed and controlled only indirectly, through opinion, their dominant cause. There is indeed only one institution discussed in *The Social Contract* that might be regarded as operating at this point on the causal chain: the censorship. But the censorship cannot in itself reform bad manners and morals; it can only preserve good ones. We shall return to this question later.

It is by operating on opinion, then, that Rousseau proposes to create the citizen. Accordingly, we must consider those institutions through which, in Rousseau's view, opinion is most effectively formed: above all, education (which, for Rousseau, is by no means confined to the school) and civil religion.

These are not institutions of the state, strictly speaking, but of what later writers (most importantly, Hegel) were to call civil

9. Rousseau's critique of existing—that is, eighteenth-century European, and particularly French—society consists, in large part, of an indictment of its prevailing opinions and opinion makers. For an extended and useful discussion that develops this thesis, see Judith Shklar, *Men and Citizens: A Study of Rousseau's Social Theory*, pp. 75–127. This theme is of course not broached directly in *The Social Contract*, where the critique of existing society is indirect, based on an implicit comparison with what a *de jure* state would be.

society. Underlying Rousseau's account of education and civil religion is an unacknowledged drama between the spontaneous institutions of civil society and the state. These spontaneous institutions are those social groups whose interest the theory of *The Social Contract* regards as private and, therefore, proscribes. Rousseau realizes, at least implicitly, that these groups do exist, that their formation is virtually automatic. The purpose of public education and civil religion is precisely to combat this automatic tendency. Opinion is the battleground; the line is to be drawn here against private interest. To this end, the state requires supervening, artifical institutions to combat those that arise spontaneously. The state must take civil society in hand, for it will otherwise be impossible to educate opinion toward that generality which is the condition for its possibility.

Education

Some writers have seen an ambivalence bordering on inconsistency in Rousseau's writings on education.[10] It is said that the theory of private education, elaborated especially in *Emile*, is incompatible with the indications Rousseau gives in his political writings of the nature and scope of public education. This alleged incompatibility is not supposed to pertain to the method of education: in each case, the educational process consists in a subtle and (to the pupil) imperceptible transformation of the will, brought about through persuasion and example, never force or coercion. Instead, the incompatibility is alleged to consist just in the question whether education should be private or public. The opening pages of *Emile* should, however, resolve the problem. Rousseau tells us there that the choice between public and private education depends strictly on the historical context in which the choice is made. Where sovereignty does not exist—as is the case, I have argued, in all existing states—to propose public education is to propose sheer foolishness. "The public institution does not, and cannot exist," writes Rousseau, "for there is neither country nor patriot. The very words should be struck out of our language."[11] But where sov-

10. See B. Groethuysen, *Jean-Jacques Rousseau,* p. 117. This view is challenged in an interesting article by M. Martin Rang, "L'Education publique et la formation des citoyens chez J.-J. Rousseau," pp. 253 ff. What follows in this section is heavily indebted to Rang's work.

11. *Emile,* trans. Barbara Foxley (London: Everyman's Library, 1913), p. 8.

ereignty does exist, there public education has its legitimate place. This is the circumstance we have to consider.

Apart from the hints given in Book 2, chapter 12, Rousseau says almost nothing about education in *The Social Contract*. The most explicit texts are the *Encyclopedia* article "On Political Economy" and chapter 4 of the *Considerations on the Government of Poland.* As neither text is readily accessible in English, it will be useful to provide rather substantial excerpts here. First, from the *Encyclopedia:*

> How can love of country grow in the midst of so many other passions that smother it? And what place remains for one's fellow citizens in a heart already divided between avarice, a mistress and vanity?
>
> It is from the first moment of life that one must learn to merit living; and, as one participates in being born in the rights of citizenship, the moment of our birth ought to be the beginning of the exercise of our duties. If there are laws for the ripe years, there ought also to be laws for childhood, which teach us to obey the others. And, as we do not allow each man's reason to be the sole arbiter of his duties, neither should we abandon to the lights and prejudices of their fathers, the education of their children—something which is in any case more important to the state than to their fathers. In the course of nature, the death of the father may rob the child of the last fruits of this education; and the country, sooner or later, feels the effects. The state remains, even should the family dissolve. How much better if the public authority were to take the father's place and charge itself with this important function, acquiring the father's rights in fulfilling his duties. Then there would be less cause for worry. In this regard, it is only necessary, strictly, to change the name, for them to have in common, under the name citizens, the same authority over their children that they exercise separately under the name fathers. They will be no less obeyed in speaking in the name of the law, than they were in speaking in the name of nature. Public education, under rules prescribed by the government, and under magistrates established by the sovereign is therefore one of the fundamental maxims of popular and legitimate government. If children

are raised in common, in the breast of equality, if they are imbued with the laws of the state and the maxims of the general will, if they are instructed to respect these above all things, if they are surrounded by examples and objects that speak to them ceaselessly of the tender mother that nourishes them, of the love she has for them, of the inestimable goods they receive from her, and of what they owe her in return, do not doubt that they will learn to cherish each other mutually like brothers and to want only what society wants; to substitute actions of men and citizens for the sterile and vain babble of the sophists, and to become one day the defenders of the fathers and of the country of which they have for so long been the children.

I shall speak a little of the magistrates destined to preside over this education, which is certainly the most important business of the state. One feels that if such signs of public confidence were lightly given, that if this sublime function were not bestowed on those who had with dignity fulfilled all the rest, who were not in that honorable and sweet repose of their old age, heaped with honors, that this enterprise would be useless and without success. For where the lesson is not supported by authority and the precept by example, instruction is fruitless. And even virtue loses its credit in the mouth of one who does not practice it. Let there be illustrious warriors, weighed down with laurels, preaching courage; let honest magistrates, draped in purple and on their tribunals, teach justice. Then they will form virtuous successors and will transmit, from age to age, to succeeding generations, the experience and talents of the leaders, the courage and virtue of the citizens, and the common emulation of everyone to live and die for the country.[12]

In this early text of 1755, following a long tradition in political thought beginning with Plato, public education is depicted as "the most important business of the state." This same theme is resumed in a text written in 1771, nine years after the first publication of *The Social Contract*, and first published in 1782, four years after Rousseau's death. This is the *Considerations on the Government of*

12. The text from which this translation has been prepared can be found most easily in volume 3 of the *Oeuvres complètes* (Pléiade edition), pp. 260–62; or in Vaughan, ed., Political Writings, 1:256–58.

Poland, of which part of the fourth chapter, entitled "Education,"
reads as follows:

> This is the important article. It is education which ought to give
> souls a national strength and direct their opinions and tastes so
> that they become patriots by inclination, passion and neces-
> sity. A child on opening his eyes should see the country and
> until his death he need see no more. All true republicans take
> in love of country with their mother's milk, that is to say, the
> laws and liberty. This love is the whole existence of the patriot.
> He sees only the country; he lives only for it. When he is alone,
> he is nothing. When he no longer has his country, he is no
> more. And if he is not dead, it is worse.
>
> National education belongs only to free men. Only they
> have a common existence and are truly bound by law. A
> Frenchman, an Englishman, a Spaniard, an Italian, a Russian
> are all more or less the same man. They all leave school
> fashioned for a diploma; that is to say, for servitude. At the age
> of twenty, a Pole ought not to be another man. He should be a
> Pole. I wish that on learning to read, he read things about his
> country; that at ten, he know all of its products; at twelve, its
> provinces, roads and cities; that at fifteen, he know its history;
> at sixteen, its laws. I wish that in all of Poland there not be a
> beautiful deed nor an illustrious man of whom he has no
> memory nor a full heart, and of which he cannot, in an instant,
> give an account. One can judge from this that it is not ordinary
> studies, directed by foreigners and priests that I want children
> to follow. The law should regulate the subjects, the order and
> the form of studies. There ought to be only Poles for teachers;
> married, so far as possible, and distinguished by their manners
> (*moeurs*), their probity, their good sense, and their lights. These
> teachers should be destined for occupations—not more impor-
> tant nor more honorable, for that would be impossible—but less
> arduous and more brilliant, when, after a certain number of
> years, they shall have had their fill. Above all do not make a
> profession of teaching. All public men in Poland should have
> no estate other than that of citizen. All the posts that they fill,
> and especially the most important, like this one, should be
> considered only a testing-ground, a degree for climbing even

higher, after having merited doing so. I exhort the Poles to pay attention to this maxim on which I often insist; I believe it to be a great strength in the state. We shall see shortly how, in my view, it can be made practicable without exception.

I do not like those distinctions between colleges and academies that cause the rich and poor nobility to be brought up differently and separately. All being equal according to the constitution of the state, all should be brought up together and in the same manner. If it is not possible to establish an entirely free public education, it ought at least to be put at a price that the poor can afford. And should we not have a certain number of entirely free places in each college, places funded by the state; what one calls in France *bourses* (scholarships)? These places—given to the children of poor gentlemen, not as charity, but as compensation for good service—would become honorable titles, and could produce a double advantage that we ought not to neglect. It is necessary that the nomination to these places not be arbitrary, but that they be made by a kind of judgment of which I shall speak later. Those who fill these places should be called "children of the state" and distinguished by some honorable sign that will give them priority over other children of their age, not excepting those of the mighty.

This public education is not to be confined to academic studies, strictly speaking. Nor is it even to be confined to the school. Public games and spectacles are of even greater importance; so much so that participation in them, in Rousseau's view, should be obligatory. The text continues:

In all schools there should be a gymnasium or exercising place for the children. This article, so neglected, is, according to me, the most important part of education; not only for forming robust and healthy temperaments, but still more for moral ends, that are now neglected or filled only by a lot of pedantic and vain precepts which are so much wasted speech. I cannot sufficiently reiterate that good education ought to be negative. Prevent vices from birth and you will have done enough for virtue. The means of doing so is the last facility of good public education: it is always to interest children, not by boring studies of which they understand nothing and which they hate, if only for being forced to remain in place, but by exercises that please, while satisfying the need of their bodies to move about as they grow, and for which the pleasure is not limited there.

One ought not to allow them to play separately, according to their fantasies, but rather together, in public, in such a way that they always have a common end towards which all aspire, and which excites competition and emulation. Parents who prefer domestic education, who would have their children brought up under their own eyes, should nevertheless send them to these exercises. Instruction can be domestic and private, but games should always be public and common for all. For it is not a question just of occupying the children, of forming a robust constitution, of making them agile and well-equipped, but of accustoming them to rules, to equality, to fraternity, to competition, to living under the eyes of their fellow-citizens and to desiring public approbation. For this end, it is necessary that the prizes and awards not be distributed arbitrarily by the exercise-masters, but by acclamation, according to the judgment of the spectators. One can count on these judgments always being just, especially if one takes care to make these games attractive to the public, if one provides such apparatus as to make the game a spectacle. Then it may be presumed that all honest men and good patriots will make it a duty and pleasure to attend.

Rousseau goes on to suggest yet other extra-scholastic state educational apparatus:

In Berne, there is a quite singular exercise for the young patricians as they finish school. It is called the mock state (*l'Etat extérieur*). It is a miniature copy of all that comprises the government of the Republic; a senate, solicitors, officers, bailiffs, orators, speeches, judgments, solemnities. The mock state even has a little government and some revenue. This institution, authorized and protected by the sovereign, is the nursery of the statesmen who will one day direct public affairs, filling the very employments that they first exercise only in a game.

Over all of this educational apparatus, the state is to exercise, through its magistrates, the very highest degree of vigilance and control:

Whatever form public education takes—and I do not undertake here to provide details—it is useful to establish a college of magistrates of the first rank who have supreme administrative authority and who name, revoke and change at will, equally, the principals and directors of the schools (who are themselves, as I have already said, candidates for the highest offices of the magistracy), and the exercise-masters, in whom one also should seek to promote zeal and vigilance. The highest places will be open or closed to them according to how well they fulfill their functions. As the hope of the Republic depends on these establishments, the very glory and fate of the nation, I find and avow them to be of an importance that I am quite astonished they are not thought to enjoy. I am distressed for humanity that so many ideas that seem good and useful to me, however practicable they be, are so far from being put into effect.

To be sure, I am only giving indications here; but this is enough for those to whom I address myself. These ideas, poorly developed, show from afar the route, unknown to moderns, along which the ancients led men to that vigor of soul, that patriotic zeal, that esteem for the truly personal qualities without regard to what is only foreign to man, which are without example among us, but for which the leaven in the hearts of all men waits to ferment, to be put into action by institutions conducive to that end. If you direct the education, the customs, the manners (*moeurs*) of the Poles in this spirit, you will develop in them that leaven which is not yet damaged by the corrupt maxims, the worn institutions, the egoistic philosophy that is preached and that kills. . . .[13]

It is interesting to note how this system of public education is imbedded in a hierarchically divided society. Only the nobility are to be educated to citizenship. And though there is to be compensation for the most gifted among the less well-to-do, there are not to be equal educational opportunities even within this estate. It is impossible to determine whether this is simply a concession to Polish reality or a more deeply held prejudice. It is, however, in no

13. See either volume 3 of the *Oeuvres complètes* (Pléiade edition), pp. 953–1041, or Vaughan, ed., *Political Writings*, 2:424–516. See the introductory essay by Jean Fabre in the Pléiade edition for the background and history of the text.

sense enjoined by the theory of sovereignty, though it is arguably consistent with it.

In any case, public education—within and without the school—is here held to be the principal means for forming opinion in such a way as to promote citizenship. Private interest is to be stifled from birth. Children are to be raised with the public interest always and foremost in mind. And this end is best served by a system of public educational institutions.

Civil Religion (4:8)

In the chapter on the legislator (2:7), Rousseau, following Machiavelli, had already depicted recourse to divine authority as a bulwark of actual states and a potential bulwark of a *de jure* state. "The legislator puts into the mouths of the immortals that sublime reason which soars beyond the reach of common men, in order that he may win over by divine authority those whom human prudence could not move" (2:7). Rousseau does not say so explicitly, but it is clear enough that this appeal to God is an example of what Plato in *The Republic* called a "golden lie," a myth advanced by the leaders of the state for purposes beneficial to the people.[14] In this case, the appeal to divine authority has as its effect the establishment of institutions conducive to the moral and rational development of the population. The sovereign is to be educated to full (practical) rationality by appeal to the extra-rational.[15]

This recourse to God is not to be limited just to that moment in the supposed historical existence of the *de jure* state where the legislator intervenes to set "the blind multitude" on the right track.

14. It is immaterial whether the leaders recognize these legitimating myths to be deceptions or whether they are themselves victims of this deception. The implication, in both Rousseau and Plato, is that at least sometimes a golden lie will be seen for what it is.
15. There is a parallel move in Kant where the existence of God and the immorality of the soul are construed as 'ideals of reason' providing the motive for an entirely secularized conception of the moral life. For an historical account of the theological background of Kantian ethics, see Keith Ward, *The Development of Kant's View of Ethics*. It should not be concluded, however, that Kant also saw the appeal to God and immortality as golden lies, nor that Rousseau's remarks on the legislator and this chapter on civil religion in any way motivated Kant's recourse to theology in his writings on morality. In this respect, Kant appears more naive than Rousseau, less Machiavellian.

In Book 4, chapter 8, the penultimate chapter of *The Social Contract*, Rousseau advocates that the appeal be on-going. There should be, he argues, in addition to the fundamental institutions of the state fashioned by the legislator, and the system of public education, a civil religion whose function is also to shape opinion—and, thereby, manners and morals and wills—away from egoism and toward that generality that is the condition for the existence of the state.[16]

Historically, Rousseau suggests, all religion was effectively civil religion; the laws of a people and their religion were integrally connected. Each state had its peculiar form of worship, just as it had its own form of government. The domains of the gods were fixed by political boundaries. Religion was one of the cements of social life.[17] Hence, despite the multitude of religions, there were no religious wars. "The god of one nation had no right over other nations. The gods of the pagans were not jealous gods; they shared among them the empire of the world" (2:8). When the Jews, conquered first by Babylon, then by Syria, refused to worship the deities of their conquerors, their refusal was for this reason taken as a kind of rebellion and suppressed as such. According to Rousseau, this is the sole instance of religious persecution before Christianity.

16. The chapter on civil religion, though prepared in rough draft as early as the composition of the first version of *The Social Contract* was added to the final version after its submission to the publisher Rey in December 1760. Some writers have suggested that this addition is symptomatic of an inconsistency in Rousseau's thought: that having advanced a rationalist and revolutionary conception of political right, he found himself—perhaps because he was himself afraid of the implications of his view—forced to retreat back into a medieval, theological conception of politics. This view is advanced most incisively by Albert Schinz in *La Pensée de Jean-Jacques Rousseau* (Paris, 1929), pp. 364–75. This same position is criticized, decisively in my view, by Robert Derathé in his notes to the Pléiade edition. As I have been arguing, the appeal to God is just one of a number of means suggested for creating in the citizens a mentality hostile to the formation of private wills and conducive to the formation of general wills.

As Derathé recounts, this chapter was frequently criticized by Rousseau's contemporaries for its apparent deviation from a purely secular treatment of political right. I would suggest, on the contrary, that Rousseau's use of civil religion is in fact integral to a purely secular account.

17. This view of the social function of religious organization was later taken up and developed by the founders of modern social theory; for example, by Emile Durkheim in *The Elementary Forms of the Religious Life*. As is well known, Durkheim considered Rousseau an important precursor of modern sociology; see Durkheim, *Montesquieu and Rousseau: Forerunners of Sociology* (Ann Arbor, 1970).

Christianity changed the pattern. Its universality and other-worldliness sundered the traditional link between church and state:

> ... Jesus came to establish on earth a spiritual kingdom, which separating the theological from the political system, destroyed the unity of the state, and caused the intestine divisions which have never ceased to agitate Christian peoples. Now this new idea of a kingdom in the other world having never been able to enter the minds of the pagans, they always regarded Christians as actual rebels, who, under cover of a hypocritical submission, only sought an opportunity to make themselves independent and supreme, and to usurp by cunning the authority which, in their weakness, they pretended to respect. This was the cause of the persecutions. [4:8][18]

The pagan suspicions were quickly realized: "the humble Christians altered their tone and soon, this pretended kingdom of the other world became, under a visible leader, the most violent despotism in this world" (4:8).

Here we have no historical accident. This transformation, in Rousseau's view, was implicit in the very politics of Christianity. Christianity claims an extra-national—indeed, an otherworldly—allegiance. The Christian's first loyalty is to the kingdom of heaven and its worldly organization. This attitude can only destroy national cohesiveness and, thereby, weaken the state. Christianity is emphatically *not* a civil religion; for this reason, it cannot serve as an adequate state religion, and "no good polity is possible in Christian states" (4:8). The inevitable jurisdictional conflicts weaken the social bond essential for cementing the population, for combatting private interest, and for forming, in each citizen, a truly general will.

These arguments are directed against all Christian formations, not just the Roman Catholic Church. However national the organization of a church, the faith remains essentially universalist. This is the reason why all the attempts at founding national churches remain nugatory. "Among us, the kings of England have established themselves as heads of the Church, and the Tsars have done

18. By far the most violent opposition generated by this chapter on civil religion came from what might be called the political right and had to do with the vehemence of Rousseau's attack on Christianity.

the same; but by means of this title they have made themselves its ministers rather than its rulers; they have acquired not so much the right of changing it as the power of maintaining it; they are not its legislators; but only its princes" (4:8). Where allegiance is claimed to an otherworldly kingdom of heaven, allegiance to the state is necessarily diminished. Where the citizenry is inclined "to render unto Caesar that which is Caesar's, and unto God that which is God's," sovereignty is threatened. In Rousseau's account of sovereignty, everything, at least in principle, is renderable unto Caesar.

On one level, then, Christianity is a threat to sovereignty, because it in effect constitutes a rival political organization, a state within the state. That Christianity is also the religion of the Gospel is, for Rousseau, equally dangerous to sovereignty, for the outlook fostered by the Gospels is inimical to that of the citizen. It is, first of all, so otherworldly as to make citizens indifferent to their social and political obligations.

> Christianity is an entirely spiritual religion, occupied solely with heavenly things; the Christian's country is not of this world. He does his duty, it is true; but he does it with a profound indifference as to the good or ill success of his endeavours. Provided that he has nothing to reproach himself with, it matters little to him whether all goes well or ill here below. If the state is flourishing, he scarcely dares to enjoy the public felicity; he fears to take a pride in the glory of his country. If the state declines, he blesses the hand of God which lies heavy on his people. [4:8]

Worse still, Christianity looks beyond national frontiers to humanity as a whole. It is thus incompatible with the kind of patriotism that Rousseau believes essential, if citizens are to aim successfully at a general interest.

Moreover, the apolitical attitude Christianity fosters has significant, negative political effects. Christianity, Rousseau argued long before Nietzsche, fosters a slave's mentality. And the citizen-slave is not inclined to resist attempts at the usurpation of sovereignty. "Christianity preaches only servitude and dependence. Its spirit is too favorable to tyranny for the latter not to profit by it always. True Christians are made to be slaves; they know it and are hardly aroused by it. This short life has too little value in their eyes" (4:8).

What, then, should the civil religion be? Rousseau answers that, above all, it should be minimal, its precise content depending, again, on the particular characteristics of the population. It should contain no more than is necessary to operate on opinion to insure national cohesiveness and civic responsibility. Its articles of faith should be few, precise, and not prone to divisive commentary.

In points of positive dogma, Rousseau suggests it need include no more than belief in God, Providence, the immortality of the soul, reward for virtue and punishment for wickedness, and, of course, the sanctity of the social contract and its laws. With the exception of this last tenet, there does not seem to be any very incisive reason for settling on these doctrines rather than others. Probably Rousseau, like Kant, thought such beliefs presuppositions of the moral life, and so of citizenship. In any case, once again, argument is lacking.

Rousseau insists, however, that anything beyond this very elementary creed (or whatever is appropriate to the population in question) should not concern the sovereign, for any very extensive public intervention in religious affairs is doomed to be divisive. Theological disputes, if they must occur at all, are within the realm of civil liberty. Where a belief is of "no moment to the community," the subject "owes no account of his opinions" to the sovereign (4:8). Though in practice there will thus be a rather wide area in which different religious beliefs and practices will be tolerated, religious tolerance is strictly limited by political requirements. The sovereign is to maintain firm control over whatever beliefs are of moment to it.

One very illiberal consequence of this position should be noted. Insofar as the dogmas of civil religion include belief in God, as Rousseau thinks they should, atheism is not to be tolerated and may even be punishable by death.

It is tempting to speculate whether, for Rousseau, the principles of positive dogma are another concession to human unreason. I am inclined to think so. Surely it is possible in principle to regard laws as obligatory without regarding them as sacred. Were human moral and intellectual capacities developed to their fullest, perhaps

Rousseau would accede to some entirely secular morality. But, of course, the moral and intellectual capacities of the people, even of citizens of a *de jure* state, are not fully developed, and what Rousseau is proposing is a kind of transitional institution for the blind multitude emerging from the state of nature. The dogmas of civil religion, then, might just be a golden lie, a legitimating myth.

In summary, the purpose of civil religion is to operate on opinion in such a way as to form general wills in citizens. So important is this generality that it requires a divine sanction, which is just one of several means to the formation of the sovereign. Presumably, when this end or some near approximation is finally attained, the means can be dispensed with. Civil religion might then be cast aside; perhaps there could even be a society of virtuous atheists.[19] But, then, as Rousseau might say, men would have no need of religion, for they would themselves be gods.

The Censorship (4:7)

The institution of the censorship differs from other institutions discussed so far in that its function is not to shape or reform opinion but to protect it from corruption. The censor "declares" public opinion: "Just as the declaration of the general will is made by the law, the declaration of public opinion is made by the censorship. Public opinion is a kind of law of which the censor is minister, and which he only applies to particular cases in the manner of the Prince" (4:7). The censorship is, in other words, a magisterial office, though it should apparently—since it is, strictly speaking, a tribunal—be separate from the government. It is the ministry of the unwritten law of public opinion. The censor, Rousseau insists, is to be not the arbiter of public opinion but its spokesman.

The existence of such an institution presupposes a far-reaching homogeneity of opinion. The censorship must, in effect, appeal to attitudes which the population would acknowledge to be its own. Rousseau suggests no method for ascertaining when or how the censorship acts legitimately. Where there are conflicting views, the censorship, as proposed, would be plainly unworkable: the validity

19. This is more an implication of Rousseau's position than a belief that can be confidently attributed to him. Rousseau apparently did believe in God, and believed that any reasonable person would do likewise; see Ronald Grimsley, *Rousseau and the Religious Quest* (Oxford, 1968).

of its judgments would be always open to question, and thus the conditions for its existence would be missing. The censorship can operate, then, only when the legislator, the public system of education, and civil religion have done their work: when the population is sufficiently formed into a sovereign with a common identity and interest. In this social context, it serves as a kind of control, a way of rooting out antisocial elements that might crop up from time to time despite a high level of moral education and social solidarity. The censorship is therefore an institution of the state at its apex: "institute censors when the laws are vigorous," Rousseau suggests; "so soon as they have lost their power all is over" (4:7).

Since the censorship is just a kind of negative check on opinion, it could be said to operate on the level of what opinion produces — manners and morals (*moeurs*). To be sure, the censorship is powerless to shape manners and morals. Such shaping is the task of the institutions that operate on them indirectly, by molding opinion; but the censorship can root out bad manners and morals and can, therefore, preserve the good results of the legislator, public education, and civil religion. In Rousseau's words: "the censorship may be useful to preserve morality, but never to restore it" (4:7).

5

Political Economy

We have seen that, for Rousseau, the *de jure* state requires legitimating myths and an elaborate state system of public education and civil religion to enforce the reign of these myths. In this respect, Rousseau stands in the venerable Platonic tradition of the "golden lie." To form the sovereign, Rousseau tells us, is to transform opinion, to develop a consciousness of social solidarity.

To do so, it is of course necessary to intervene directly on the level of opinion; but this action will not be sufficient. Ultimately, "consciousness arises out of life" (in Marx's words). For a collection of individuals to become a community with a single will, aiming (successfully) at a general interest, *there must be a general interest to be discovered.* And this supposes an integrated society, where divisions pose no threat to the generality of the will.

What renders this view of society fanciful or utopian is, above all, the division of society into classes. For the theory to become fully *practical,* class divisions must be taken into account and treated (that is, transformed) accordingly.

For this reason, it is not enough just to intervene on the level of opinion. Indeed, this is the reason why interventions on the level of opinion are doomed to fail, unless the golden lie is somehow made true; for what divides society thereby divides opinion also, at least tendentially. Rousseau's proposals for public education and civil religion can counteract this tendency only to a certain point. Even the assault on opinion requires an assault on what divides opinion, the division of society into classes.

This assault constitutes the end point of Rousseau's practical argument. It will be remembered that Rousseau assimilates class interests to private interests, effectively denying in this way the very existence of social classes and their interests. However, social classes do exist. I have tried to show how all Rousseau's measures concerning opinion are attempts to mitigate this stubborn, re-calcitrant fact. Now we see that this attempt requires, finally, the literal suppression of what the theory does not countenance. Classes are to be eliminated, not just in their effects (on the level of opinion), but in themselves. The *de jure* state is to be grounded in a classless economic structure.

This is the closest Rousseau comes to arguing *for* the central tenet of his theory of political right and obligation: the existence of a general interest. It is significant that when Rousseau finally does broach this question directly, the discussion shifts from moral philosophy to political economy. Determinant economic institu-tions and policies must be implemented to overcome private inter-est and to *create* a general interest. Does this move not concede that in fact (on the level of appearance), the general interest does *not* exist?

Equality (2:11)

Although all citizens are equal members of the sovereign, Rous-seau does not envision anything like strictly equal income distribu-tion. Equality of income and wealth (and even of power, insofar as it is a consequence of unequal wealth) is neither possible, in Rous-seau's view, nor even desirable. Such equality is incompatible with the division of labor and private ownership, practices and institutions Rousseau never questions. What sovereignty does re-quire, however, is a certain limit on unequal distribution. Specifically:

> If we inquire in what precisely the greatest good of all consists, which ought to be the end of every system of legislation, we shall find that it is reduced to these two principal objects, *liberty* and *equality*. Liberty because any individual depen-

dence is so much force taken away from the body of the state;
equality because liberty cannot subsist without it.

. . . With regard to equality it must not be understood by
this word that the degrees of power and wealth be absolutely
the same, but that, as to power, it should fall short of all
violence and never be exercised except by virtue of rank and
the laws; while as to wealth, *no citizen should be rich enough to
be able to buy another, and none so poor as to be constrained to
sell himself.* This supposes moderation in property *(biens)* and
influence *(crédit)* on the part of the great; and on the part of
ordinary citizens, moderation of avarice and covetousness.
[2:11, italics mine]

A measure of equality is enjoined, then, not as an end in itself, but
because "liberty cannot subsist without it"; it is a means for
insuring sovereignty. Too unequal a distribution of power would
be fatal to sovereignty; on the other hand, a strictly equal distribution is impossible.[1] The solution lies in setting bounds to inequalities: if no one is rich enough to be able to buy another or
poor enough to need to sell himself, liberty can subsist.

I have said that this formula aims at the suppression of social
classes, but it does not do so expressly. What Rousseau wants to
suppress or at least to mitigate is the division of society into estates
based on wealth and status (rich / poor), not class divisions growing
out of differential relations to the means of production (lord / serf,
capitalist / worker, and so on). He does admit differential social
ranks, as we have seen; and in explaining why a measure of
equality is necessary for sovereignty, he remarks: "Do you then
wish to give the state stability? Bring the two extremes [rich / poor]
together as nearly as possible; tolerate neither the opulent nor
beggars. These two states, naturally inseparable, are equally fatal
to the general welfare; from the one springs supporters of tyranny,
from the other, tyrants. It is always between these two that the
traffic in public liberty takes place: the one buys, the other sells"
(2:11 n). Rousseau seems here, once again, to have in mind ancient

1. The unequal distribution of power to which Rousseau refers in the second
paragraph quoted above is that which grows out of unequal income
distribution (wealth = power) and the division of society into different
estates or "ranks." Provided this greater or lesser power is used lawfully
and "falls short of all violence" it poses no special problems for sovereignty.

Rome, that historical approximation of a *de jure* state, undone by an increasingly unequal distribution of wealth resulting first in corruption (the degeneration of manners and morals, the decline of sovereignty) and finally in tyranny (sovereignty's fall).

But the letter of Rousseau's formula and the spirit that underlies it point in a different direction: not backward to antiquity but forward toward the emerging capitalist organization of Europe. Rousseau is not so much drawing a lesson from the Roman past as warning against the European future.

It is even fair to conjecture that his description of admissible inequalities ("no citizen should be rich enough as to be able to buy another, and none so poor as to be constrained to sell himself") is *expressly* anti-capitalist: that it aims to proscribe the essential characteristic of the capitalist mode of production, the wage bargain in which the worker (reduced to a propertyless proletarian) exchanges his capacity to labor for a fixed period in return for a wage, supplied by the capitalist. I think a literal reading of Rousseau's formula on admissible inequalities supports such a conjecture. This surmise would be entirely corroborated if it could be shown that the wage bargain is an illegitimate contract in the sense of Book 1, chapter 4—specifically, a pact of voluntary submission. Since it is motivated by inequality (the worker *is* so poor as to be constrained to sell his capacity to labor; the capitalist *is* rich enough to buy what is sold), and since it does involve a kind of forfeiture of self-determination (for the duration of the agreement, subject of course to legal restraints), the wage bargain does appear to differ significantly from a simple and unobjectionable agreement to perform a service (in accordance with one's duty). But there are differences, too, from paradigm cases of slavery: in the wage bargain, one alienates only one's capacity to labor, not one's self, and one does so for only a limited period.[2]

On this question, finally, one can only speculate. My suspicion

2. With the emergence of the capitalist system, and the consequent generalized transformation of human relations into exchange relations, it does become plausible, as anti-capitalist critics have pointed out repeatedly, to identify one's self with one's capacity to labor (for a wage). In the same vein, it could be argued that the limited term of the wage contract, far from mitigating slavery, actually works to insure subordination, subject to the requirements of capitalist production. Capitalism requires a mobile labor force, free from legal ties to land or even to specific enterprises. A short, but renewable, wage contract encourages the formation of such a labor force.

is that Rousseau does not have wage labor in mind (nowhere does he proscribe it explicitly), but that a confirmed Rousseauean could, with not too much ingenuity, argue against capitalism on these grounds.

Rousseau's more telling anti-capitalist argument is less direct. Briefly, the contention is that the background conditions for sovereignty very likely cannot be sustained in a world where the wage bargain prevails. Capitalism, as Rousseau could foresee, leads to the concentration of population in industrial centers and to pronounced social inequalities. It promotes urban over rural values and encourages idle and useless consumption (for the few). In short, it contributes to a general decline in civic virtue. The *de jure* state, as we know, depends on civic virtue absolutely. It therefore requires simplicity of manners and relative equality, the dominance of the countryside over the towns and of rustic virtue over urban corruption and luxury. Whether or not capitalist social relations are legitimate in principle, their practical effects—on the level of opinion and *moeurs*—are overwhelmingly debilitating to the proper exercise of the general will.

Rousseau's anti-capitalism is, then, at once utopian and regressive. As a warning for the future, it points backward to Europe's past (or toward an idealization of that past), backward to a golden age. Indeed, is this not just the old dream of economic independence, the dream of the craftsman and independent producer, of the merchant and, above all, the peasant farmer? Rousseau's vision of the *de jure* state rests, ultimately, on a longing for what Adam Smith was to call "that early and rude state of society" where (as in capitalism), commodities are exchanged at their value but where (as is not the case in capitalism) producers *owned* their means of production.

Rousseau knows that this longing is a dream, a utopia: "This equality, it is said, is a chimera of speculation which cannot exist in practice. But if the abuse is inevitable, does it follow that it is not necessary even to regulate it? It is precisely because the force of things tends always to destroy equality that the force of legislation should always tend to maintain it" (2:11). Legislation must go against "the force of things"; it must counteract what is, in effect, an intractable tendency to destroy equality and, therefore, liberty. Rousseau virtually admits such efforts of legislation can hardly succeed. His vision is, thus, of utopia.

It is important not to lose sight of the reciprocal and comple-
mentary connection between this utopian economic program and
the measures Rousseau proposes on the level of opinion. Public
education and civil religion cannot function effectively as tools for
the formation of the sovereign unless they are grounded in an
economic structure that prevents the formation of overriding class
interests. This structure, for Rousseau, requires free relations between relatively equal and independent producers, each owning
their means of production and exchanging the products of their
labor in the marketplace. Rousseau appreciates the inherent instability of these market relations; he acknowledges the tendency
toward the concentration of wealth and the consequent
(re)emergence of class interests. Thus, the economic structure of the
de jure state requires extensive operations on opinion to counteract
these tendencies. Moral education is to be grounded in the free
market; the laws of that market are to be counteracted by moral
education.

Viewed historically, this reciprocal connection is highly tenuous and even paradoxical. The call for public education and civil
religion was a battle-cry for the ascending bourgeoisie, insofar as
these institutions, in Rousseau's time, were progressively national-
ist and anti-feudal. This side of Rousseau's practical program was
taken up by the French revolutionaries, above all by Robespierre.[3]
On the other hand, the economic measures Rousseau proposes are
clearly retrogressive in the face of an emerging capitalism. In this
way, his thought reflects the contradictory tendencies of a disin-
tegrating feudal society.

Community

However utopian and historically tenuous Rousseau's political
economy may be, it does provide an important, if indirect, lesson
for his successors and even for us today.

As we have seen, sovereignty, in Rousseau's analysis, requires
the thoroughgoing subordination of individual, private interest to
the interest of "the whole community," the general interest. For
Rousseau (given his analysis of the condition of man in the state of

3. For an account of Rousseau's influence on the thought of French revolutionary leaders, see Albert Soboul, "Jean-Jacques Rousseau et le jacobinisme," pp. 405-24. A more sceptical account in English is J. McDonald's
Rousseau and the French Revolution, 1762-1791.

nature), each person's *real* interest is that of the whole community of which he is (or, better, should become) an integral part.

However, as I have pointed out, Rousseau says nothing whatever to establish the existence of this interest. He has only inferred its necessity as a condition for the possibility of (political) right and obligation. The theory of government, an attempt to show how the general will can be put into effect, maintained, and protected from degeneration, also effectively presupposes the general interest. However, in discussing interventions on the level of opinion and manners and morals, and even on the general shape of the laws (in the chapter on the lawgiver), the account takes a different turn. In a sense, the point of these chapters is just to create the psychological conditions for the general will to be discovered. (In this connection I said earlier, in more traditional philosophical terminology, that the general will exists for Rousseau in *reality*, but not always empirically, on the level of *appearance*. The general interest, at this point, is an idea of reason; but it is not yet a "fact.") It is evident that the implementation of these psychological conditions amounts to no less than the *creation* (in fact, on the level of appearance) of the general interest itself. In effect, Rousseau's response to the obvious need to defend the assumption on which the theory of sovereignty rests—that there is a general interest to be discovered by deliberation and voting, and to be executed by the prince—is to deny the question at the level on which it is posed, and to move from one sort of discourse to another, from moral philosophy to moral "education," from the discourse of (ideal) reality to the discourse of (empirical) fact. With the shift to political economy, Rousseau's "defense" is complete.

The general interest exists (empirically) insofar as it is *continually constituted* by the practice of each citizen and by the institutions of society—above all, by its economic institutions. This, finally, is the condition for the possibility of the general will. It is the condition for the escape from the state of nature and the full recovery of each person's autonomy. The collective task, far from being agreement to a single "social contract," is the creation and re-creation of "the whole *community*."

This task requires, as we have seen, *both* the vigorous suppression of whatever divides society (above all, of social classes) and the positive introduction of *community*, of a shared historical and affective experience. Only then will the world conform to the theory, and the general will *exist*. Rousseau's proposals for the formation of the sovereign, seen in this light, are really proposals for the constitution of a general interest. But the condition for these proposals—the condition for community and, ultimately, even sovereignty—is economic. "Equality [is necessary] . . . because liberty cannot subsist without it" (2:11). Even if Rousseau understood this equality to refer only to degrees of wealth, the equality he speaks of really amounts, if I am right, to the absence of class divisions. The *de jure* state can only be classless.

To be sure, Rousseau's conception of classlessness is historically inadequate and not even very satisfactory internally. In a society of free, independent producers, where the products of labor are exchanged on the market as commodities, an *obstacle* to community is of course eliminated; there are no longer class divisions. But relations between individuals remain competitive, not cooperative; and private interest still holds sway outside the political sphere, in civil society (above all, in the market place).[4] Private interest is not so much eliminated as displaced. And this situation can occur only to the detriment of community and all that depends on it.

But the essential point remains: sovereignty requires community, which, in turn, requires classlessness. These connections are not so much logical as psychological: resulting from the all-too-human, but intractable, tendency for private interest to dominate and direct human action, "Taking men as they are," as Rousseau proposes in the introductory note to Book 1, laws can be made such that "administration is legitimate and certain" only on condition that these practical measures are implemented.

Thus, Rousseau developed the theory of sovereignty (as radical democracy) and sketched its dependence on moral education and political economy. He is hardly to be blamed if, decades before the full development of a working class anywhere in Europe, he did not also properly theorize the connection between radical democracy and socialism, a *cooperative* classless society, building on the

4. As noted earlier (see p. 24, n. 13), this is in essence Marx's criticism of the French (bourgeois) revolution and also of Rousseau, whom he regarded, more or less, as its theoretician. For Marx, the state of nature is merely displaced onto and intensified in the free market; see "On the Jewish Question" (1843), a text of Marx's youth that bears crucial insights for the evaluation of Rousseau's thought.

achievements of capitalist industry and not pointing back to "the early and rude state of society." Rousseau laid the groundwork for others, later, to make these connections. And most important of all, he focused sharply on what is vital and too often overlooked, even by his socialist successors: the absolutely central importance, in both theory and practice, of community.

Individualism

Still, no matter how far Rousseau's emphasis on community, in both theory and practice, overcomes the atomic individualism of so many of his predecessors, contemporaries, and successors (above all, in the liberal tradition), a profoundly individualist strain remains. This residual individualism is implicit in the very goal of political association: the full realization of autonomy or *self*-determination. As we have seen, for Rousseau, the condition for achieving this goal is the establishment of community and the corresponding development of individual *virtue*. As is appropriate for a writer immersed in the classical and republican tradition, an acknowledged disciple of Montesquieu, Rousseau depicted community on the model of the Greek *polis* or city-state, and conceived virtue as *civic* virtue. Sparta is the ideal, and the virtuous man in the *de jure* state is just the good citizen.

But there is, at the same time, an influence Rousseau was intent on acknowledging in nearly all his writings: the example of Geneva, his native city.[5] As a true citizen of Geneva, Rousseau conceived political association as, in fact, less classical than Protestant or, more exactly, Calvinist; though, of course, Rousseau's Calvinism is thoroughly secularized. The achievement of *de jure* political institutions remains, essentially, an individual task and responsibility. To be sure, the form of that association can only be communal: the individual's *private* will must be fully subordinated to the *general* will, the will of "the whole community." But this subordination of the will and the implementation of the general will in the institutions of society are conceived as the *true* interest of each person as a *potentially* moral agent. Community and virtue, in the end, are motivated by the quest for individual (moral) "salvation."

5. For example, on the title page of *The Social Contract*, Rousseau signed his name "J.J. Rousseau, citoyen de Genève."

This point of view is nowhere more evident than in Rousseau's account of virtue. The object is always to become a moral person, to become autonomous. Civic virtue is a means, but not the only one, to achieve this end. This is the reason why, as Rousseau argues in *Emile* and elsewhere, a non-civic virtue is possible and indeed obligatory, wherever—as may be inevitable everywhere—*de jure* political institutions are lacking. Private virtue is an unfortunate second best, but it is a viable option. If one cannot be a citizen, one can at least be a man. For Aristotle, and perhaps for Rousseau's idealized Spartans as well, this option does not exist. In the classical view, community is not the supersession of atomic individualism, for atomic individualism itself is inconceivable. Man is essentially and always a *political animal;* and community—far from being a human contrivance, a covenant, for the realization of *self*-determination—is natural, indeed inevitable, for such political animals as we are. Private virtue, as discussed in *Emile,* is an absurdity, as is the very ideal of self-determination. Rousseau's classicism is thus deceptive. In the end, as he is wont to admit, he is more the offspring of the Genevan theocracy, of the emerging Swiss bourgeoisie, than of the Greek *polis.*

For Rousseau, the individual is sovereign, both within the political sphere established by the social contract and outside that sphere, in civil society, where the sovereign "takes no interest." For this reason, Rousseau's political economy, while not strictly entailed by theoretical exigencies, is natural and appropriate. A more profound historical judgment (or perhaps a better social psychology) might enjoin the suppression of private interest everywhere and not just its "displacement." But this move would jar with that profoundly *moral* individualism (which Kant was later to explore), according to which the self, in the final analysis, is the ultimate constituent of the moral world order. This is "the moral view of the world" (in Hegel's expression) that Rousseau "discovered." It is a deeply Protestant vision of the good society, a vision that gives Rousseau's thought its timely, historical appeal and its inner coherence.

Politics

Could this Protestant vision, presenting itself from a universal point of view, beyond classes and their interests, possibly express a class point of view? I think Rousseau's political economy—in its natural coherence with his various "superstructural" proposals and with the notion of autonomy itself—indicates that a class position is expressed.

Briefly, *The Social Contract,* in its vision of the good society, expresses the interests of those "intermediary strata" brought into prominence by the emergence of capitalist social relations but, at the same time, threatened by the very development of capitalism. It expresses the interests of the small producer, the independent bourgeois, the small-scale artisan, and the free peasant farmer. *The Social Contract* is anti-aristocratic and anti-capitalist, but also implicitly, though compassionately, anti-plebian. The good society is a solidary, homogeneous, communitarian *market* society where citizens (as producers, but not as legislators) are relatively self-sufficient and independent. It is appropriate, I think, to call this vision petit-bourgeois.

Like any serious political philosophy, Rousseau's is a political intervention, with real effects in the unfolding course of history, the history of class struggle. Its very classlessness is partisan, but partisan toward a class that is highly transitory in outlook (and composition) and thoroughly unstable. On the eve of the French Revolution, the petit-bourgeoisie was in general a progressive force against feudalism. It is not surprising, in those circumstances, that Rousseau's thought, the most developed theoretical expression of the petit-bourgeois class position, should become a revolutionary weapon. Nor is it surprising, in different historical circumstances, that Rousseau should appear reactionary—advocating romantic escapism, pastoralism, and anti-industrialism—or conservative—upholding the sanctity of tradition and (established) authority.

That Rousseau's politics includes these tendencies (and many others) is the key to understanding the history of *The Social Contract,* the history of its reception and (political) impact. Perhaps no other political thinker has spoken so clearly, and yet been understood so variously, and always with good reason. Rousseau's politics is polyvalent and contradictory. But this should not surprise us either, for it reflects exactly the situation of the class whose interests it expresses.

Conclusion

I think this reading of *The Social Contract* does establish, indirectly, the conceptual warrant for the historical thesis of Hegel, Cassirer, and many others, including Kant himself: that an important motivation of Kantian moral philosophy was to conceive the foundations for this "regional" investigation of political right and obligation; that Rousseau "discovered" the world Kant later, more profoundly, "explored." Both thinkers occupy a conceptual space structured, in effect, by the central oppositions of Kantian moral philosophy: autonomy / heteronomy, person / thing, (practical) reason / (private) interest or prudence. There is, between Rousseau and Kant, a profound conceptual affinity. However, when we reflect on this affinity, a striking and extremely revealing difference suggests itself.

In Kant's attempt to envisage the foundations of Rousseau's philosophy of the state, the very idea of the state disappears! There is no notion of external coordination, no "legitimate" monopoly of the means of violence. The Kantian equivalent of Rousseau's *de jure* state, the "kingdom of ends," is not a state at all but an *internally coordinated association* of "harmonious," rational wills.[1] No one is "forced to be free" because everyone, by hypothesis, is already

1. See *The Foundations of the Metaphysics of Morals,* pt. 2, secs. 428–41.

free, already self-determined, already (in the Kantian sense) rational.

Within the conceptual framework shared by Rousseau and Kant, the idea of the state, of *external coordination,* can only be a concession to unreason, to human recalcitrance, to private interest. Where (practical) reason is in control, as Kant realized, the state disappears as unnecessary.

It is tempting to attribute a theory of "the withering away of the state" to Rousseau, but such ascription would be misleading. The *de jure* state does not become *less* a state as its subjects become more fully "citizens." The *de jure* state does not admit of degrees. Either the general will is sovereign or it is not. If it is sovereign, the state, as an apparatus of external coordination and control, is unnecessary. Thus, the *de jure* state becomes a (Kantian) "kingdom of ends."

Robert Paul Wolff has argued that Rousseau poses "the fundamental problem" of political philosophy (the reconciliation of authority and autonomy), correctly, but that this problem has no solution, that authority and autonomy cannot be conceived together.[2] For this reason, he concludes, substantive political philosophy, the theory of the *de jure* state, is impossible; for there is no *de jure* state. Philosophical anarchism is the only rational option. However, it is now clear that this conclusion follows *even if* authority and autonomy *can* be conceived together. For then we would have an account not of a state, strictly speaking, but of the philosophical anarchist's ideal: an internally coordinated, harmonious association of persons. Philosophical anarchism is implicit in "the fundamental problem" itself.

However, it does not follow from this conclusion that anarchism is the only viable philosophical position. For even if the fundamental problem is correctly posed, it is posed within a specific, conceptual framework that cannot grasp the specificity, the *autonomy,* of politics. Within this framework, the theory of the state is possible only insofar as the state ceases, so to speak, to be a state. Political philosophy has no "object"; it passes into moral philosophy without a trace. This fact by itself should impugn the adequacy of Rousseau's (and Kant's) way of thinking about politics, and it should impugn the consequences that follow from this way of

2. *In Defense of Anarchism.*

thinking. We need not become anarchists because a conceptual framework that is, in the final analysis, defective for theorizing politics compels that conclusion.

Indeed, we should go a step further, I think, and realize that it is Rousseau's residual individualism, his Calvinism, and, ultimately, his class position that result in this vision of the state as a community of morally autonomous persons; thereby making the dissolution of political philosophy into moral philosophy inevitable, and a proper theory of the state impossible.[3]

Nevertheless, as we know, Rousseau is, above all, a political writer. And Kant, too, has a great deal to tell us about politics.[4] Kant's political writings deserve very careful attention, especially for their realism and *distance* from moral philosophy. This distance is evident in many of Rousseau's political writings also: for example, "The Considerations on the Government of Poland" and "The Project for a Constitution for Corsica." That Rousseau's timely political interventions fall far short of the ideal set forth in *The Social Contract* reflects on one level, no doubt, a pessimism about the possibility of achieving *de jure* institutions in a Europe already corrupt beyond salvation. Rousseau, the realist, is prepared, soberly, to accept much less than the ideal. On a deeper level, these texts and (less blatantly) even *The Social Contract* itself evidence a certain (unconscious) refusal by Rousseau to pursue his thoughts to the limit, to the moral world order investigated in Kantian moral

3. It is significant and worthy of much further investigation that Marxist writings on the state effectively *transform* the traditional (and "natural") order of disciplines: the theory of the state is severed from moral philosophy and becomes a relatively independent branch of a more general theory of history (historical materialism) that *also* includes, at least programmatically, a theory *of* ideology and, thereby, *of* moral philosophy.

As I have already suggested, Rousseau's account of *community*, extricated from its specific, conceptual context, remains an invaluable and barely exploited source of insight for historical materialism. To this day, the Marxist theory of the state—in a word, as an *apparatus* for organizing *class domination*—remains vastly underdeveloped, despite the important contributions of Lenin (in *The State and Revolution* and elsewhere) and Gramsci. Gramsci is the first Marxist thinker to explore mechanisms of class domination along the lines opened up, in a different context, of course, by Rousseau's account of the formation of the sovereign. See *Selections from the Prison Notebooks* (New York, 1971), particularly those texts where Gramsci develops the concept of 'hegemony'.

4. See the collection *Kant's Political Writings*, ed. Hans Reiss.

philosophy. In this sense they represent a denegation of the Kantianism that is the condition of their possibility.

But this very Kantianism is also the condition for the impossibility of properly conceiving politics. We can thus only be grateful that Rousseau did not pursue his thoughts to the limit. For however inadequate his grasp of the concept of the state, Rousseau's political insight surpasses even the discovery of that moral world order that is the supra-political culmination of the politics of autonomy. What we learn along the way may prove more valuable, finally, than the destination.

Selected

Bibliography

Editions of *The Social Contract*

There is no entirely satisfactory English translation. Of the many versions available, I recommend in descending order:

> *The Social Contract and Discourse on the Origin of Inequality.* Translated by Henry J. Tozer. Edited with an introduction by Lester G. Crocker. New York: Washington Square Press, 1967.

> *The Social Contract.* Translated with an introduction by Maurice Cranston. London: Penguin Books, 1968.

> *The Social Contract and Discourses.* Translated with an introduction by G.D.H. Cole. London: Dent, 1913. Reprint. London: Everyman's Library, 1966.

There are many excellent editions in French. The definitive one since its publication is the text established by Robert Derathé:

> *Oeuvres completes de Jean-Jacques Rousseau.* Edited by B. Gagnebin and Raymond. Paris: Bibliotheque de la Pléiade, Vol. 3, *Du Contrat social: Ecrits politiques*, 1964.

Derathé's introduction and notes are invaluable. His edition effectively supersedes the once-standard collection of Rousseau's political writings edited by C.E. Vaughan:

The Political Writings of Jean-Jacques Rousseau. 2 vols. Cambridge: At the University Press, 1915. Reprint. Oxford University Press, 1962. (The final version of *The Social Contract* is in vol. 2.)

Also, for its helpful introduction and notes (in English), see:

Du Contrat Social. Edited with an introduction and notes by Ronald Grimsley. Oxford: Oxford University Press, 1972.

Secondary Works on Rousseau and Political Philosophy

Of the articles on Rousseau and political philosophy on which I have drawn extensively, many can be found in three important collections:

Etudes sur le 'Contrat Social' de Jean-Jacques Rousseau. Actes des journées d'étude organisées à Dijon. Paris, 1964. (Hereafter listed as *Etudes.*)

Annales de philosophie politique. Vol. 5, *Rousseau et la philosophie politique,* 1966. (Hereafter listed as *RPP.*)

Hobbes and Rousseau: A Collection of Critical Essays. Edited by M. Cranston and R.S. Peters. Garden City, N.Y., 1972. (Hereafter listed as *HR.*)

Althusser, L. "Sur le *Contrat Social* (Les Décalages)." In *Cahiers pour l'analyse,* no. 8, *L'Impensée de Jean-Jacques Rousseau.* Paris, n.d. Translated as "Rousseau: The Social Contract." In Althusser, *Politics and History.* London, 1972.

Barry, B. *Political Argument.* London, 1965.

Barth, H. "Volonté générale et volonté particulière chez J.-J. Rousseau." In *RPP,* pp. 35–50.

Bastid, P. "Rousseau et la théorie des formes de gouvernement." In *Etudes,* pp. 315–27.

Burdeau, G. "Le citoyen selon Rousseau." In *Etudes,* pp. 219–26.

Burgelin, P. *Le Philosophie de l'existence de J.-J. Rousseau.* Paris, 1951.

———. "Le social et le politique chez Rousseau." In *Etudes,* pp. 165–76.

Cassirer, E. *Philosophy of the Enlightenment.* Translated by F. Koelln and J. Pettegrove. Boston, 1955.

_____. *The Question of Jean-Jacques Rousseau*. Translated and edited by Peter Gay. Bloomington, 1954.

_____. *Rousseau Kant Goethe*. Translated by James Gutmann, P.O. Kristeller, and John Herman Randall, Jr. Princeton, 1945.

Charvet, J. "Individual Identity and Social Consciousness in Rousseau's Philosophy." In *HR*, pp. 462–83.

Chevallier, J.J. "Le mot et la notion de gouvernement chez Rousseau." In *Etudes*, pp. 291–313.

Cobban, A. *Rousseau and the Modern State*. London, 1934. 2nd rev. ed. 1964.

Colletti, L. *From Rousseau to Lenin*. London, 1972.

Cotta, S. "La position du problème de la politique chez Rousseau." In *Etudes*, pp. 177–90.

_____. "Théorie religieuse et théorie politique chez Rousseau." In *RPP*, pp. 171–94.

Cousin, J. "J.-J. Rousseau interprète des institutions romains dans le *Contrat Social*." In Etudes, pp. 12–34.

Crocker, L.G. "Rousseau et la voie du totalitarisme." In *RPP*, pp. 99–136.

_____. *Rousseau's Social Contract: An Interpretive Essay*. Cleveland, 1968.

Davy, G. "Le corps politique selon le *Contrat Social* de J.-J. Rousseau et ses antecedents chez Hobbes." In *Etudes*, pp. 65–93.

Dehaussy, J. "La dialectique de la souveraine liberté dans le Contrat social." In *Etudes*, pp. 65–93.

Derathé, R. "L'homme selon Rousseau." In *Etudes*, pp. 203–17.

_____. *Jean-Jacques Rousseau et la science politique de son temps*. Paris, 1950. Reprint. Paris, 1970.

_____. "Les rapports de l'executif et du legislatif chez Rousseau." In *RPP*, pp. 153–69.

Durkheim, E. *Montesquieu and Rousseau: Forerunners of Sociology*. Ann Arbor, 1960.

Einaudi, M. *The Early Rousseau*. Ithaca, N.Y., 1967.

Fetscher, I. "Rousseau, auter d'intention conservateur et d'action revolutionnaire." In *RPP*, pp. 51–75.

_____. *Rousseaus politische Philosophie: zur Geschichte des demokratischen Freiheitsbegriffs*, Neuwied, 1960.

Françon, M. "Le Langage mathematique de J.-J. Rousseau." In *Cahiers pour l'analyse*, no. 8, *L'Impensée de Jean-Jacques Rousseau*. Paris, n.d.

Friedrich, C.J. "Law and Dictatorship in the *Contrat Social*" In *RPP*, pp. 77-97.

Gagnebin, B. "Le role du legislateur dans les conceptions politiques de Rousseau." In *Etudes*, pp. 277–90.

Gilliard, F. "Etat de nature et liberté dans la pensée de J.-J. Rousseau." In *Etudes*, pp. 111–18.

Godechot, J. "Le *Contrat social* et la revolution occidentale de 1762–1789." In *Etudes*, pp. 393–403.

Gough, J.W. *The Social Contract: A Critical Study of Its Development*. 2nd ed. Oxford. 1957.

Green, T.H. *Lectures on the Principles of Political Obligation*. Ann Arbor, 1967.

Grice, R. *The Grounds of Moral Judgement*. Cambridge, 1967.

Groethuysen, B. *Jean-Jacques Rousseau*. Paris, 1949.

Hendel, C.W. *Jean-Jacques Rousseau, Moralist*. 2 vols. Cambridge, 1934.

Hoffman, S. "Rousseau on War and Peace." *American Political Science Review* 57 (1963): 54–87.

Jouvenel, B. de. "Rousseau, évolutioniste pessimiste." In *RPP*, pp. 1–19.

———. "Rousseau's Theory of the Forms of Government." In *HR*, pp. 484–97.

Kelly, G.A. *Idealism, Politics and History: Sources of Hegelian Thought*. Cambridge, 1969.

Lacherrière, R. de. "Rousseau et le socialisme." In *Etudes*, pp. 515–35.

Launay, M. *Jean-Jacques Rousseau, écrivain politique (1712–1762)*. Cannes, 1972.

———. *Rousseau*. Paris, 1968.

McDonald, J. *Rousseau and the French Revolution, 1762–1791*. London, 1965.

Masters, R.D. *The Political Philosophy of Rousseau*. Princeton, 1968.

Millet, L. *La Pensée de Rousseau*. Paris, 1966.

Pateman, C. *Participation and Democratic Theory*. Cambridge, 1970.

Plamenatz, J. " 'Ce qui ne signifie pas autre chose, sinon qu'on le forcera d'être libre.' A commentary." In *RPP*, pp. 137–52. Also in *HR*, pp. 318–32.

_____. *Man and Society.* Vol. 1. London, 1963.

Polin, R. *La politique de la solitude, Essai sur J.J. Rousseau.* Paris, 1971.

_____. "Le sens de l'égalité et de l'inégalité chez J.-J. Rousseau." In *Etudes*, pp. 143–64.

Rang, M. "L'éducation publique et la formation des citoyens chez J.-J. Rousseau." In *Etudes*, pp. 253–75.

Rawls, J. *A Theory of Justice.* Cambridge, Mass., 1971.

Rawson, E.R. *The Spartan Tradition in European Thought.* chaps. 15 and 16. Oxford, 1969.

Redpath, T. "Reflexions sur la nature du concept de Contrat social' chez Hobbes, Locke et Rousseau." In *Etudes*, pp. 55–63.

Shklar, J.N. *Men and Citizens: A Study of Rousseau's Social Theory.* Cambridge, 1969.

_____. "Rousseau's Images of Authority." In *HR*, pp. 333–65.

Soboul, A. "Jean-Jacques Rousseau et le jacobinisme." In *Etudes*, pp. 405–24.

Soto, J. de. "La liberté et ses garanties." In *Etudes*, pp. 227–52.

Starobinski, J. "Du *Discours de l'inégalité* au *Contrat social.*" In *Etudes*, pp. 97–109.

_____. Jean-Jacques Rousseau, la transparence et l'obstacle. 2nd ed. Paris, 1971.

Strauss, L. "On the Intention of Rousseau." In *HR*, pp. 254–90.

Talmon, J.L. *The Rise of Totalitarian Democracy.* Boston, 1952.

Tussman, J. *Obligation and the Body Politic.* Oxford, 1960.

Volpe, G. Della. "Critique marxiste de Rousseau." In *Etudes*, pp. 503–13. Translated as "The Marxist Critique of Rousseau." *New Left Review*, no. 59 (January-February 1970).

_____. *Rousseau e Marx.* Rome, 1956.

Vossler, O. *Rousseaus Freiheitslehre.* Gottingen, 1963.

Weil, E. "J.-J. Rousseau et sa politique." *Critique* 56 (January 1952): 3–28.

Wolff, R.P. *In Defense of Anarchism.* New York, 1970.

Kant

Those who wish to acquire some familiarity with Kant's moral philosophy should read, at the very least, parts 1 and 2 of *The Foundations of the Metaphysics of Morals*. Kant's major work in moral philosophy is *The Critique of Practical Reason*. His political writings have been collected in a single volume:

> *Kant's Political Writings*. Translated by H.B. Nisbet. Edited with an introduction and notes by Hans Reiss. Cambridge, 1970.

Access to Kant's moral philosophy will be facilitated by the following secondary sources:

> Korner, S. *Kant*. Baltimore, 1950.
>
> Ward, K. *The Development of Kant's View of Ethics*. New York, 1972.
>
> Wolff, R.P. *The Autonomy of Reason*. New York, 1974.
>
> Patton, J.J. *The Categorical Imperative: A Study in Kant's Philosophy*. London, 1947.
>
> Beck, L.W. *A Commentary on Kant's Critique of Practical Reason*. Chicago, 1960.
>
> Vlachos, G. *La pensée politique de Kant*. Paris, 1962.

Collective Decision Making

Arrow has written a relatively non-technical account of his work:

> "Values and Collective Decision-making." In *Philosophy, Politics and Society*, 3rd series, edited by Peter Laslett and W.G. Runciman. New York. 1967.

An earlier version of that paper and comments by Richard Brandt and Paul Samuelson may be found in:

> Hook, S., ed. *Human Values and Economic Policy*. New York, 1967.

Of the more technical literature, among the most important works are:

> Arrow, K.J. *Social Choice and Individual Values*. 1951. 2nd ed. New York, 1963.
>
> Black, D. *The Theory of Committees and Elections*. Cambridge, 1958.
>
> Murakami, Y. *Logic and Social Choice*. London, 1968.

Pattanaik, P.K. *Voting and Collective Choice.* Cambridge, 1971.

Rothenberg, J. *The Measurement of Social Welfare.* Englewood Cliffs, N.J., 1961.

Sen, A.K. *Collective Choice and Social Welfare.* San Francisco, 1970.

Index of Names

Library of Congress Cataloging in Publication Data
Levine, Andrew, 1944-
    The politics of autonomy.
    Bibliography: p.
    Includes index.
    1. Rousseau, Jean Jacques, 1712-1778. Contrat
social. I. Title.
JC179.R9L53   320.1   76-8757
ISBN 0-87023-215-0